UNSAFE AT ANY SPEED

by Ralph Nader

PB Special
Published by Pocket Books
New York
1966

Copyright, ©, 1965 by Ralph Nader

All rights reserved

A **PB Special,** published by Pocket Books, a division of Simon & Schuster, Inc., 630 Fifth Avenue, New York, N.Y. 10020, and on the same day in Canada by Pocket Books of Canada, Ltd., Richmond Hill, Ontario

Printed in the U.S.A.

To Frederick Hughes Condon

Preface

For over half a century the automobile has brought death, injury, and the most inestimable sorrow and deprivation to millions of people. With Medea-like intensity, this mass trauma began rising sharply four years ago, reflecting new and unexpected ravages by the motor vehicle. A 1959 Department of Commerce report projected that 51,000 persons would be killed by automobiles in 1975. That figure will probably be reached in 1965, a decade ahead of schedule.

A transportation specialist, Wilfred Owen, wrote in 1946, "There is little question that the public will not tolerate for long an annual traffic toll of forty to fifty thousand fatalities." Time has shown Owen to be wrong. Unlike aviation, marine, or rail transportation, the highway transport system can inflict tremendous casualties and property damage without in the least affecting the viability of the system. Plane crashes, for example, jeopardize the attraction of flying for potential passengers and therefore strike at the heart of the air transport economy. They motivate preventative efforts. The situation is different on the roads.

Highway accidents were estimated to have cost this country in 1964, $8.3 billion in property damage, medical expenses, lost wages, and insurance overhead expenses. Add an equivalent sum to comprise roughly the indirect costs and the total amounts to over two per cent of the gross national product. But these are not the kind of costs which fall on the builders of motor vehicles (excepting a few successful law suits for negligent construction of the vehicle) and thus do not pinch the proper foot. Instead, the costs fall to users of vehicles, who are in no position to dictate safer automobile designs.

In fact, the gigantic costs of the highway carnage in this country support a service industry. A vast array of services—medical, police, administrative, legal, insurance, automotive repair, and funeral—stand equipped to handle the direct and indirect consequences of accident-injuries. Traffic accidents create economic demands for these services running into billions of dollars. It is in the post-accident response that lawyers and physicians and other specialists labor. This is where the remuneration lies and this is where the talent and energies go. Working in the area of prevention of these casualties earns few fees. Consequently our society has an intricate organization to handle direct and indirect aftermaths of collisions. But the true mark of a humane society must be what it does about *prevention* of accident injuries, not the cleaning up of them afterward.

Unfortunately, there is little in the dynamics of the automobile accident industry that works for its reduction. Doctors, lawyers, engineers and other specialists have failed in their primary professional ethic: to dedicate themselves to the prevention of accident-injuries. The roots of the unsafe vehicle problem are so entrenched that the situation can be improved only by the forging of new instruments of citizen action. When thirty practicing physicians picketed for safe auto design at the New York International Automobile Show on April 7, 1965, their unprecedented action was the measure of their desperation over the inaction of the men and institutions in government and industry who have failed to provide the public with the vehicle safety to which it is entitled. The picketing surgeons, orthopedists, pediatricians and general practitioners marched in protest because the existing medical, legal and engineering organizations have defaulted.

A great problem of contemporary life is how to control the power of economic interests which ignore the harmful effects of their applied science and technology. The automobile tragedy is one of the most serious of these man-made assaults on the human body. The history of that tragedy reveals many obstacles which must be overcome in the taming of any mechanical or biological hazard which is a by-product of industry or commerce. Our society's obligation to protect the "body rights" of its citizens with vigorous resolve and ample resources requires the precise, authoritative articulation and front-rank support which is being devoted to civil rights.

This country has not been entirely laggard in defining values relevant to new contexts of a technology laden with risks. The postwar years have witnessed a historic broadening, at least in the courts, of the procedural and substantive rights of the injured and the duties of manufacturers to produce a safe product. Judicial decisions throughout the fifty states have given living meaning to Walt Whitman's dictum, "If anything is sacred, the human body is sacred." Mr. Justice Jackson in 1953 defined the duty of the manufacturers by saying, "Where experiment or research is necessary to determine the presence or the degree of danger, the product must not be tried out on the public, nor must the public be expected to possess the facilities or the technical knowledge to learn for itself of inherent but latent dangers. The claim that a hazard was not foreseen is not available to one who did not use foresight appropriate to his enterprise."

It is a lag of almost paralytic proportions that these values of safety concerning consumers and economic enterprises, reiterated many times by the judicial branch of government, have not found their way into legislative policy-making for safer automobiles. Decades ago legislation was passed, changing the pattern of private business investments to accommodate more fully the safety value on railroads, in factories, and more recently on ships and aircraft. In transport, apart from the motor vehicle, considerable progress has been made in recognizing the physical integrity of the individual. There was the period when railroad workers were killed by the thousands and the editor of *Harper's* could say late in the last century: "So long as brakes cost more than trainmen, we may expect the present sacrificial method of car-coupling to be continued." But injured trainmen did cause the railroads some operating dislocations; highway victims cost the automobile companies next to nothing and the companies are not obliged to make use of developments in science technology that have demonstrably opened up opportunities for far greater safety than any existing safety features lying unused on the automobile companies' shelves.

A principal reason why the automobile has remained the only transportation vehicle to escape being called to meaningful public account is that the public has never been supplied the information nor offered the quality of competition to enable it to make effective demands through the marketplace and through government for a safe, nonpolluting and efficient automobile that can be produced economically. The consumer's expectations regarding automotive innovations have been deliberately held low and mostly oriented to very gradual annual style changes. The specialists and researchers outside the industry who could have provided the leadership to stimulate this flow of information by and large chose to remain silent, as did government officials.

The persistence of the automobile's immunity over the years has nourished the continuance of that immunity, recalling Francis Bacon's insight: "He that will not apply new remedies must expect new evils, for time is the greatest innovator."

The accumulated power of decades of effort by the automobile industry to strengthen its control over car design is reflected today in the difficulty of even beginning to bring it to justice. The time has not come to discipline the automobile for safety; that time came over four decades ago. But that is not cause to delay any longer what should have been accomplished in the nineteen-twenties.

Contents

The three diagrams in Chapter 3 are taken from:

"Four Proposals for Improving Automobile Crashworthiness" by Robert A. Wolf, Transportation Research Department, Cornell Aeronautical Laboratory, Inc., Buffalo, New York, 14221.—being an address given on September 22, 1964 before the annual meeting of the American Automobile Association, Miami Beach, Florida.

UNSAFE AT ANY SPEED

1
The sporty Corvair:
The "one-car" accident

John F. Gordon did not become president of the world's largest manufacturing company by using strong words. But on October 17, 1961, as the keynote speaker before the annual National Safety Congress, the head of General Motors was among friends—"professionals" from the National Safety Council and other organizations that make up the closely knit traffic safety establishment. Mr. Gordon saw "diversionary forces" undermining safety progress. "The traffic safety field," he declared, "has in recent years been particularly beset by self-styled experts with radical and ill-conceived proposals. . . . The general thesis of these amateur engineers is that cars could be made virtually foolproof and crashproof, that this is the only practical route to greater safety and that federal regulation of vehicle design is needed. This thesis is, of course, wholly unrealistic. It also is a serious threat to a balanced approach to traffic safety. To begin with, it is completely unrealistic even to talk about a foolproof and crashproof car. This is true because an automobile must still be something that people will want to buy and use. . . . We can only design into it the greatest degree of safety that is consistent with other essential functional characteristics. Beyond that, we must depend on intelligent use. The suggestion that we abandon hope of teaching drivers to avoid traffic accidents and concentrate on designing cars that will make collisions harmless is a perplexing combination of defeatism and wishful thinking."

Mr. Gordon finished his address, entitled "Safeguarding Safety Progress," amid enthusiastic and confirming applause. It was a rare occasion for a top auto executive to speak about vehicle safety design in any vein, even in an argumentative context of raising and demolishing straw men. The national media gave wide circulation to his criticism of "self-styled experts" and, in subsequent months, General Motors management made sure that every GM dealer received copies of the address to distribute throughout the local community.

Mrs. Rose Pierini did not read about Mr. Gordon's complaints. She was learning to adjust to the loss of her left arm which was severed two months earlier when the 1961 Chevrolet Corvair she was driving turned over on its top just beyond the San Marcos overpass on Hollister Street in Santa Barbara, California. Exactly thirty-four months later, in the same city, General Motors decided to pay Mrs. Pierini $70,000 rather than continue a trial which for three days threatened to expose on the public record one of the greatest acts of industrial irresponsibility in the present century.

Mrs. Pierini's experience with a Corvair going unexpectedly and suddenly out of control was not unique. There simply are too many Corvairs with such inclinations for her case to be singular. What was distinctive about the "accident" was the attempt to find the cause of it on the basis of investigation, instead of resorting to the customary, automatic placing of blame on the driver.

As described by a California Highway Patrol officer, John Bortolozzo, who witnessed the flip-over while motoring in the opposite direction, the Pierini vehicle was traveling about thirty-five miles per hour in a thirty-five mph zone in the right lane headed toward Goleta. He saw the car move toward the right side of the road near the shoulder and then "all of a sudden the vehicle made a sharp cut to the left and swerved over." Bortolozzo testified at the trial that he rushed over to the wreck and saw an arm with a wedding band and wristwatch lying on the ground. Two other men came over quickly and began to help Mrs. Pierini out of the vehicle while trying to stop the torrent of blood gushing forth from the stub of her arm. She was very calm, observed Bortolozzo, only saying that "something went wrong with my steering."

After helping Mrs. Pierini to the ambulance, the officer made a check of the vehicle while it was on its top. He noticed that the left rear tire was deflated because of an air-out. Looking at the road, he noticed some gouge marks made by the metal rim of the left rear tire. He gave his opinion at the trial that the distinctive design features of the Corvair caused it to go out of control and flip over as had other Corvairs in accidents he had investigated. It was during the cross-examination of Officer Bortolozzo by defense lawyers that General Motors decided to settle the case.

Up to this point no engineering experts had been called to testify by plaintiff Pierini, but already the case had been going badly for General Motors. Two members of the respected California Highway Patrol had taken direct aim on the Corvair design. One of them, Charles Hanna, mentioned a confidential circular put out by the highway patrol dealing with handling hazards of certain rear-engine cars, including the Corvair. Hanna, a fourteen-year veteran of the patrol who had investigated over four thousand accidents, testified that "I have had many, many chances to observe accidents involving this type of vehicle. And they all have the same type of pattern."

Mr. James A. Johnson, service manager of Washburn Chevrolet Company, where the Pierini Corvair was purchased, told the court that his company sold an accessory specially designed for the Corvair by a nearby manufacturer. Attached underneath the vehicle to each end of the lower control arms, this accessory reduced excessive caving-in, or tuck-under, of the rear wheels on cornering or other stress situations.

The dealership's proprietor, Shelton B. Washburn, confirmed that as early as 1961 General Motors provided dealers with regular production option 696, which they could sell to Corvair owners. RPO 696 included heavier suspension springs and shock absorbers, a front stabilizer bar, and rear-axle rebound straps to reduce tuck-under. This RPO was a factory installed kit and not openly advertised. It was intended to meet the demands of the most knowledgeable Corvair owners who take their cornering seriously.

Mr. Johnson, in reply to questioning by plaintiff's counsel, stated that he had been at a General Motors training center at Burbank in 1959 to receive instructions and training about the new Corvair model. There, General Motors personnel told him that the differential tire pressures, front and rear, in Corvair automobiles were a critical factor in their stability. There followed these exchanges:

Counsel: Were you instructed by your superiors to tell members of the public that tire pressures on the Corvair were vital, important, crucial, and critical?

Johnson: No.

Counsel: Did you instruct your subordinates to tell members of the public and customers of Washburn Chevrolet that tire pressures on the Corvair were vital, important, crucial, or critical?

Johnson: We didn't tell the public this, no.

Counsel: Is it true that tire pressures on a Corvair are a must: they have got to be just right for the stability of the car?

Johnson: Yes.

Further indications as to how General Motors alerted its dealers are provided in this questioning of Washburn:

Counsel: When did you first learn that you were to sell Corvair automobiles?

Washburn: Oh, it was sometime during the year 1959. I don't recall the exact month.

Counsel: Did General Motors or the Chevrolet division advise you about the engineering of the Corvair at any time before you started selling that car to the public?

Washburn: The only things that I had seen from Chevrolet Motors Division was what we call sales training films which we use, before we have a new car announcement, to train our salesmen. And they had films on the Corvair in it, in this kit which we get every year to train the salesmen on the new product.

Counsel: But there was nothing in the films that you saw about the engineering of the Corvair, was there?

Washburn: No.

Counsel: The Chevrolet division shipped those cars, those Corvairs, to you without giving you any information about the engineering; correct?

Washburn: That is correct.

Counsel: And you started selling those to the public without having any engineering information on the car, true?

Washburn: Yes, yes; well, with the exception of this one school that Mr. Johnson attended.

The plaintiff's case was just warming up. Still to come were the engineering specialists and the reading into the record of depositions of leading GM personnel responsible for the making of the Corvair, from the drafting board to the production line. But then General Motors called a halt and settled. Judge Percy C. Heckendorf appeared as one summarily deprived of a great drama. He told the court: "I am disappointed from your standpoint, members of the jury, that you are not going to be able to see both sides perform and hear their arguments and go into it. It is a real experience and I would love to have heard that."

The notoriety attached to the Corvair would have soiled the General Motors' image of product leadership carefully shaped over the years by a superbly managed program of public relations. For a car to have gone on trial and have been struck down by "twelve men good and pure" would have profoundly shaken even this goliath of American industry. And finally, what about the possible spillover into that dreaded chasm, public regulation? What would legislators think—men long nourished on the diet that "it's all because of the nut behind the wheel"—when court-sanctioned investigations of evidence brought out into the open the facts about an American car that abruptly decides to do the driving *for* the driver in a wholly untoward manner? Against such prospects of ill omen, the alternative—pay and delay—was much more attractive.

Delay can do many things when a large corporation is doing battle with an injured person. The corporation can hang on much longer. Furthermore, the offending Corvairs—primarily 1960-1963 models—can only diminish in number with each passing month; the cause of their collisions and waywardness can continue to go undetected by victims, next of kin, accident investigators, and lawyers.

By October 1965, more than one hundred suits alleging instability in the Corvair had been filed around the country. In the summer of 1965, three of them were decided in court. General Motors denied the charges, and instead blamed the accidents involved on driver negligence. In one case brought in Chicago, the trial court, in a default judgment, decided against GM when the company repeatedly failed to comply with court orders to make available test and engineering information on the car. In two other cases (brought in California and Florida), jury verdicts were in favor of the company's argument that the drivers were careless. In none of the three suits, whatever their resolution may be on appeal, did General Motors reveal the technical data and test results that would have placed before the public the full facts about the Corvair.

The Corvair's peculiar friskiness did not escape the notice of the automobile writers and editors who put out those sprightly car magazines that fill shelves in drugstores. To this animated cult of auto lovers, the introduction of the "Waterless Wonder from Willow Run" into a world of automobile design, mired for three decades in the rut of follow-the-crowd compromises, was a dream realized. The Corvair was different. It was the first modern American automobile to offer a swing-axle independent rear suspension with an aluminum, air-cooled engine mounted in the rear. This was news, challenge, and controversy—the combination that makes for good copy and lively reading. Immediately following the car's introduction in September 1959, the articles began pouring forth on the Corvair road tests, on its rear engine placement and its suspension system. By 1963, sports car racer and writer Denise McCluggage could begin an article on Corvair handling idiosyncrasies with words that assumed a knowing familiarity by her auto buff readers: "Seen any Corvairs lately with the back-end smashed in? Chances are they weren't run into, but rather ran into something while going backward. And not in reverse gear, either."

Then Miss McCluggage went on to describe a phenomenon she termed a "sashay through the boonies, back-end first." "The classic Corvair accident is a quick spin in a turn and swoosh!—off the road backward. Or, perhaps, if half-corrective measures are applied, the backward motion is arrested, the tires claw at the pavement and the car is sent darting across the road to the other side. In this case there might be some front-end damage instead."

Was Miss McCluggage trying to frighten anyone? Not in the least. Such frolics, she confided, were manageable if not avoidable and she went on to develop the "art of driving the Corvair" for the reader's benefit and, perhaps, life. The vehicle's provocative movements were not to be viewed pessimistically as a danger, but merely as a challenge to driving expertise. The Corvair on a sudden detour could be "brought back" before reaching the point of no return, according to the author, given know-how, anticipation and concentration.

Not all this country's ninety-five million drivers, however, could qualify for the Shell 4000 Rally. For the over 99 per cent residuum not in Miss McCluggage's class, the automobile "after-market" entrepreneurs provided other remedies. Hardly had the first Corvair hit the highway in 1959 before an enterprising company in Riverdale, California, EMPI, realized the economic opportunity in the Corvair's engineering lack. The company developed, tested and began to sell an accessory rear stabilizer called the EMPI Camber Compensator that was specially designed for installation beneath the rear suspension control arms of Corvairs. Quite simply, it was a bar to help keep the wheels in optimum contact with the roadway.

EMPI advertised broad claims for its device: "keeps wheels on the ground," "designed and engineered to correct oversteer," "increases stability in winds," "reduces body sway," "lowers roll center," "reduces lean on turns." In 1961, EMPI began selling an accessory front anti-sway bar that, it claimed, gave "added stability" and "greatly improved the handling of the Corvair." The more significant of the two devices was the rear-end camber compensator. Estimates of its effectiveness in meeting all of EMPI's declared objectives varied, but there was a solid consensus that these objectives defined very real Corvair problems. And there was widespread endorsement that the compensator was a sizeable step forward in safety. *Sports Car Illustrated*, after observing Corvair test runs in 1961, took note of the "irrefutable evidence that the EMPI Camber Compensator does indeed do much to reduce oversteer and smooth out the unstable rear-end breakaway."

Ocee Ritch, a well-known California auto specialist who has tested and treated almost every Corvair line (thirty-six of them through 1963), states that the camber compensator "limits positive camber [tuck-under of the rear wheels] to a great extent and changes weight transfer characteristics of the car."

EMPI was not the only company offering stabilizing equipment for the Corvair. Several competitors entered the field as the commentary began to build up from the auto magazines. In the area of suspension changes for safety, said Ritch in 1963, the Corvair owner "has more choices than a bull elk in mating season." Ritch might have added, "if he carefully reads the auto magazines." A reader of such magazines who owned a Corvair could well become interested in such equipment after seeing such reports as:

—"The car can be a handful if the driver doesn't understand its peculiarities."

—The rear weight bias and independent springing together "give the car rather unsettling properties at higher speeds. Take cornering, for example. The rear starts to swing outward. The rear tires dig in but the shift in weight places them at rather odd angles relative to the the pavement. These angles are great enough to increase steering force and, suddenly, the car is negotiating a tighter curve than intended. The phenomenon of oversteer has intruded into the scene."

—Another problem with the Corvair is "extreme sensitivity to cross winds. If a sudden gust hits the car, it causes the rear to sway rather severely."

Ritch commented in 1963, after three years of empirical research trying to come up with the best advice and equipment for "the Corvair enthusiasts" (among which Ritch included himself), that "with the Corvair's center of gravity and high roll couple of the suspension, body lean becomes a considerable force acting to tuck both wheels under in a cornering attitude. This results in loss of adhesion because of lowered tire surface contact. The sudden breakaway which has been experienced by every Corvair driver comes when a slight irregularity in the surface destroys the small amount of adhesion remaining."

At the Riverside race course in California there is a curve having an increasingly sharp corner and a downhill exit—all made further unpleasant by a bump just past the apex. "Fortunately," says Ritch, "the approach is relatively slow and there is lots of warning, so in racing it seldom claims any victims. But similar configurations occur in mountainous country, particularly in the Rockies, and, for the stranger, at least, there are no shutoff markers. A Corvair driver could innocently lead-foot it into one of these curves and take up sky-diving, complete with car."

The veteran "car doctor," Bill Corey, working out of his shop in Pasadena, California, has diagnosed the Corvair's ills and put the "raw" vehicle through an improvement course; then he sells it as the "Corey Corvair." In addition to the usually prescribed treatments for what Corey calls the "Corvair's unconventional handling, to say the least," he recommends stronger shock absorbers and higher quality tires than those offered the ordinary purchaser.

John Fitch, formerly a highly successful racing driver and consultant to General Motors, early saw in the Corvair substantial "leeways for modifications" that would improve the vehicle's performance. His approach was comprehensive. Out of his Lime Rock, Connecticut, workshop has come the Sprint, which is a converted Corvair Monza designed to improve the engine and handling performance. People who like the basic Corvair design but want something better and safer simply have a regular new Corvair delivered to Fitch, who works it over functionally and adds a few appearance extras. In describing the kind of Corvair he turns out, Fitch made it clear what market he was catering to: "I didn't want a race car," he said: "if I did, I'd buy something for that purpose. But I did want to feel more confident when behind the wheel that the car would go where I pointed it."

The foregoing comments are made by men who know the Corvair and are enthusiastic about the relative newness of its engineering as far as mass-produced American cars are concerned. They work at the Corvair as a labor of love and their criticisms are made in that framework. These criticisms are serious and are meant to be taken as such by their authors. But critics are not necessarily crusaders. They never indulge in commentary about the kind of engineering and management operations within General Motors which led to such an unsafe vehicle in handling. In the automobile magazine world such commentary is considered poor taste. It may also be indiscreet. One concentrates on the vehicle, not on its makers.

Most of the auto-buff magazines are run on a shoestring with a small group of car-infatuated, articulate people editing or writing the copy. The general tone is laudatory, but to hold their readers, there are substantial amounts of crisp criticism concerning vehicle deficiencies. However, an unwritten rule is that you never "straight-arm" a vehicle or its manufacturer, nor enter the territory of muckraking. To use terms such as "dangerous handling," or "irresponsibility of manufacture" would hit the industry too close to home. Far better to talk about "road adhesion qualities" or "problems of quality control." These magazines need the automobile company advertising, but probably more important, they require the technical assistance of company liaison men for pictorial materials and the loan of cars which they test-drive and write about each month.

But the auto magazines and the Corvair specialists did have an effect on General Motors and its Chevrolet division. Not that any defects in the vehicle's handling were suddenly revealed to Chevrolet's engineers. Whatever the independent specialists could do by way of testing and modifying, Chevrolet could do better, if only by virtue of its vastly superior resources. What the modifiers and accessory suppliers did was to provide a yardstick which measured the production model Corvair and showed it to come out seriously wanting. When a prosperous business being done by small companies can be built up on the basis of making Corvairs safer, top management takes notice. Obviously, selling greater safety for Corvairs implies that the factory models are dangerous, and implication might seep beyond the tight little world of auto fans and magazines. It took General Motors four years of the model and 1,124,076 Corvairs before they decided to do something for all unsuspecting Corvair buyers by installing standard equipment to help control the car's handling hazards.

For the 1964-model year, Chevrolet decided that any buyer of a Corvair deserved an anti-sway bar between the front wheels and a single-leaf transverse spring under the rear end to perform a function similar to the EMPI Camber Compensator. The 1965 Corvairs borrowed concepts from the Corvette Sting Ray's rear suspension. Out went the swing axles, pivoting only at the differential case, and in came a four-link suspension with universal joints at each end of the axle half-shaft. (See diagram p. 13) In addition there are two lateral stabilizer rods mounted in the rear ahead of the lower link. Other changes in the front suspension assembly, steering, and tire tread had the handling problem in mind. All were changes that the automotive engineer of the nineteen thirties would have seen the need for. (See Fig. 1)

The response from the automobile press was prompt and full of praise. Even the hard-bitten test drivers of Consumers Union reported in the widely circulated *Consumer Reports* that, compared with previous models, there was a very marked improvement in handling.

The auto magazines generally were ecstatic but they used their lavish compliments of the 1965 model as a permissive relief against which to uncover their long-contained fury over earlier Corvair breeds. In an article entitled "Chevy's All-New Corvair, We Love It!", *Car and Driver* wrote: "Despite a widespread mis-

FIGURE 1

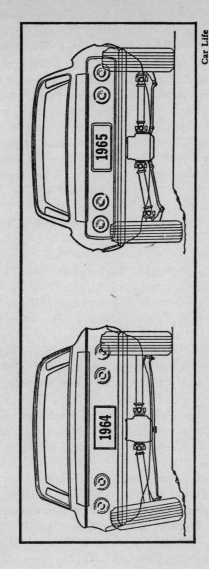

Car Life

Rear Suspension action, comparing 1964 and earlier swing-axle systems to the 1965 full independent axles. Note that as the rear wheels move down into an unevenness or bump, the wheels do not change camber as they did with the older system.

conception that the old Corvair was 'almost' a sports car, it was one of the nastiest-handling cars ever built. The tail gave little warning that it was about to let go, and when it did, it let go with a vengeance few drivers could cope with. The rear wheels would lose traction, tuck under, and with the tail end jacked up in the air, the car would swing around like a three-pound hammer on a thirty-foot string. This is not to say that the car was unstable within the limits of everyday, fair-weather driving—just that those limits were none too clearly posted and, once transgressed, you were in pretty hairy territory indeed. The new Corvair handles altogether differently from its predecessors. Final oversteer is still evident (as it must be in every rear-engined vehicle), but getting there is now half the fun, and it's by a new route."

Car Life, in describing the 1965 Corvair's better road manners, began their test drive apprehensively: "We approached this new Corvair with caution, as we have always had to approach Corvairs because of their somewhat unusual handling characteristics." A new and promising car magazine called *Road Test*, which accepts no automobile advertising, commented: "Previous to 1965, the car was probably the worst riding, worst all-around handling car available to the American public with the exception of the original Pontiac Tempest. Corvairs have a reputation of being 'tricky' cars to drive. Many have been involved in one-car accidents such as [the one] in which television comedian Ernie Kovacs lost his life." *Road Test* called the 1965 Corvair "one of the sweetest handling automobiles we have ever tested. The new line incorporates modifications the Corvair specialists such as Bill Corey, Bill Thomas and John Fitch have advocated for years."

Ever since the Corvair was introduced, General Motors' official reaction to criticisms has been silence. The handling hazards of Corvairs did not proceed from engineering mysteries or the prevalence of one technical 'school of thought' over another. The Corvair was a tragedy, not a blunder. The tragedy was overwhelmingly the fault of cutting corners to shave costs. This happens all the time in the automobile industry, but with the Corvair it happened in a big way. What was there for General Motors to say?

The tragedy of the Corvair did not begin that thirtieth day of September in 1959 when it went on display in dealer showrooms. Nor did it begin when Ford test drivers got hold of two Corvairs somewhat prematurely from a dealer in early September and lost control of them at the company's test track. It began with the conception and development of the Corvair by leading GM engineers—Edward Cole, Harry Barr, Robert Schilling, Kai Hansen and Frank Winchell.

Cole, now a General Motors' executive vice-president, provided the managerial ignition. He was an old devotee of rear-engined cars and right after World War II became involved with a short-lived experimental Cadillac having a rear engine. A prototype, ponderously bedecked with dual tires at the rear for stability, was soon shelved. To Cole, however, the idea of a rear-engined car remained attractive and he carried it over with him to Chevrolet and developed a project proposal as he rose in that division's hierarchy. In 1955, as chief engineer of Chevrolet, Cole saw a market for a small, "compact" car. Already an unpretentious import with a rear, air-cooled engine and independent suspension was "pre-testing" the American market with rising commercial success. But Cole and his associates were not in any mind merely to produce an American stereotype of the Volkswagen. This was to be a brand-new kind of car utilizing the lessons of past models and the advances of the latest automotive technology. When he rose to head Chevrolet division in the summer of 1956, Cole put some of his finest engineering talent to work on preliminary design work. In the spring of 1957, Barr, Schilling, and Hansen made formal presentations before the top-level GM engineering policy committee and the executive committee. It was then that the official go-ahead to build the Corvair was given to Chevrolet. Kai Hansen was made head of the project.

A small, light car project naturally would look to the European experience. This is what Hansen and his associates did before coming up with the Corvair design. To aid in such an evaluation, they had the benefit of one of GM's most creative engineers, Maurice Olley. Originally hailing from Rolls Royce, Olley was a prolific inventor with over twenty-five U.S. patents issued in his name and assigned to General Motors. His field of specialization was automobile handling behavior. In 1953 Olley delivered a technical paper, "European Postwar Cars," containing a sharp critique of rear-engined automobiles with swing-axle suspension systems. He called such vehicles "a poor bargain, at least in the form in which they are at present built," adding that they could not handle safely in a wind even at moderate speeds, despite tire pressure differential between front and rear. Olley went further, depicting the forward fuel tank as "a collision risk, as is the mass of the engine in the rear." Unmistakably, he had notified colleagues of the hurdles which had to be overcome.

Hansen's group was familiar with the risks of its appointed task. Its members knew well the kinds of priorities which would force them to dilute their engineering standards. First, the new automobile had to sell well and make a "target rate of return" on investment, according to GM's unique and well-established policy of guaranteed profits. The way to do this, General Motors' management decided, was to make a small, lighter car, with fuel economy, which would seat six passengers comfortably and give a ride comparable to a standard Chevrolet passenger sedan. Given the goal of designing a much lighter vehicle, this was no routine task. If these objectives could be achieved, the quest for profit maximization would have reached new frontiers. An automobile representing a reduction of 1,332 pounds of material, or more than one-third the weight of a standard 1960 Chevrolet, that could sell for only about $200 less than standard models would constitute a marvel of production cost efficiency and sales ingenuity.

In January 1960, Hansen told a meeting of the Society of Automotive Engineers: "Our first objective, once the decision was made to design a smaller, lighter car, was to attain good styling proportions. Merely shortening the wheel base and front and rear overhang was not acceptable. To permit lower overall height and to accommodate six adult passengers, the floor hump for the drive shaft had to go. Eliminating the conventional drive shaft made it essential then that the car have either rear-engine, rear-drive or front-engine, front-drive. Before making a decision, all types of European cars were studied, including front-engine, front-drive designs. None measured up to our standards of road performance."

Chevrolet engineers decided that the best and most "esthetically pleasant" utilization of passenger space dictated the use of a rear-engine, rear-drive design. This decision presented the problem, according to Hansen, of successfully applying the arrangement to a chassis that combines stability with a good ride and easy handling qualities. Hansen's job was to get the various factors working for safer handling—principally, front and rear weight-distribution, tire-pressure differentials and tire design, suspension geometry, and relative dynamic behavior in the front and rear—and still keep a soft ride and maximum cost reduction possible.

Hansen and his fellow engineers could not have been under any misapprehension as to the magnitude of the handling challenge before them. They had to deal with by far the heaviest rear-engined automobile in the western world, having between sixty and sixty-three per cent of its weight on the rear wheels. This fact alone posed handling problems considerably in excess of those afflicting the smaller and lighter rear-engined European cars. Ocee Ritch describes the consequences of this weight and size difference between rear-engined cars by way of simple analogy: "If you swing a bucket at the end of a short rope and accidentally hit your brother in the head, is he more apt to suffer a concussion if the bucket is empty or full? Similarly, if you increase the length of the rope and swing it at the same speed, will it cause more damage? Right on both counts. The more weight or the longer the arm, the more force is generated. In the case of the automobile, deviating from a straight line is the equivalent of swinging the bucket."

Automotive engineers will say, in defending their performance, that every car is a compromise with economic and stylistic factors. This statement, if true, is also meaningless. For the significant question is, who authorizes what compromises of engineering safety? Hansen has never publicly revealed what choices he would have preferred to take had he been given more authority against the erosive demands of the professional stylists and the cost department. The secret world of the automobile industry does not encourage free and open engineering discussion of alternative courses of action. But on occasion there is an exposition of what was actually done. Before a meeting of the Society of Automotive Engineers on April 1, 1960, in Detroit, Charles Rubly, a Chevrolet engineer who worked on the Corvair, gave his colleagues the practical considerations: "One of the obvious questions is: 'If you wish more of the roll couple to be taken on the front wheels, why did you leave the stabilizer off?' First, we felt the slight amount of gain realized did not warrant the cost; secondly, we did not wish to pay the penalty of increased road noise and harshness that results from use of a stabilizer. Another question that no doubt can be asked is why did we choose an independent rear suspension of this particular type? There are other swing-axle rear suspensions, of course, that permit transferring more of the roll couple to the front end. Our selection of this particular type of a swing-axle rear suspension is based on: (1) lower cost, (2) ease of assembly, (3) ease of service, and (4) simplicity of design. We also wished to take advantage of coil springs . . . in order to obtain a more pleasing ride . . ."

Mr. Rubly's four reasons could be reduced to one: lower cost. Having made such concessions, the Corvair engineers had to compensate for the strong oversteering tendency of the design. This was done by recommending to the Corvair owner certain critical tire pressure differentials which he should maintain between front and rear wheels. Corvair buyers received this advisory near the end of the owner's manual: "Over-steer problems may also be encountered with incorrect pressures. Maintain the recommended inflation pressures at all times."

No definition of "over-steer" is given in the manual. The recommended pressures are fifteen psi (pounds per square inch) on the front wheels and twenty-six psi on the rear wheels when cold (defined as "after car has been parked for three hours or more or driven less than one mile") and eighteen psi front and thirty psi rear when "hot." According to the Chevrolet division, such pressure differences promote vehicle stability by introducing proper steer characteristics.

It is well established that cornering stability can be improved with any weight distribution, front or rear, by manipulating tire inflation pressures. (Equally inflated tire pressures, front and rear, says Professor Eugene Larrabee of the Massachusetts Institute of Technology, makes the Corvair dangerous to drive.) But any policy which throws the burden of such stability on the driver by requiring him to monitor closely and persistently tire pressure differentials, cannot be described as sound or sane engineering practice. The prominent automotive engineer Robert Janeway expressed a deeply rooted technical opinion in engineering circles when he evaluated the use of this human expedient: "Instead of stability being inherent in the vehicle design, the operator is relied upon to maintain a required pressure differential in front and rear tires. This responsibility, in turn, is passed along to service station attendants, who are notoriously unreliable in abiding by requested tire pressures. There is also serious doubt whether the owner or service man is fully aware of the importance of maintaining the recommended pressures."

Corvair dealers and salesmen also have widely varying opinions about what are the best tire pressures. It is unusual to find one who adheres to or agrees with the owner's manual recommendations, although recently Chevrolet directives have reiterated the need for following the manual's figures. The apathy among dealers about the function of proper pressures for Corvair handling is quite unsettling. Dealer employees have routinely suggested to inquirers equivalent or near-equivalent tire pressure between front and rear. A Washington, D.C., dealer advised with assurance, "Carry twenty-four pounds in the front tires and twenty-six pounds in the rear." The owner's manual was wrong, he said, and concluded with the aside, "Cars are like women. They're all different." Whether it be in Los Angeles, Atlanta, St. Petersburg, New York, or Detroit, Corvair owners have been exposed to this kind of random and varying advice.

There is considerable dispute among automotive experts whether Chevrolet's recommended differentials of twenty-six and fifteen pounds per square inch are adequate. In a deposition of tire specialist Raymond B. Stringfield, taken on behalf of General Motors in one of the Corvair cases, the witness stated: "The Corvair recommends fifteen pounds in the front wheels. . . . Fifteen is dangerous under any circumstances for any purposes."

Ocee Ritch states flatly that the "suggested fifteen psi front, twenty-six psi rear (cold) or eighteen psi and thirty psi (hot) is far too low for high-speed driving or cornering." His recommended course of action requires a constant attention by the operator which proper vehicle design should have rendered wholly unnecessary. "Our prolonged experiments indicate that pressures should be increased until the tires begin to lose adhesion, then reduced slightly . . . a trial-and-error process, since production units are fitted with at least three brands of tires, each differing slightly from the other, plus the fact that loading and any suspension changes make significant differences."

The Corvair driver becomes puzzled on confronting such a range of advice. If he writes to the Chevrolet division for clarification, he receives a reply assuring him that the manual's recommendations are the optimum tire pressures and were derived after exhausting research and testing. But clearly a more heavily loaded Corvair, such as one with five passengers, requires different tire pressures to minimize differences in tire deflections front and rear. Corvair engineers knew about this problem and considered raising the recommended rear tire pressures. Once again, however, they succumbed to the great imperative—a soft ride. Rubly recounts it plainly enough: "The twenty-eight psi would reduce the rear-tire deflection enough but we did not feel that we should compromise ride and add harshness because under hot conditions tire pressures will increase three to four psi." Remarks such as these make it difficult to give full credence to company claims and advisories dealing with automotive safety. For behind the façade of engineering authority is the reality of the "trade-off"—auto industry cant for the bare-bones concessions to the cost and style men. The engineering assurances can not be taken at face value in such a context of undisclosed adulteration.

Another area intimately related to Corvair stability is the load-carrying capacity of the tires. According to the Tire and Rim Association, a tire industry standards group, the maximum permissible load capacity of the size tire used on the Corvair is 835 pounds per tire at twenty-four psi. These maximum permissible loads are derived after compromise between the tire manufacturers and the automobile companies. Yet even under these less than stringent standards, the rear tires of the Corvair are ordinarily overloaded with two or more passengers. Stringfield stated that four passengers would definitely overload the tires. During his deposition, he was questioned about the tire air-out * during the vehicle's cornering. His reply: "The Corvair is, with any passengers at all, very near the maximum-rated load on the rear tires and a sudden thrust [as when a wheel slides while cornering] is capable of forcing the bead inward, unless the air pressure is sufficiently high to resist it; and a tubeless tire is more dangerous in that respect than a tire with an inner tube, because the inner tube prevents the escape of air, if there is only a slight movement, and forces the bead back into place."

"Under-tired" vehicles are not new to the automobile industry. Since the end of World War II, progressively shaving costs off tires has been one of the cost department's most successful triumphs. A multiplier is operating here; a saving on one tire means

* A sudden loss of air around the tire rim without the tire being punctured.

savings on all five tires. But although it is not uncommon for other vehicles, overloading tires on the Corvair, in combination with its other unique features such as weight distribution, is particularly hazardous.

With such precarious weight distribution and tire load, Chevrolet division's relocation of the spare tire from the front, where it was in the 1960 Corvair, to the rear for the 1961 Corvair Monza was greeted with sheer incredulity by independent Corvair specialists. The reason for the switch was to increase the luggage space in the front "trunk." This switch not only added to the rear-end weight but exposed the tire in the engine compartment to possibly harmful temperatures. Also, there is a hidden danger to the uninitiated driver who takes out this warm spare tire, fills it with the prescribed air pressures, and mounts it on his vehicle. As the tire cools, the air pressure diminishes. The driver is neither given nor advised to carry a tire gauge. Nor is there a tire pressure alarm to warn drivers when a tire is under-inflated, though such a device is available as a truck accessory. But he is urged to purchase an air conditioner, which involves placing about 105 pounds of extra equipment in the rear-engine compartment, further exacerbating weight imbalance.

It would not be fair to say that the Corvair engineers designed a vehicle but forgot about the driver. They knew the risks in a design where the car usurps the driving task under certain expected stresses of highway travel. These stresses occur not just in high-speed emergency conditions but in ordinary driving situations within legal speed limits. The combination of factors which leads to the critical point of control loss may occur with a statistical infrequency, but the traditional integrity of automotive design has been to embrace just such situations. Stability limitations, for example, must be evaluated under the most unfavorable loading conditions—six passengers with luggage in the case of the Corvair even though most mileage registered by Corvairs will be with fewer passengers.

When it serves their promotional interests, the automobile manufacturers show great concern about the most infrequently occurring situations. A continuing illustration is the elaborate defenses which they make for producing vehicles with up to four hundred horsepower and a speed capability reaching 150 miles per hour. Is such power and speed hazardous? Not at all, claim the companies, for they provide an important margin of safety in emergency conditions. Apparently emergency conditions include speeds up to and over 100 miles an hour.

The men who headed the Corvair project knew that the driver should be given a vehicle whose handling is both controllable and predictable. They knew that impossible demands could be placed upon the driver by an inherently oversteering vehicle. For the past thirty-five years, American cars have been designed so as to be basically understeering. The Corvair was the first mass-produced exception. Dr. Thomas Manos, the highly respected automotive engineering professor at the University of Detroit, is not teaching Hansen's group anything they do not know when he states his judgment about oversteering automobiles: "The driver must become aware that he has to continually fight the wheel or continuously correct because he is the factor which makes the vehicle a stable piece of equipment." Hansen's group didn't forget about the driver. They did not have the professional stamina to defend their engineering principles from the predatory clutches of the cost-cutters and stylists. They did not forget the driver; they ignored him.

There is no dispute in automotive engineering literature that an oversteering, rear-engined vehicle demands more attention on the part of the driver during cornering and other situations where centrifugal forces come into play. The reason for this is plain. General Motors' John Gordon's explanation is helpful. "If you're making a right-hand turn, there's a tendency for the car to move more to the right than you will anticipate it would in relation to the amount of movement you put on the steering wheel." The driver must *let up* on the steering wheel to correct the tendency of the rear end of the car to run outward more on a curve than the front end. But steering the front wheels away from the inside of the curve becomes more difficult with increasing speeds of forty, fifty, or sixty miles per hour. Robert Janeway, former director of Chrysler's dynamic research department, holds that an oversteer condition "is both disconcerting and dangerous except to an expert driver of sports cars or racing cars. The required reversal of steering-wheel direction after initiating the turn is an unstable situation that is difficult for the ordinary driver to handle without overcorrection, with potentially dangerous swings on both sides of the proper curved path. From the standpoint of safety, oversteer is an intolerable condition and has always been recognized as such by the industry in the U.S."

Compared with oversteering, an understeering condition is an inherently stable one. On a curve, the front end tends to run wide and in order to negotiate the curve the driver has to steer inward even more sharply. This is a naturally predictable, automatic response. An understeering car, in John Fitch's words, "responds to the instinctive reaction of the driver," particularly the unskilled driver.

Instability of rear-engined oversteering vehicles on a straight road when there are crosswinds is a well-known phenomenon. The light front end tends to make the vehicle's directional path conform with that of the wind forces. Corvair drivers have often had the feeling of the wind pressing their car toward the side of the road. Serious accidents can result from a car's vulnerability to crosswinds.

During the design stage, Hansen's group tried to counteract the Corvair's inherent oversteer by employing wider wheel rims for increased tire cornering power and by building some understeer into both front and rear suspension systems according to well-known principles. But it is clear that they were not permitted to go as far as their engineering integrity should have dictated. The type of swing-axle rear suspension used on the 1960-1964 Corvairs is simple and cheap to manufacture and assemble. But it contained a hazard that was quite independent of the engine location. The rear wheel is mounted on a control arm which hinges and pivots on an axis at the inboard end of the arm near the center of the vehicle. This design is inordinately encouraging to tuck-under of the outside wheel on cornering which, of course, reduces the wheel's cornering capability and aggravates the oversteer effect. The limitation of this swing axle setup is described in a patent filed in 1959 by a Chevrolet suspension engineer, Johannes W. Rosenkrands and assigned to General Motors. Until the 1964 Corvair, the only component limiting downward wheel travel was the shock absorber—a function which shock absorbers are not designed to serve.

What most sets the 1960-1963 Corvairs apart from light foreign vehicles with comparable percentages of weight distributions and swing axles is the sudden onset of the critical point at which the vehicle goes out of control and frequently flips over. This point

FIGURE 2: UNCONTROLLED SWING AXLE ACTION IN ONE TYPE OF CORVAIR INSTABILITY. SEEN FROM REAR.

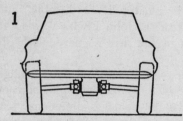
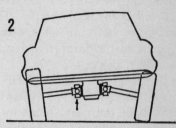

1. *Moderately loaded car on straightaway (slight positive camber)*

2. *Moderate right turn. Left axle angle allows centrifugal force of turn to cause beginning lift at arrow.*

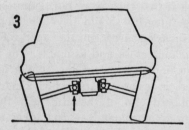
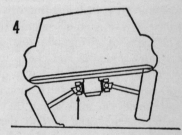

3. *Critical right turn with tuck under—approaching rear end breakaway slide. Axle angle causes aggravated lift.*

4. *Breakaway, extreme tuck-under, and incipient rollover.*

is reached by any number of combinations of vehicle speed, radius of the curve, and tire inflation pressures. For example, tests have shown a Corvair moving out of control at about twenty-two mph, with twenty-six psi in front and rear tires, and turning on a fifty-degree radius of curvature. At higher speeds, a less sharp curve is required to achieve the same rear-end breakaway. But passing maneuvers on a highway could easily involve a severe turn during the swing out and in. Janeway points out that what is most significant is that "critical speeds can occur in the normal driving speed range on sharp curves even at moderate degrees of oversteer." Other makes of vehicles can be made to oversteer through drastic tire inflation differentials, or very heavy loading, but as the forces produced mount toward the critical point, they give a warning to the driver in the "feedback" he receives through the steering wheel, if indeed he is not forewarned by the under-inflated tires before or as he gets underway. (See Fig. 2)

The Corvair is different in the 1960-1963 models and to a lesser extent in the 1964 model. At a critical point of lateral acceleration (or centrifugal force), there is a sudden rear-wheel tuck-under. Technically, the positive camber increases radically 4° to 10° or 11° camber—a horrifying shift causing violent skidding, rear-end break-away or vehicle roll-over. The change occurs without any warning and in an instant. A variety of disturbing forces may cause this sudden tuck-under—tire side skidding, gusts of crosswind, the second leg of an S-shaped curve or a comparable cornering maneuver. All these are conditions that the engineer should take into account during his advance analysis of vehicles for potential design faults. Near the critical point, it takes an expert driver to provide the corrective steering action—assuming highway conditions permit and there are no obstructions, such as another vehicle or a tree.

But the Corvair was not built to be sold only to champion racing drivers. And when the critical point is reached, even Dan Gurney would be unable to control the Corvair. The car was built and sold as "easy handling," as "a family sedan," as a car that "purrs for the girls," according to some of the General Motors' advertisements. Understanding the way it was built during the first four years of the model provides in turn a better understanding of General Motors' great emphasis on "defensive driving" when it exhorts the drivers of this country to be more careful.

In ways wholly unique, the Corvair can become a single-minded, aggressive machine. One factor has been noticed in many single-car Corvair upsets. This is where the rear wheel tucks under so far that the rim touches the roadway. When this occurs no driver can control the vehicle, which will be lifted up and very likely turn over. Rim scrapings or gouge marks on the road have become the macabre trademark of Corvairs going unexpectedly out of control.

Derwyn Severy has been working in the field of automobile collision research for fifteen years at U.C.L.A.'s Institute of Transportation and Traffic Engineering. He has received state, federal, and automobile industry grants for his collision testing, experiments acclaimed by industry and non-industry engineering colleagues. General Motors, Ford, Chrysler and American Motors have all had their automobiles privately evaluated at various times by Severy's group. Since 1959 Severy has been aware of and deeply disturbed by the Corvair's handling characteristics. He has found the vehicle, because of its directional instability, to demand more driving skill in order to avoid collision than any other American automobile.

Does he know of any other domestic car with recommended tire pressure differentials—front and rear—of such magnitude? Severy says he does not. If passengers occupy the rear seat area of these Corvairs, would it increase the oversteer characteristics? "Yes," he replied. Must certain pressures be maintained to reduce somewhat the vehicle's inherent directional instability? "Yes." Is the use of a technique that places the continuous responsibility on the driver a safe procedure to follow? "No." He elaborates: "Where the public at large is expected to maintain this tire pressure understanding, then I'd say it becomes a dangerous situation to the extent that the vehicle is sensitive to oversteer or directional instability from variations in tire pressure."

The Corvair tragedy consisted of a series of lost opportunities. When the vehicle was being designed and tested in prototype quantities, the Chevrolet division had fully developed and rigorous proving ground, laboratory, and theoretical tests for determining vehicle handling characteristics and directional stability. Proving ground facilities were equipped with instrumentation for evaluating the sensitivity of a vehicle and its tendencies to oversteer under a wide range of conditions. At the same time, General Motors had instruments which could have programed even steering responses of the driver and determined the extent of "feedback" that the operator depends upon from the handling behavior of the vehicle to govern his driving actions. As far back as 1953, Lyle A. Walsh of the GM engineering staff was writing in the *General Motors Engineering Journal* about well-established techniques of putting a car's suspension system under the scrutiny of scientific laboratories while the car was in action. In 1958 the same journal contained a report by Chevrolet engineers Robert Graham and Ronald Shafer about a new simulator to test vehicle suspensions. A year later, Chevrolet's Max Roensch described the four-year-old Chevrolet engineering laboratory, including the elaborate test and development techniques available to supplement the findings of the General Motors' proving ground under actual vehicle driving conditions. He listed the basic responsibilities of the laboratory:

(a) To evaluate the performance and durability of proposed designs, using established test standards;

(b) To establish test standards;

(c) To correlate laboratory investigations with both field experience and GM proving ground test findings;

(d) To supply test data that document and supplement vehicle road tests;

(e) To study all vehicle characteristics or problems under controlled conditions;

(f) To accelerate test results by duplicating actual conditions more quickly than is possible in normal vehicle use or test driving;

(g) To build, adjust, measure, and record all vehicle components before tests, to analyze and record test results;

(h) To provide advance test and development before complete assemblies or vehicles are available.

Taken even at face value, this is a formidable obstacle course through which the handling deficiencies of the Corvair could not have passed undetected.

Mathematical techniques for analyzing vehicle handling qualities were available to General Motors since the first "Cornell equations" were developed under General Motors' sponsorship at the Cornell Aeronautical Laboratory in Buffalo, New York, between 1953 and 1955. The engineering mechanics department of GM research laboratories further advanced this theoretical research. Basically, the Cornell equations show how a vehicle should behave, given certain combinations of variables, each of which affects control and stability. Computers then analyze the control and handling performance of a vehicle as it would be affected by these variables.

Obviously, proving grounds, laboratory and theoretical testing and analysis provided the Corvair engineers with the data to document thoroughly the design limitations of the Corvair before it went into production. The drastic tuck-under hazard, for example, is easily determined by a study of the dynamic "moments" of the rear wheel cornering forces about the universal joint's pivot point for each swing axle in the rear-suspension system. Professor Manos, who views the tuck-under problem as the most serious defect of the 1960-1963 Corvairs, has said that he would flunk any student who would not work this calculation out in any automotive engineering course. It is just that elementary and crucial a calculation to vehicle safety.

Yet a safer Corvair suspension system was not forthcoming—not in 1960, not in 1961, not in 1962 and not in 1963. With the receipt of hundeds of written complaints sent to General Motors by people whose Corvairs had suddenly gone out of control, and the real threat of many lawsuits which must have been anticipated by company lawyers, the absence of any corrective action year after year can only be explained by bureaucratic rigidities and the abject worship of that bitch-goddess, cost reduction.

But at last Chevrolet moved to improve the 1964 models. The engineers at GM are very obedient. Given the green light, they did what they long knew could and should be done. A transverse leaf spring in the rear and a front anti-sway bar were included as standard equipment for 1964 models. The leaf spring served much the same function as the EMPI Camber Compensator and substantially reduced the tuck-under hazard. The 1965 Corvair came out with a more fundamental change in the form of a link-type suspension with dual control arms. These improvements represented new company policy, but not engineering innovations. They drew on well-developed knowledge that went back into GM's empirical work during the thirties and extending to the experimental rear-engined race car developed after World War II by Chevrolet's key suspension engineer, Zora Arkus-Duntov.

It was no longer necessary to rely upon outside evidence to establish the risky gaps in pre-1964 Corvair engineering. General Motors provided the proof with its 1964 and 1965 model modifications. A way was found to overcome the problems of ride and cost which Chevrolet's Rubly found so insistent during the making of the Corvair.

While General Motors may have finally lumbered into engineering improvements, it would be corporate heresy for the proud industry leader to worry about the hundreds of thousands of Corvairs waiting for the law of averages to catch up with them on some S-curve or breezy straightaway. After all, those Corvairs were already sold.

At the May 1965 annual shareholders' meeting in Detroit's vast Cobo Hall, Dr. Seymour Charles, a General Motors' stockholder and the founder of the Physicians for Automotive Safety, rose to plead with management to call back to dealer stations all remaining 1960-1963 Corvairs in order that life-saving stabilizing components might be installed. Dr. Charles was not able to arrive at a cost estimate since there is no way of knowing how many such Corvairs are still roaming the highways. (*Motor Trends'* technical editor, Jim Wright, noted in 1963 that the "wrecking yards have a good selection these days.") But assuming that 750,000 cars have survived, the most money that such a recall would cost would be $25 million: equivalent to under a half-day's gross sales, or less than five days net profits (after taxes) to General Motors. This sum would include instructing owners, far more clearly than by placing a note in the little-read and often lost owner's manual *, about the importance of tire pressure differentials and about the meaning of oversteering in terms of driver response.

On the platform in front of Dr. Charles were General Motors' board chairman, Frederic G. Donner and its president, John F. Gordon. Mr. Donner was presiding over the meeting. He deflected the request by inviting Dr. Charles to come up after the meeting to discuss his problems with several of the executives.

Mr. Gordon sat impassively watching Dr. Charles become the first shareholder ever to raise openly at a General Motors' annual meeting the question of specific unsafe vehicle design. The presi-

---

* William F. Sherman, technical director of the Automobile Manufacturers Association, was speaking for the industry when he said in 1961, "We've long since given up on the idea that the motorist will read the owner's manual."

dent of General Motors really knew very little about the Corvair or the trouble it has caused its victims—and his own company's lawyers. At the time of GM approval of Chevrolet's Corvair design in 1957, Gordon was group vice-president of the body and assembly divisions. This entitled him to membership on both the top-level engineering policy group and the executive committee which approved the Corvair design. He was one of the five men responsible for the final approval of the most "revolutionary" automotive package which GM had ever presented to the domestic market. As an automotive engineer with several patents to his credit, Mr. Gordon might have been expected to interest himself in this substantial debut. Yet on April 10, 1965, under deposition, Mr. Gordon stated that he did not recall the Corvair design being presented to the engineering policy group. He admitted that he did not know what kind of rear-end suspension was on the Corvair design that was approved for production by his committees.

Gordon became president of General Motors in 1958. In the ensuing seven years he ordered no inquiry into the Corvair design in spite of rising and unprecedented litigation, owner complaints and detailed confidential company-sponsored investigations of Corvair accidents involving directional instability. He said he had never heard of the stabilizing equipment produced especially for the Corvair by other, smaller manufacturers.

In his defense, Gordon says his duties were primarily administrative and that he relied on subordinates with technical competence. One such technical subordinate was Charles Chayne, vice-president of engineering. Until his retirement in 1963, Mr. Chayne was a prolific writer and speaker about engineering excellence and safety, addressing professional, trade, and legislative audiences. In the May-June 1956 issue of the *General Motors Engineering Journal,* he wrote that the function of the engineering policy group was to review "proposed major departures from current engineering practices suggested by the divisions and also make final recommendations on any new major engineering programs, such as new car models." Mr. Chayne went further to describe in detail a primary objective of General Motors' product engineering organization: "To keep informed on behavior of our products in the hands of our customers so that improvements and corrections can be made if required." He then stated a key principle of General

Motors' operating philosophy: "Coordinated control refers to the formulation of overall policy and control of the flow of information. A two-way flow of information exists at each level of management—the downward flow from authority and the upward flow from initiative."

In the making of the Corvair, there was a breakdown in this flow of both authority and initiative. Initiative would have meant an appeal by the Corvair design engineers to top management to overrule the cost-cutters and stylists whose incursions had placed unsafe constraints on engineering choice. There are, however, deterrents to such action that regularly prompt the design engineer to shirk his professional duty. It is to the keepers of those most sacred totems—cost reduction and style—that corporate status and authority accrue. Anyone skeptical about the role of pennies in the production of America's most expensive durable consumer product should listen to Buick's Edward Ragsdale tell about putting a new car into production: "Cost estimates are given the closest possible scrutiny, and they frequently are calculated to the fourth and fifth decimal place. The difference of just two cents per car doesn't sound like very much—but at current production rates, two cents a car may mean $10,000 for the model run. Hence the cost decision has a great bearing upon all proposed changes."

With a spectacular profit record and over 50 per cent of the domestic automobile market, General Motors is least vulnerable to competitive pressures that might have been the reason for cutting costs at the expense of Corvair safety. It is not commonly realized that General Motors' return on invested capital and its net income as a percentage of its sales are about double those of its nearest competitor—the Ford Motor Company. In 1964, for example, Ford had a net income, as a percentage of sales, of 5.6% and an 11.3% return on invested capital. The comparable General Motors figures were 10.2% and 20.4% respectively. These are remarkable differences in American industry for the two leading companies in a highly concentrated product line such as automobiles. It may not be surprising, if still shocking, to have a Corvair-type tragedy issue from an auto manufacturer whose declining sales and high costs were driving it to the wall. But coming from General Motors, such behavior—and the fact that it is tolerated—is a syndrome of a much deeper malaise that radiates beyond corporate borders and into society.

On May 18, 1956, almost a year before the Corvair project was launched, the former head of research and development for the Chevrolet Division, Maurice Olley, filed a patent application (issued as #2,911,052 on November 3, 1959) where he said what he thought of the Corvair-type suspension: "The ordinary swing axle, under severe lateral forces produced by cornering, tends to lift the rear-end of the vehicle so that both wheels assume severe positive camber positions to such an extent that the vehicle not only 'oversteers' but actually tends to roll over. In addition, the effect is non-linear and increases suddenly in a severe turn, thus presenting potentially dangerous vehicle handling characteristics."

Olley's judgment was ignored.

2
Disaster deferred:
Studies in automotive time bombs

The American automobile is produced exclusively to the standards which the manufacturer decides to establish. It comes into the marketplace unchecked. When a car becomes involved in an accident, the entire investigatory, enforcement and claims apparatus that makes up the post-accident response looks almost invariably to driver failure as the cause. The need to clear the highways rapidly after collisions contributes further to burying the vehicle's role. Should vehicle failure be obvious in some accidents, responsibility is seen in terms of inadequate maintenance by the motorist. Accommodated by superficial standards of accident investigation, the car manufacturers exude presumptions of engineering excellence and reliability, and this reputation is accepted by many unknowing motorists.

How many victims of Corvair tuck-under—those who survived —know why their vehicle suddenly went out of control? General Motors' Charles Chayne can say, with little fear of contradiction by consumers, that "excellence of automotive engineering is almost taken for granted by the public." Beggars at the trough have no alternative.

Mr. Chayne had occasion to appear before legislative committees between 1956 and 1963 as General Motors' chief safety spokesman. Between his long and well illustrated presentations of company policy and performance, and his guided tours of legislators around company proving grounds, he was never asked about the matter of the 1953 Buick Roadmaster. The Roadmaster episode, unlike other operating failures, became a matter of public record only because of a private lawsuit—scarcely the best means for informing the public about a booby trap that suddenly leaves a two-ton automobile without brakes.

Robert Comstock, a veteran garage mechanic at the Lawless Buick Company in Ferndale, Michigan, found out what a brakeless Roadmaster felt like. On the morning of January 18, 1954, he was putting a license plate on another car inside the garage when a Roadmaster driven by Clifford Wentworth, the assistant service manager, ran into his leg and crushed it. Wentworth had taken the car from its owner, Leon Friend, a few minutes earlier. Friend was complaining that the day before he had experienced a sudden and total loss of braking power, luckily at a very low speed. When Wentworth got into the car to move it to a service stall, he forgot there were no brakes and rammed into Comstock. Wentworth was shaken deeply enough by this tragedy to leave his job. But the story he told the Wayne County Circuit Court when Comstock and his workmen's compensation carrier sued him and General Motors was a horror tale of larger proportions than this single case.

Here are Wentworth's exchanges with Comstock's lawyer and the judge:

Counsel: Now, did you find any complaints or anything wrong with the power brake units in the 1953 Buick automobiles?
Wentworth: Yes sir.
Counsel: When did you first discover anything wrong?
Wentworth: Shortly after the cars began using power brake systems.
Counsel: And can you tell us about when these 1953 Buicks with power brakes came out?
Wentworth: It would be in the fall. I don't know the exact date.
The Court: Fall of 1952?

Wentworth: Yes, I believe so.

Counsel: And about how soon after that did you begin to find trouble?

Wentworth: A matter of weeks, I believe. Loss of fluid and failure of the brakes. The "O" ring sealer would fail and fluid would be sucked into the engine and burned with the gasoline.

Counsel: Do I understand correctly in a power brake unit you have a master cylinder with fluid in it?

Wentworth: Yes sir.

Counsel: You have a sort of plunger, is that right?

Wentworth: That is right.

Counsel: You press the brakes, the plunger goes down and puts the fluid under pressure?

Wentworth: That is correct.

＊ ＊ ＊

Counsel: This fluid is distributed by pipes to the four wheels of the car, is that correct?

Wentworth: Yes.

Counsel: And that pressure is distributed to each of the four wheels where it operates on each one of the brakes?

Wentworth: Yes, sir.

Counsel: The "O" ring sealer would be what?

Wentworth: A sealer between the vacuum cylinder and master cylinder.

＊ ＊ ＊

Counsel: Now, the motor sucking the fluid out of the cylinder would cause the fluid to disappear, is that correct?

Wentworth: That is correct.

Counsel: And when the fluid disappeared, what happened to the brakes?

Wentworth: The brakes were lost immediately.

＊ ＊ ＊

Counsel: Did the Lawless Company sell many cars equipped with this kind of unit?

Wentworth: Many cars.

Counsel: How frequently did the buyers complain?

Wentworth: Well, I don't know the exact number, but we couldn't get parts fast enough to repair them, sir.

＊ ＊ ＊

Counsel: How is it you say two or three weeks or months after, a month or two after the model was out you got word from General Motors to get all these cars in, and they were worried about it, and ten months went by before anything was ever said to Mr. Friend?

Wentworth: I could not attempt an active mailing campaign to get these customers in. People as they came in were told.

The Court: You called him, didn't you?

Wentworth: He contacted me first with brake trouble. Then there were telephone conversations.

The Court: You mean in that ten months' time you hadn't ever called him up?

Wentworth: I could have.

* * *

The Court: You said Buick was very much disturbed about this and wanted to get in touch with everybody immediately?

Wentworth: This is correct.

The Court: Ten months went by and you never did anything about this?

Wentworth: Because I was not allowed a campaign to call these people or mail anything to them.

The Court: They asked you to call them.

Wentworth: They said to get these cars whenever you could get your hands on them. When a customer didn't come around I couldn't look up the thing. I thought it was Buick's responsibility. . . .

The Court: Who said you couldn't send letters?

Wentworth: The Service Department at Buick. It was a hush thing. They didn't want the public to know the brakes were bad and they were very alarmed.

* * *

The Court: If you don't mind I would like to ask a question. You said you were notified shortly after this model was out that when anybody brought their car in to make sure they didn't go out without having the brakes fixed?

Wentworth: We were notified to get these cars in, but I couldn't get parts, sir, so it dragged on and on.

The Court: What happened when cars came in?

Wentworth: They sat, usually.

The Court: What if somebody came in, did you tell them?

Wentworth: No. I was looking after the best interests of my boss and General Motors. I certainly didn't want to ruin their sales.

The Court: If a man came in with these kind of brakes, the brakes that were on this 1953 model, you said they told you it was a dangerous condition, and any time they came in to see that the brakes were fixed, or tell them about it?

Wentworth: If I told the man I couldn't fix it I was in a lot of trouble. What could I do? We couldn't get parts.

The Court: You mean even if he came in to have his 1,000 mile check-up, like Mr. Friend in June, or came back after his vacation in July or August, you didn't say anything to him about it because you did not have the parts?

Wentworth: That is right.

The Court: Even though you knew it was a very dangerous condition and people might be killed?

Wentworth: Like everything else, and you can get testimony from any of the boys working with me that I was terribly alarmed. . . . I don't run General Motors.

On the witness stand Wentworth displayed strong concern that the Buick division could not supply him with parts to repair the brake defect. It was not until November 1953—well over a year after the offending 1953 Roadmasters were placed on the market —that Buick began to ease this anguish of its dealers. Elmer Krause, the general service manager of Buick, testified that replacement kits for the defective parts were at that time manufactured. He declared that Buick made 7,988 of these kits available to its dealers in the fourth quarter of 1953, and that 44,126 such kits were produced in the first quarter of 1954. In addition, Buick sent to its dealers throughout the country a special bulletin entitled "Empty Power Brake Reservoirs: 1953 power brake-equipped Buicks." The date of the bulletin was November 2, 1953. Along with the failure of the "O" ring seal in the master brake cylinder, this bulletin revealed another cause of the Roadmaster's brake failure: "This trouble has been diagnosed as a poor fit between the base of the hydraulic cylinder casting and the vacuum can. . . . This then does not permit equal pressure to the "O" ring seal between the two surfaces and allows vacuum to pull oil from the reservoir pipe past the threads of the retainer holding the seal and primary cup—then into the can, up the vacuum pipe, and into the engine."

But the principal defect—the failure of the "O" ring seal—was identified by Charles Holton, Buick's brake engineer. It was this failure which, without warning, would find the driver pressing his brake foot pedal clear to the floor boards without any braking power resulting. Apparently, to Buick's way of thinking, the manufacturer of such a vehicle was not under any obligation to warn its car buyers of this hazard. Mr. Krause's testimony is right to the point:

Counsel: Mr. Krause, did the Buick Motor Division ever contact the owners of these cars?

Krause: No, sir.

Counsel: Didn't advertise what the conditions were?

Krause: No, sir.

Counsel: Were any parts ever sent to a dealer as replacement unless he asked for them?

Krause: No, sir.

Counsel: I take it nothing was done at all by the Buick Motor Company or Buick division of General Motors unless and until the parts were asked for and then they were given, if possible?

Krause: The parts were ordered by the dealer and shipped to the dealer by us.

Counsel: That is all the Buick Company did?

Krause: Well, other than put out the technical information such as the bulletin you just read there.

Judge Thomas Murphy pressed this inquiry further:

The Court: You didn't call them up and say, get all these cars in and have them repaired?

Krause: No, sir.

Counsel: Why not?

Krause: Well, in the first place that is the obligation of the dealer, and in the second place we don't know who all the owners are or where they are.

Counsel: Did they ever do anything to find out?

Krause: We have no right to tell the dealer how to run his business. He is an independent businessman.

Counsel: But did you do anything to find out?

Krause: No.

In view of the notorious pressure and manipulation of automobile dealers by car manufacturers, Mr. Krause's interposition of dealer independence as a defense for Buick's irresponsibility seems less than charitable. His statement that Buick did not know who all the owners were is hardly straightforward; dealers have lists of all new car buyers, and their addresses are available to the company. While a small percentage of new Buick resales by their original owners might have made location of these second owners difficult, the overwhelming majority were within reach of the mails. But knowing the names of the owners was not really the problem. The obstacle was, as Charles Holton conceded in court, that Buick does not under any circumstances send letters directly to owners. Nor, according to Mr. Krause, did the Buick division ask its dealers to get these automobiles back for repair. This statement contrasts with Mr. Wentworth's testimony that Buick did request such action, but only on condition that the owners were not made aware of the problem.

The evidence seems to favor Mr. Wentworth's version. Testimony in his case showed that the replacement unit provided by Buick was without charge to the owner and that Buick paid the labor cost of installation.

In spite of all the evidence pointing to the negligence of General

Motors, Mr. Comstock lost his case. Lawyers for General Motors asked and received a directed verdict right after the plaintiff rested his case. In his opinion, Judge Murphy said it was his belief that General Motors was negligent in not notifying Mr. Friend to have the brakes repaired. But he thought that Mr. Wentworth's action of driving the car without brakes into Comstock's leg was "a new and independent proximate cause of the injury," which superseded the negligence of General Motors.

Comstock appealed to the supreme court of Michigan and set the stage for a memorable opinion by a unanimous court. Justice Edwards rendered a decision overruling the trial judge and sending the case back for a new trial. His words defined certain standards which seem almost elementary, yet which do not operate today:

The braking system is obviously one of the most crucial safety features of the modern automobile. The greatly increased speed and weight of a modern automobile are factors which must be considered in relation to the care which would be reasonable for a manufacturer to use in designing, fabricating, assembling, and inspecting a power brake. A modern automobile equipped with brakes which fail without notice is as dangerous as a loaded gun. . . .

Defendant's Buick division warned its dealers. It did not warn those into whose hands they had placed this dangerous instrument and whose lives (along with the lives of others) depended upon defective brakes which might fail without notice.

In our view, the facts in this case imposed a duty on defendant to take all reasonable means to convey effective warning to those who had purchased '53 Buicks with power brakes when the latent defect was discovered. . . .

If such a duty to warn of a known danger exists at point of sale, we believe a like duty to give prompt warning exists when a latent defect which makes the product hazardous to life becomes known to the manufacturer shortly after the product has been put on the market. This General Motors did not do. . . .

This record shows that Friend took good care of his automobile. Prompt warning to him would in all likelihood have meant repair before any brake failure occurred. Prompt warning could easily have prevented this accident.

Justice Edwards' opinion, rendered on November 25, 1959, sent the case back for a new trial. But General Motors was in no mood to risk another trial against the background of the stinging rebukes and strict guidelines of the supreme court of Michigan. The company settled with Comstock for $75,000 as compensation for the loss of his leg.

The Comstock case brought out facts revealing the utter abdication of responsibility and a deliberate withholding of lifesaving facts that would have prompted, in other fields of public safety, an investigation by authorities. But the Comstock decision had no impact on public policy. General Motors later settled a case in Pennsylvania involving an engineer whose Roadmaster brakes failed on a hill and sent him to his death. Beyond these two cases, the company emerged unscathed. There was no publicity.

However neglected the lesson of Comstock has been by public agencies, it has become a keystone case for attorneys representing the car manufacturers. Recently, these lawyers seem to have made their voices heard at Chrysler and Ford to the point where the watchword has become, "Automotive danger requires warning." In October 1964 the Ford Motor Company mailed a letter to some 30,000 owners of the 1965 full-sized Fords. The letter said: "In order to provide you with the highest quality product available, the Ford Motor Company has decided to improve the rear suspension arm attachment by adding a reinforcement bracket to each side. . . . We would like you to bring your Ford car up to current specification and appreciate your cooperation in making your car available to your Ford dealer for that purpose."

These are soothing words, more attuned to the ear of a fastidious car owner than to the motorist who might simply want to stay alive. They hardly convey the disaster which might occur if a suspension arm were to break loose from the chassis frame and lead to the vehicle's veering wildy out of control. When asked for further elaboration by the *Chicago Daily News,* R. C. Graham, national service operations manager of Ford division, replied: "We do not consider the modification a safety factor." Another Ford spokesman, responding to a similar inquiry by Consumers Union, described the offered improvement as nothing more than a refinement to preserve "a quiet ride." The same spokesman said that he did not know how many of the 30,000 Fords which slipped past factory inspectors have had their rear suspension arms reinforced.

In November 1964, Chrysler Corporation sent only to its dealers a bulletin urging them to recall for inspection certain 1965 Plymouth Furys, Chryslers, and full-sized Dodges (denoted by serial numbers) to determine whether the bracket holding the steering gear needed rewelding. As in the Ford case, some 30,000 cars were involved. To Chrysler's credit, it admitted that safety was a consideration in sending out its bulletin. After all, a vehicle's handling could become somewhat difficult should the steering gear break loose. But the company made no attempt to get in touch directly with the car buyer or find out how many unmodified cars were not brought back to dealers.

Consumers Union's automotive consultants considered the Ford case more serious than the Chrysler one. Yet Ford stuck to its story that the letters were sent for the purpose of preserving "a quiet ride."

The fact that automobiles are produced with faulty features or components is commonplace knowledge to those working in the industry. Although he tried later to qualify his statement in an interview with the *Wall Street Journal,* L. Ralph Mason, manufacturing manager of the Chevrolet division, stated unequivocally in a written message to Chevrolet plant supervisors, "I am deeply concerned about the quality we are building in our cars today." He had good reason to be. The industry's 1965 models fell to new depths of shoddy workmanship. *Consumer Reports* summarized for its readers the findings of its automobile testing specialists: "The condition of the 1965 cars Consumers Union has bought for test is about the worst, so far as sloppiness in production goes, in the whole ten-year stretch of deterioration that began in 1955, the first year in which U.S. new car sales first approached eight million. Complaint in the trade about the condition of the cars as delivered began to get bitter then and it has continued to be bitter ever since."

Tests of the 1963 models purchased at random by Consumers Union had resulted in thirty-two of thirty-two cars displaying troubles in the first 5000 miles of driving. The defects included rain leaks, a window running out of its channel, door handles that fell off, a broken distributor cap, a speedometer needle that fell back to zero and remained there, a broken seat adjuster, an ignition lock that wouldn't lock, a door that wouldn't latch, engines that leaked oil, directional signals that wouldn't cancel, a grossly inaccurate gas gauge, front wheels out of alignment, and headlights, as the late Mildred Brady of Consumers Union put it, "that aimed at the ground or at the eyes of approaching motorists or at the birds in trees."

Consumers Union's testing facilities in Connecticut are thorough as far as they go, but they are limited by the budgetary considerations of an organization whose only income is subscription payments for its magazine. Each car is tested for a few thousand miles at most. The more latent defects, such as early metal fatigue of suspension arms or rusting-through of hydraulic lines, that would appear on cars driven by ordinary motorists, are not likely to show up and be recorded for the public's safety information.

Some of the most detailed documentation publicly available about defective vehicle construction comes out of litigation against the manufacturer by injured parties. Highly persuasive evidence leading to settlements or verdicts against car makers has involved new cars with headlight failures, leakage of gasoline fumes causing an explosion, a dangerously positioned petcock leading to brake failure on a bus, stuck accelerators, hood latch defects allowing the hood to rear up and slam back through the windshield, defectively designed brakes and steering wheels, door latch and door hinge failure. Other cases have come to final judicial decision or have been settled in favor of the plaintiff before the end of trial.

The issue in these cases revolved around either negligent design or negligent construction by the manufacturer. Consequently, these individual cases centering on a particular defect of a particular model cannot be simply dismissed as non-recurring single instances. A "design defect" by definition occurs on all vehicles of that make or model; a "construction defect," arising out of a mass production assembly line, points to a substantial number of vehicles similarly afflicted—as illustrated above by Ford's rear suspension arm and Chrysler's steering wheel bracket.

A count of court decisions certainly does not constitute a representative sample either of the kind or frequency of vehicle defects. The formidable course that ends with a jury verdict is only taken in cases that are lucky enough to have extant physical evidence, an intransigent defendant, imaginative counsel and, in most instances, little or no insurance coverage. But the fact that so many of the design defects that *are* revealed must come to light in court is a severe commentary on how superficially our society evaluates the vehicle's role in accidents and injuries. It contrasts sharply with rail, air and marine design hazards which are meticulously investigated and publicly documented by government authorities.

The Senate hearings on automobile safety held in July 1965 elicited testimony from the manufacturers that indicated frequent written notification of dealers concerning defective conditions of new cars, together with corrective instruction and repair kits. (In the past it has been customary for the manufacturer to give the dealer *oral* notice, especially when the defect was serious and latent.)

Only in a few instances have the manufacturers aimed these "campaigns" directly toward the new car owners. There is no evidence that the manufacturers keep records concerning the number of car owners whose cars are not corrected. A substantial number of motorists are never reached by the dealers, who do not relish advertising any defects of their cars in the local community and who often are instructed by the companies only to make the correction if the customer brings his car in on another matter.

With every new model year, it must be presumed, on the basis of the evidence dealing with breakdowns in product quality, thousands of drivers are driving defective new cars that are likely to be involved in accidents. Hundreds of dealers know this, but are either obeying company orders or are protecting their own interests by remaining silent.

The 1953 Roadmaster case, the Ford suspension arm, and the Chrysler steering wheel bracket are evidence of breakdown in production quality control. Even more insidious are hazards that are the products of *design*. Born of deliberate knowledge, these hazards are far less likely to be admitted by car makers when they are confronted with substantial evidence of their danger. And, of course, motorists are not warned of these hazards in owner's manuals.

The connection between design defects and driver misjudgment or uncontrollable vehicle behavior is so subtle that neither the accident investigator nor the operator is aware of this connection in collisions. Automatic transmission defects illustrate this point with spectacularly tragic consequences. With more and more vehicles employing automatic transmissions, the occurrence of the "engine-powered runaway accident" is rising alarmingly. These accidents display a similar pattern. A vehicle starting from a stand-still or at a very low speed careens or lurches completely out of control with startling unexpectancy. For example:

—A young lady enters her garage and gets into her car to go to work. An instant later the car plummets in the wrong direction straight through the back end of the garage.

—A middle-aged woman is maneuvering her car out of a parked position on a busy main street; suddenly the car shoots forward across the street over the sidewalk and crashes fifty feet through a store window, narrowly missing a number of pedestrians and store clerks.

—An automobile is coming out of a parking garage; abruptly it lurches forward and then careens wildly, killing or injuring pedestrians and patrons of a restaurant.

—A woman shopper is trying to back up her car from a street parking area. The automobile's front wheels are against the curb. On pressing the accelerator to ease out backward, the vehicle does not respond; the driver presses down further on the gas. The car jumps the curb, crosses an alley to a nearby house and kills a couple sunning them-selves in their own back yard.

—A couple drives into a lumber yard. The husband gets out of the car and notices that his wife has stopped three feet short of a marked area. He asks her to pull up the required distance. She shifts to what she thinks is the for-ward gear. (The car door is open, and he is guiding her.) The car backs up instead; the open door knocks him down and the car runs over him and kills him.

These are actual cases illustrating the common transmission-induced accidents which trap the driver. They occur because of negligent design of the automatic transmission shift patterns. The driver is charged with reckless driving or negligent manslaughter. Rarely does the police officer recognize that the accident he is investigating proceeded from a built-in design hazard that ma-terialized.

In many instances these "drivers' errors" are the result of con-fusion over the bewildering variety of automatic shifting devices offered in different makes and models of automobiles.

It is about such design faults that a leading specialist in human engineering, Harvard's Professor Ross McFarland, says, "If defects are present, it is only a matter of time before some driver 'fails' and has an accident." ("Human engineering" tries to identify, in advance of manufacture, difficulties in the interaction of man and automobile, so as to permit the safest and most efficient operation of the vehicle by the driver.) Some of this advance design analysis is pretty difficult work. But it takes no science and little foresight to condemn accurately a particularly dangerous transmission shift pattern—the P N D L R gear quadrant common to Cadillacs, Buicks, Oldsmobiles, Pontiacs, Studebakers and Ramblers over the past ten years. This pattern places the reverse and foward low positions next to each other without separation and frequently with such a slight angular difference that it cannot be detected by feel at the knob end of the lever. The driver is forced to *look* at the shift lever for confirmation of the gear in use. The driver has to lift the lever to go into reverse. Should he not lift it enough, the car will remain in forward low while the driver is looking backward and expecting the car to move in that direction.

The design of automatic transmissions departed from long accepted principles of all types of mechanical controls (whether on machine tools, hoists, or automobiles) to place neutral between the reverse and forward gears. According to an automotive transmission engineer, Oscar Banker, there was a mechanical situation in the Hydramatic transmission which made the placement of forward adjacent to reverse less costly. By 1956, he said, elimination of this requirement rendered such a shift pattern wholly inexcusable. Still the manufacturers, with one exception, refused to eliminate this hazard. (That exception was Chevrolet division which dropped it in 1957.)

About this time, the Society of Automotive Engineers began to consider the desirability of standardizing the shift pattern. This was the obvious thing to do. The years wore on without any action. At the annual SAE meeting in January 1961, a General Motors' engineer delivered a paper on the new 1961 model Hydramatic. When he finished, several engineers asked him why the hazardous control pattern was not changed and when the various General Motors' divisions intended to replace it. He replied,

"Never. We now have ten million cars running with it. The die is cast; the rest of you will have to adopt the pattern."

This reaction angered Mr. Banker. He wrote to General Motors' president, John F. Gordon, who replied, "The matter of transmission shift sequence has been discussed on several occasions and we can assure you that the proponents of the two sequences currently used on our cars are equally vehement in their support of what they are now using. Both groups bring forth equally valid reasons for continuing their present practice. . . . After each review of the situation, our conclusion has been and very probably will continue to be that we will make no change in our present practice." Gordon's letter was dated May 17, 1961. Three years later, GM's representatives offered no objection whatever when the General Services Administration asked for comments about requiring a standard gear quadrant (P R N D L). Included in the GSA standard was the sentence, "In no case shall any forward drive be adjacent to any reverse drive position." General Motors found itself without this split of engineering opinion alluded to by Gordon. The various divisions decided to change over, after nearly a decade of unconscionable delay.

Each year that had passed meant that a new investment could be postponed. As the runaway accidents piled up and federal government insistence loomed on the horizon, the offending car makers relented. All domestic 1966 models have neutral placed between the forward and reverse drive positions.

From instrument panels to windshields, the modern automobile is impressive evidence that the manufacturers put appearance above safety. When it comes to vision, the car makers seem to value their concept of appearance over the driver's right to see.

The least to which any motorist should be entitled is a visual environment that permits him to see the road clearly. But it is highly doubtful whether any driver today, regardless of his visual acuity, could meet the standards of state licensing laws if he had to take the test sitting behind his steering wheel under normal day and night conditions. He would be confronted by interferences that range from irritating and fatiguing eyestrain to total obstruction.

A common complaint by a driver who has struck a pedestrian or another vehicle is, "I didn't see him." The fact is that, in many such instances, he was prevented from seeing because months before his accident the automobile stylists were fashioning his vehicle as if they thought that visibility had nothing to do with driving.

Professor Merrill Allen of Indiana University has shown the utter carelessness of such designers with a vivid demonstration. Sitting in a vehicle about fifteen feet in front of which a man stood on a tree-lined street in broad daylight, Dr. Allen photographed the scene twice. In the first picture, the pedestrian was completely invisible to any driver because of the reflection of the dashboard on the windshield. In the second picture, by simply placing black velveteen on the dash top as a light-absorber, the pedestrian became clearly visible. Few pedestrians ever suspect how frequently their position is entirely beyond the visual range of drivers bearing down on them because designers do not make dash panels and other reflective surfaces glare-free.

With funds from the American Optometric Foundation and the federal government, Professor Allen has been surveying automobiles from the standpoint of adequate visibility. In 1963 he reported the results of a study of fifty-six models of automobiles: "Not a single automobile manufactured in America and neither of the two European products tested could provide a suitable visual environment for daytime driving."

His criteria for such a suitable environment are: (1) that the driver be able to see through the windshield without reduction in contrast or serious reduction in brightness; (2) that he be able to read the instrument panel with a minimum of time away from watching the highway; and (3) that the automobile be free of sources of glare or unnecessary obstructions in the field of view.

As recorded by university specialists in optometry and human engineering, the more serious features which hamper driver vision are:

1. Distortions, waves, ghost images and poor surface polish on windshields and rear and side windows. Most blatantly hazardous is the plastic "rear window" employed on convertibles which is never clear to begin with, scratches easily and progressively discolors to a brownish opaque tone.

2. Windshield wiper blades and defrosters which do not provide an adequate clear windshield area.

3. Rear-view mirrors with waves and irregularities, often of inadequate size and in improper locations both inside and outside the vehicle. (Until the 1966 models, outside rear-view mirrors were not even standard equipment on the vast majority of models.)

4. Windshield wiper assemblies and other chromium ornamentation on corner posts, horn ring, steering wheel, hood, and fender that provide reflecting surfaces which direct the sun's rays directly into the driver's eyes, cause a serious visual disability that amounts to blindness in some situations. William I. Stieglitz, a prominent aviation safety specialist, describes how one car, which has a bright, shiny chrome hub of the steering wheel with two spokes that come out to the side districts, irritates and fatigues him. The sun reflects off the steering wheel to a bright spot on the top of the windshield and visor. Each time he turns the wheel, this light flashes back and forth before his eyes. "I have to fight it to keep my eye on the road," he says.

5. Dash panel visibility, frequently impaired by the use of low contrast markings, excessive shading in daylight by the hood, or poor night illumination. The design and location of basic controls and instruments, varying according to no rational standards and determined as if their main purpose is to give individuality to a particular model car, confuse the driver and divert his attention from the road. Stieglitz sees such chaos as entirely inexcusable. "Research in aviation," he says, "has proved the value of shape-coded knobs and standard location of controls in minimizing operator errors; none of this has been applied to automobiles. We come out with slogans on the radio: 'Never take your eye off the road,' and then we give the driver a car in which we defy him to turn on a windshield wiper, turn on his lights, turn on a heater or a defroster, without taking his eye off the road to look and find the controls."

6. Many automobiles which persist in using glossy and/or light colors on the dash board below the windshield. This causes dangerous veiling glare on the inside of the windshield, which causes the driver to look *at* the windshield as well as *through* it.

7. Front and rear turn signals, taillights, and brake lights

not always visible throughout a full one hundred and eighty degrees at full effective brightness because they are often buried in bumpers, are shielded by fender or bumper extensions and/or are too small and have inadequate light distribution. Dr. George E. Rowland, a consultant in human engineering, commented on this aspect during a recounting of observations at the 1964 New York Automobile Show for *Product Engineering:* "Virtually all the rear-end lighting arrangements seen in the show employ lighting first and foremost as a decorative gimmick, with lighting size, shape, and intensity forming a pattern which the stylist hopes will serve as a kind of 'make-identity.' An alarming number of the longest cars shroud their front and rear lights with sheet metal. They may well be invisible from the side under a variety of night-time and bad-weather driving conditions."

An English optometrist, J. B. Davey, writing in the November 1964 issue of *The Ophthalmic Optician,* expresses concern over the exporting of some of these hazards: "In spite of their traditional flamboyance," he declares, "American cars at night are difficult to see from the side. Regrettably Vauxhall is following the practice of the parent (General Motors) company and masking front and rear lamps. To distort an American saying, 'What is good for GM is not necessarily good for Great Britain.' Both the BMC 1800 and the Triumph 2000 have fitted 'repeaters' for the flashing turn indicators so that the driver or rider who is alongside can know when a turn is intended."

8. Windshield corner posts which are still excessively thick and provide dangerous and unnecessary obstruction of vision, particularly on the left side. Professor Allen says: "It would be quite easy, while turning left, to run down a pedestrian, or to be in collision with another car that was approaching on a collision course from the left, and for the driver not to see the hazard until too late, due to the left corner post obstruction." The Road Research Laboratory of the British Government has shown with precise measurements how the field of view can be obscured at a given angle, speed and distance. Also in England, the Society for Motoring Manufacturers and Traders has established that

the corner post should not be nearer than twenty-five degrees from the straight ahead position and at twenty-five degrees the maximum permissible obscuration is about four degrees, which is increased by one degree for each five degree increase in the angular distance from straight ahead. No American automobile meets the SMMT standard for the left corner post. This is an especially sharp commentary since European cars—with two or three exceptions, such as the Rover 2000—are not noted for many safety features superior to American vehicles.

(The lack of interest of the auto makers in defining and overcoming poor visibility characteristics of the vehicles they sell is well illustrated by the "hidden child" problem that plagues postal drivers. For years, the post office department has been troubled by deaths and injuries to small children who wander close to the front end of postal vehicles close to the curb. The driver, in his stop-and-go delivery routine, is often not aware of their presence. The post office tried every style and type of traffic mirror available commercially but none provided maximum front view vision close to the vehicle. In 1962, a postal worker, Harry M. Knarr, Jr., of Sarasota, Florida, came up with the idea of using an ordinary steel saucepan cover—a pot lid. The full curvature of the polished stainless steel reflecting disc, without the rim employed for the conventional glass surface mirror, provided the driver with a full view of the entire front of his vehicle down to bumper level. Although this mirror design is unpatented and in the public domain, no vehicle manufacturer has yet offered this safety device, estimated by postal authorities to cost $1.70, as standard equipment for its trucks.)

9. The tinted windshield—an option that is being vigorously promoted by the auto makers. Numerous research projects financed by federal grants have shown conclusively that tinted windshields interfere with night driving in particular and that, contrary to popular impression, the tint does not relieve glare from oncoming headlights as much as it reduces light available to the driver. In addition, there is a cruel twist to this optional feature. Since aging decreases

visual acuity, the older driver requires more light for seeing as clearly as he did at a younger age. Drivers past forty-five are the car buyers best able to pay for such options as the tinted windshield, captivated as they may be by smooth assurances that this will help them see better. They are being deceived. Studies in this country, reported by Professor McFarland of Harvard, have shown that ordinary windshields absorb twelve per cent of the light; tinted windshields absorb thirty per cent. Similar findings were registered by the Road Research Laboratory.

Drawing on his own work, on that of Doctors Barry King, P. J. Sutro and R. G. Domey, and on other research sponsored by the Armed Forces Epidemological Board, Professor McFarland makes this judgment on the use of tint: "In the valuation of tinted windshields the age of the driver is an extremely important factor, since it has been established that with increasing age there is a decrease in the retina's sensitivity to light under low levels of illumination. If during night driving [when accident rates are three times higher than in the daytime] this decrease in light sensitivity is combined with the reduced transmission of light through tinted glass, a serious safety problem may arise. . . . Studies have indicated that at any age the effect of the tinted glass at night is a reduction in the visibility of lights and other objects near the threshold of perception."

Dr. McFarland is a pioneer in the science of designing motor vehicles to fit the operational needs and safety of drivers and passengers. He has written scores of professional articles in the restrained, severe style of the detached scientist. His assessment of tinted windshields constitutes an expression of deep concern over industry neglect.

Dr. Allen sums up the case of vision specialists against the industry: "The blame for the thousands of lives lost each year lies in part at least with the automobile manufacturers, for not a single visual handicap engineered into modern automobiles needs to be there. There are some good visual aspects to each manufacturer's products, but the faults in each are so serious as to make it seem that the good points must have been accidental. Indeed, the good features one year are often replaced in the next year's production by glaringly poor ones." *

It is clear that the reason for such apparently random fluctuations is that design decisions belong to the stylists. Almost every vision engineering defect can be eliminated by the car makers both easily and economically. The knowledge, standards and instruments have long been available to do the job. There need be no aesthetic penalty, only a reduction in garishness.

The car industry's response to criticism of the poor visual environment provided by their vehicles was silence. Non-industry research findings were ignored; no contact has been established for the meaningful dialogue. The companies make no attempt to contribute to a meaningful scientific literature on this subject.

Motorists who write to the companies complaining about glare from glossy surfaces and asking why something can't be done about it receive the reply that available remedies would interfere with the decor of the rest of the vehicle.

In testimony before the House Subcommittee on Health and Safety in 1959, the usual "we are doing research on the problem" and "the consumer wouldn't like it" combination that has become the standard industry response, was tendered by Paul Ackerman, a Chrysler vice-president and official spokesman for the Automobile Manufacturers Association.

Representative Paul Schenck said to him, "Many of us have had a great deal of difficulty driving toward the sun from the reflection from the hood, dash, and other chrome parts of the car. I wondered about that." Ackerman answered, "That, sir, is a problem. The reflection from the hood and from the interior surfaces in the windshield is a thing that we do not like. We haven't found a satisfactory solution to it. I would say that if we were, if it would be acceptable to the people who buy our products, to have hoods and the upper portion of the instrument panel with a very dull nonreflective surface that looks pretty bad but is pretty effective in reducing the reflection, some good can be done."

Schenck asked him if Chrysler was working on it, and Ackerman said, "Yes, we have developed many types of finishes trying to find an acceptable one."

A few minutes later, in response to a question from Representa-

---

* See Appendix I on how to rate your automobile for visually safe design.

tive Lawrence Brock, Mr. Ackerman assured the subcommittee that he did "not want to leave the impression here that we put ornamentation or chrome on the cars at the expense of any known improvement to safety."

Mr. Ackerman assumed that American industrial ingenuity had not and could not up to that time produce nonglare finishes that would not incite a consumer revolt. This assumption was unchallenged by the numerous suppliers who could have easily provided such finishes. Suppliers to the auto industry have long since learned the penalties of pricking the absurd balloons that the industry proffers as rationalizations for dangerous designs. And Mr. Ackerman did not explain to the Congressmen why it took "more research" to bring finishes back to the lower glare levels of automobiles built a decade or two previously.

Five and a half years after the 1959 hearings the industry apparently was still trying to develop the proper type of finish while their vehicles proliferated in glints, gleams, and glares. In November 1964, when the General Services Administration began working on the safety standards for federally purchased passenger vehicles (as stipulated by Public Law 88-551) there was a rare occasion to learn of the industry's view. Industry sources notified GSA officials that it would cost the government additional money to buy cars *without* existing glare! There was no elaboration of the remarkable implication that glare was an economy move. When GSA persisted in formulating a glare-reducing standard, the industry advisory committee to GSA tried to make sure the standard would be easy for industry to tolerate. It was. Besides watered-down standards, all parts of the vehicle except for the instrument panel and the windshield wipers were excluded. Nonindustry advice to apply the standard to all other surfaces such as steering wheel, horn ring, hood, cowl, fenders and hood ornaments was rejected by GSA officials on industry's insistence. Ford's Alex Haynes said, "It was not practical in the way of manufacturing processing."

Willis MacLeod, chief of GSA's standardization division, asked the industry representatives whether they could provide for the 1967 models (as the law designates) a no-glare windshield wiper arm to replace chrome-plated types. Chrysler's Roy Haeusler replied, "Without any question. That could be available in two years." Nobody bothered to ask why they have not been available right from the beginning.

At the same November specification development conference held by GSA, the subject of tinted windshields came up briefly. MacLeod asked the industry's leading safety engineers around the conference table whether or not a standard should specify the inclusion of tinted windshields as a relief to the human eye. This was an honest inquiry to engineering experts by MacLeod and his colleagues who were just getting their feet wet in the area of automobile design safety.

Larry Nagler of American Motors promptly replied: "We would be glad to sell them." MacLeod then asked, "If it is a useful safety device, why isn't it standard?" William Sherman, the silver-tongued spokesman of the Automobile Manufacturers Association, answered as if the matter were wholly one of personal consumer taste instead of objective scientific study: "I think this is one of those things that if anyone believes that it is worth while, it can be specified and provided, like some of these others. If you desire it, it can be specified."

Not a single industry representative made any mention of the deleterious effects on vision so long documented and so well known to them. GSA was to be "sold," not informed.

The record did not show the reason for Mr. Sherman's reluctance to admit the visual hazards of tinted glass. Mr. Sherman is the self-styled "world's greatest advocate of air conditioning in automobiles." Tinted glass reduces heat transmission into the automobile, thus creating a more hospitable environment for air conditioning, the most expensive option in automobile history.

It is not only in connection with visibility characteristics that the automobile companies have so flagrantly neglected to design vehicles in terms of human capabilities and limitations. Across the entire range of vehicle-man interaction, the companies have shown little interest in systematic analysis of automotive features involving the physical and psychological response of the driver. General Motors, for example, claims to have twenty-five thousand scientists and engineers on its employment rolls. Yet it is doubtful whether any full-time human engineering specialists are employed to determine the design faults which place strains on the driving task. Without such a concept of design, and meticulous attention to its implementation, haphazardness of style will continue to be the order of the day in laying out vehicle work space, designing controls, instruments, and window areas, and in providing a physical environment for the driver.

The problem is stated succinctly by Dr. McFarland: "In general, any control difficult to reach or operate, any instrument dial of poor legibility, any seat inducing poor posture or discomfort, or any unnecessary obstruction to vision may contribute directly to an accident."

In addition, McFarland and his associates at Harvard have done ground-breaking human engineering analyses of dozens of passenger cars and trucks since 1950. These studies have produced highly usable data on existing vehicle designs in terms of the operational requirements of the driver and his seating comfort. They also provided standards and criteria for improvements in the design and location of steering wheels, controls, instruments and workspace for virtually all drivers, no matter what their size.

The findings by McFarland's group were not trivial. For example: "In several of the commercial vehicles [trucks] evaluated, only five per cent of the drivers could comfortably reach and operate the hand brake. In other vehicles, only sixty per cent of the drivers could be accommodated for knee height between the pedals and the steering wheel. Many tall drivers were unable to adjust their sitting positions to obtain maximum visibility in relation to their instruments and the road ahead. . . . Probably the most striking defect was that the front of the seat could not be lowered without excessive pressure under the knees. Some of the medical problems frequently observed in truck drivers are believed to be related to poor seat design and to failure to provide adequate shock absorbers.

"When one truck model was evaluated, it was discovered that the taller drivers could not operate the foot brake when the gear lever was in either of the two left positions. It was impossible for a large driver to put his foot on the brake pedal without first shifting gears. This defect should have been eliminated in the pre-production stages of the vehicle.

"One serious accident resulted when a driver, while proceeding at high speed in a modern car, shut off his headlights in the belief that he was operating the cigarette lighter. The knobs for these two controls were identical in shape and size and were located near each other on the dash board.

"The brake and accelerator pedals in some vehicles are so placed that the driver must make lengthy movements in three directions before the brake can be activated, i.e. up, over, and down. Sometimes the two pedals are of identical design and material, and therefore it is impossible for the driver to distinguish the pedals by touch alone. Undoubtedly this defect has been responsible for many critical situations, especially with drivers new to the vehicle, and has probably caused a number of accidents."

Dr. Richard Domey, a research associate of MacFarland's, stated the objective of the Harvard research: "The design of seats, work space layout, reach and effort requirements and spatial locations must be carefully controlled if fatigue, monotony, and errors are to be reduced and comfort, safety, and efficiency are to be increased. Machines should be designed for the people who use them and for the environment in which both are expected to function. . . . There is no evidence that a design cannot be developed that would accommodate all the driver population, perhaps with the exception of anthropometric oddities."

The Harvard research provided data of undeniable practical value free of charge to the automobile industry. But the industry did not respond. According to Dr. Domey, the Harvard researchers have been discussing the problem with the automobile companies for over a decade, pleading with them to look at the data and consider them, but to no avail.

Until mid-1965, the automobile companies did not feel it necessary even to reply to criticisms of their products by competent scientific and engineering critics. The ability to ignore criticism, rather than to meet the issues raised, is one measure of the immunity to public responsibility that has characterized the automotive industry's position on safety matters. However, there was a conference on passenger car design held at West Point in 1961, where industry representatives were asked point-blank why automobile design for human safety had remained so aloof from known principles and remedies applied to other transport machines and equipment. Chrysler's long-time safety engineer Roy Haeusler replied, "Safety considerations are far from the only ones which determine whether knobs are chrome or black, whether they are completely recessed or partially exposed, whether they are uniformly located and of different shapes. I think this is simply an obvious indication that there are other factors governing the decisions, and other factors might not, in my estimation at least, be half so important as safety considerations."

Haeusler must have felt subdued at that point in the conference. Just a few minutes before, Robert Janeway, who had finished a long career of engineering research with Chrysler, gave an illustration from Chrysler experience that showed how many safety design improvements had absolutely nothing to do with added cost: "I have two automobiles that are just one model-year apart, made by the same manufacturer, in which pushbutton controls are completely reversed. Let alone not having standardization *among* manufacturers, here is the same manufacturer switching controls from one year to the next, and when I get into one car I have to straighten myself out on reverse, neutral, and forward positions. There's certainly no excuse for that, and I think most of these things are pretty glaring examples of just, you might say, indifference."

The car makers display no such indifference to human engineering principles when they want to use them as a basis for obtaining patents to inventions. Securing a strong patent position is apparently a much stronger motivation than the safety of motorists. A case in point is patent number 2,929,261, issued in 1960 to GM vice-president Charles Chayne and assigned to his company. It notes that for vehicle controls to be acceptable, "they must not only be easily operated but also accessible to the operator with a minimum of inconvenience." The driver, Mr. Chayne informs us, "should not be required to reach any substantial distance to operate a particular control. Furthermore, safety is a concern since the control must be of the type that an operator would not inadvertently operate under normal conditions." Persuasive words for the patent examiner at the United States Patent Office. But not persuasive at all, apparently, as far as General Motors' designers are concerned. The 1964 Buick Electra 225 has the power brake pedal and gas pedal so close together and so close to the same level that drivers have inadvertently hit both pedals simultaneously. In the same model year, Buick advertisements urged the consumer to appreciate the consideration behind Buick's stickshift, which "was planned that way to put the adventure back into driving." The reader might not know of another General

Motors promotional brochure which a few years before boasted about the safety advance brought about by the replacement of the stick shift with the steering column shift.

Another GM patent, number 3,097,542, states that "in recent years, traffic density and high speed operation of vehicles has greatly increased the need for minimizing the time required in application of the brakes. In emergency situations, delays of even small fractions of a second in elapsed time may make the difference between a successful stop and a disastrous accident." Solicitude for these fractions of seconds seems to have been shunted aside by the designers of chrome trim around the edges of the pedals that is beginning to appear on some of the more expensive cars, called "GT" models. Such metal trim increases the risk of one's foot slipping off the pedal in the process of braking or clutching.

More important than brake application is how efficiently brakes perform when called upon to do their task—a task that has grown more demanding with increasing speeds, greater horsepower, and the fact that automatic transmissions have limited retarding ability on hills. The improvement of braking systems has miserably failed to keep pace. Dangerous brake fade persists. Even under single-stop conditions at ordinary turnpike speeds, some models are incapable of braking efficiently, and swerve dangerously when making an emergency stop. The men responsible for American automobile design cannot provide the flimsiest excuse for the gap between the accelerating momentum of passenger cars and trucks and their relative braking ability. There were European solutions available which American manufacturers could have copied faster than they have done in the past. Disc brakes—universally acclaimed as superior over conventional brakes—were available on some European cars over a decade ago. On some 1965 models in this country, disc brakes were gingerly introduced (mostly as an option, on two wheels), in accord with the domestic policy of putting key safety features on the same level as luxurious items or trivial gewgaws.

Anti-skid braking systems for optimum traction have been developed in Europe as well. A 1959 Commerce Department report emphasized the need for incorporating such systems in motor vehicles. It added: "Anti-locking devices are used on aircraft; the ingenuity of the motor vehicle designer is adequate to give similar safety to the automobile user in this important area." This prerequisite for safe brakes still has not been adopted to give motorists protection in common sudden-stop situations.

The wide variety in quality of brake linings and brake fluids also provides a grisly risk for the lives of thousands. The problem of adequate brakes for trucks and buses is further complicated by the designers' reliance on the rated gross vehicle weight of the particular vehicle size. Loads beyond such a limit obviously have an adverse effect on brake performance. No other vehicle design feature is so frequently a hidden factor in auto casualties as brakes. Unused brake technology remains on the shelf at the automobile plant, while inadequate brake design continues to be a prime example of vehicle failure being interpreted as driver failure.

The singular ineffectiveness of incriminating data and critical analyses of automobile design by sources outside the industry during the last twenty years has been strongly sustained by the protective anonymity given makes and models of automobiles involved in that data.

In 1965 the mask of anonymity began to be lifted. For the first time in television history, a program titled "Death on the Highway," shown on National Educational Television stations, connected specific design hazards with car models—Pontiac Tempest, Chrysler Newport, Ford Mustang and others. Newspapers, after ignoring for months the volume of Corvair litigation, began to mention it in their columns. *Consumer Reports* and *Consumer Bulletin* no longer were the only segment of the communications media which linked hazards with brand names.

A fundamental basis for this tradition of anonymity has been the practice of academic and commercial compilers of data to refrain from naming makes and models. The popular media had little specific nourishment for its copy.

For example, none of the voluminous reports by the McFarland group contained vehicle names. In 1959 to 1960, other federally financed research at Dunlap and Associates of Stamford, Connecticut, to study the differences in accident experience of various makes of automobiles produced reports entirely devoid of vehicle names. In May 1964 *Popular Science* reported the results of brake tests for leading American car makes. Stopping distance at sixty-five miles per hour ranged from 170 feet to 359 feet. One leading make required more than twice the stopping distance of another popular make. No names were mentioned. Again in 1964, the National Association for Stock Car Advancement and Research (NASCAR) conducted evaluation tests on nineteen brands of replacement brake linings. The NASCAR report concluded, "These tests indicate a vast difference in brake lining quality. Only five of the nineteen brands tested met minimum traffic safety code specifications. The public should exercise utmost caution when their cars need brake service. It is strongly advised that motorists seek out only the best linings obtainable. NASCAR findings indicate that the use of inferior brake lining products could be extremely hazardous." NASCAR never identified the brands tested.

John Fitch, the automotive specialist from Lime Rock, Connecticut, noted with careful anonymity in 1961, "Before 1955 we had a phenomenon in our cars which was very serious. No one even talked about it and they don't talk about it now, although a few cars still have it. I'm referring to rear leaf-spring wind-up, where the rear spring, in reaction to braking torque, actually takes the shape of a flat 'S.' Now, when the tire breaks traction from the road, that spring snaps back to near its original shape and it sets up an oscillation in which both rear wheels jump off the ground, bounce back down, and the car is practically uncontrollable. This happens only under servere braking, but every now and then severe braking is necessary, and whenever it happens you can almost say that the car is out of control." Mr. Fitch's comment was made at the aforementioned West Point conference attended by twenty-one specialists from various disciplines inside and outside the industry. The papers and discussion were very specific—except for naming makes and models. Mr. Janeway managed to deliver a long paper on vehicle design aspects of safe handling containing a deadly criticism of the Corvair-type design but never mentioning the car by name. It simply wasn't cricket to do so. Anonymity gave the Corvair a valuable windfall of many months before a critical focus began to sharpen on its handling hazards.

Even Consumers Union succumbs once in a while to the habit. "A popular 1956 upper-medium priced model of American manufacture had a defect so basic that a large number of owners were stranded by complete transmission failure in the early months of ownership," said one of its reports.

The anonymity perpetuated by specialists outside the industry undermines the principle of informed consumer choice and industrial competition which form the bedrock of enterprise economy. It does to the economy what censorship of ideas does to a democracy. No other consumer product has enjoyed such immunity of specific criticism. The automobile, by brand name, stands as a sacred cow.

In July, 1965, before the Senate committee inquiring into traffic safety, Senators Abraham Ribicoff and Robert Kennedy confronted General Motors chairman Frederic Donner and president James Roche with a November 1964 Cornell report showing a much greater door hinge failure by General Motors cars than by Ford or Chrysler vehicles. For the first time in twelve years (with one insignificant exception) Cornell had named vehicle makes and the relative performance of one common design feature.

Yet secrecy still remains the order of the day. The files of the Association of American Railroads contain reports of about one hundred and seventy rail crossing accidents involving an unnamed make of American automobile manufactured in the 1961 model-year. The first 82,000 of these automobiles, it seems, were built with no skid plate, thus allowing the front cross member to dig into the road, given a certain undulation such as occurs when crossing some railroad tracks. The car would go end over head or roll over, or simply dig in while the passengers continued right through the windshield. The most serious injuries and deaths were recorded in these single-car upsets at speeds between fifteen and thirty miles per hour. Apparently later production runs of this model corrected the defect, but many buyers of the first 82,000 found out the hard way about designers' omissions. This tragic episode, also well known to several insurance companies who have documented street accidents in their files, still remains a classical example of the anonymity that has cloaked the designed-in dangers of the American automobile.

3

The second collision:
When man meets car

In the fall of 1917, two Canadian "Jennies"—small airplanes technically known as JN-4's—collided seven hundred feet above a small Texas airstrip. Of the four flyers who were manning the two-seated planes, the only survivor was a young air cadet named Hugh De Haven.

As he lay in the hospital recovering from serious internal injuries—caused, paradoxically, by a poorly designed six-inch-wide seat belt with a six-inch bronze buckle—he wondered why he had not been killed. When he recovered he inspected the wreckage of the two planes and observed that, of the four cockpits, the one in which he had been seated had remained substantially intact, while the other three had disintegrated.

From this one man's sense of wonder evolved a major life-saving concept of the twentieth century: that the human body can withstand tremendous decelerative forces inflicted by crashes or falls.

To be capable of tolerating such impacts in transport vehicles the human needed a "crashworthy" structure around him.

For the next twenty years De Haven could not find anyone who agreed with him. In this interval, while free-lancing as a successful designer of automatic equipment, he continued to press his belief that accidents can be made far safer through rational investigation of the mechanisms of injury in air crashes, many of which occurred during this period at speeds well under one hundred miles per hour. De Haven was turned away repeatedly by government and university people who called him a "crackpot." In the twenties and thirties, he recalls, "The saying used to be, 'If you want to be safe, don't fly.'"

De Haven's curiosity was not dampened. He began to study cases of spectacular suicide plunges or accidental falls by people who "miraculously" survived.

A forty-two-year-old woman jumped from the sixth floor of a building and fell fifty-five feet onto fairly well-packed earth in a garden plot. The building superintendent rushed over to the victim right after she struck the ground, saw her raise herself on her elbow and remark, "Six stories and not hurt." A subsequent examination showed no evidence of material injuries or shock.

A man fell 108 feet from a tenth-story window and landed on the hood and fenders of an automobile, face downward. He bounced off the car to the pavement. His chief injury was a depressed frontal fracture of the skull. He did not lose consciousness and recovered in short order.

A twenty-seven-year-old man jumped from the roof of a fourteen-story building, falling 146 feet onto the top and rear of the deck of an automobile and landing in a semisupine position. He suffered numerous fractures but did not lose consciousness and incurred no chest or head injuries. Two months later he was back at work.

A woman fell 144 feet from a seventeenth floor and landed on a metal ventilator box. She crushed the structure up to a depth of eighteen inches, fractured both bones of both her forearms and the bone of her left upper-arm, and injured her left foot. She sat up and asked to be taken back to her room. Subsequent examination revealed no other internal injuries or fractures.

Hugh De Haven pointed out that any of the injuries suffered in these documented cases could have been the results of a five-foot fall. He saw these cases of survival as evidence that the objects and surfaces struck by the body do less damage if the forces involved are spread over time and area. This is elementary physics. A fall on a surface that "gives," such as a pile of hay, spreads the force over time. Poking someone with the end of a baseball bat instead of an ice pick spreads the force over area. Dr. Carl Clark of The Martin Company put the distinction neatly: "Damage is done not by the force, but by the distortions produced as a consequence of this force."

This relationship between the surface hit and the injury that results was recognized by Hippocrates in about 400 B.C. In his treatise on head injuries he wrote, "Of those who are wounded in the parts about the bone, or in the bone itself, by a fall, he who falls from a very high place upon a very hard and blunt object is in most danger of sustaining a fracture and contusion of the bone, and of having it depressed from its natural position; whereas he that falls upon more level ground, and upon a softer object, is likely to suffer less injury in the bone, or it may not be injured at all . . ." From his own studies and these basic principles, De Haven concluded, "A person who escapes in a high speed crash, fatal to many others, owes his life to some decelerative interval and to a favorable distribution of pressure. . . . It is significant that crash survival without injuries in aircraft and automobiles occurs under conditions which are seemingly extreme and that fatal injuries are often sustained under moderate and controllable circumstances. It is reasonable to assume that structural provisions to reduce impact and distribute pressure can enhance survival and modify injury within wide limits in aircraft and automobile accidents."

Centuries ago, men had put these principles into practice in preparing for combat and in transporting fragile goods. They used shields and armor to dissipate force, and spears and knives to concentrate it. For carrying pottery and porcelains over great distances and rugged terrains by ships and caravans, they used effective packaging techniques to avoid "crash impacts."

But something happened to men's rationality when they placed themselves in vehicles—chariots, wagons, carriages, boats, trains, automobiles and aircraft. Death and injury from crash impacts in these carriers were called "acts of God" or "bad luck;" escape from casualties in accidents was called "a miracle." Even people whose training should have made them receptive to empirical explanations believed that forces involved in automobile or air crashes were too severe for the human body to absorb under any circumstances. So they concentrated on preventing accidents rather than on preventing injuries when accidents do occur.

The advent of World War II provided a little more receptive climate for De Haven's findings, especially as they might be applied to aircraft. With the strong backing of Dr. Eugene D. DuBois of the Cornell University Medical College, De Haven began a study of the causes of injury in aircraft accidents. He found that wounds of the heart and lungs, punctured by fractured ribs, and brain damage with and without skull fracture were prominent categories of injuries. Such injuries were sustained not just in completely disintegrated aircraft, but also in cockpits and aircraft cabins which had remained intact with little damage. De Haven called the latter kind of crashes "survivable accidents" in order to focus attention on the need for deliberate engineering for crash-survival. The first important outcome of his work was the development of improved restraining equipment to keep the pilot from striking rigid metal surfaces and instruments inside the cockpit. Aircraft manufacturers producing war planes began to pick up the safety implications of De Haven's work. Under the leadership of such dogged safety engineers as Republic Aviation's William Stieglitz and Douglas Aircraft's A. M. Mayo and John R. Poppen, fighter and light civil aircraft began to appear with more strongly moored seat structures, less lethal instrument panels, and more crash-resistant cockpit and cabin structures.

Stieglitz described the crash of a fighter airplane which went off the end of the runway at about 170 knots, flew for about 1200 feet, hit the ground, skidded for about 500 feet, and then went nose first into a six-foot earth embankment, cartwheeled, and disintegrated. The pilot crawled out by himself and rolled on the ground to put out the flames of his burning flying suit. Aside from minor burns, his total physical injury consisted of a cut on his little finger. Inspection of the wreckage showed the plane to be sheared off right down the back wall of the cockpit. But the cockpit had remained intact and the pilot, who had been restrained only by a standard lap seat belt and shoulder harness, was flying again in three months.

Dr. John Lane of the Australian Department of Civil Aviation, a pioneer in the field of crash protection, told a group of crash specialists in 1961, "We have a whole stack of thoroughly investigated accidents (involving military and light aircraft), thoroughly documented, in which the aircraft will do something like this: they will run through a power line—a high tension line—catch fire in the air, and impact the ground vertically at something on the order of seventy or eighty knots. The pilot will emerge from the debacle and simply go to call up and say, 'Send me a new aircraft.'"

De Haven was sure that if collision protection engineering could be so effective in aircraft design, it would also be applicable to the automobile. During the late forties, substantiation of his belief was furnished by others. A perceptive Indiana state policeman, Sergeant Elmer Paul, thought of it as the problem of the "second collision." In his analysis, most accident situations involved the impact of the vehicle with whatever it hit (the first collision), followed instantaneously by the impact of the occupants with the inside of the vehicle (the second collision). This second collision was what caused killing and maiming. To find out what objects inside the vehicle were responsible for injuries, and in what severity and frequency, Paul persuaded the Indiana authorities to establish the first systematic investigation of injury occurrence in automobiles wrecked on the state's highways. Close contact was established with De Haven's Cornell crash injury research project, which was beginning to turn its attention to automobile accident injury problems. The Cornell project unfortunately was plagued by the lack of financial support. Since it focused on vehicle design, it involved evaluating the products of Detroit, and this was dangerous territory, not trespassed for nearly half a century. But in 1951 the Air Force made a simple statistical comparison which revealed that it was losing more men—dead and injured—in automobile accidents than in combat in Korea. Other branches of the armed forces looked over their rolls and found similarly shocking comparisons. So the first grant to the Cornell project came in 1953 from the Army under the technical guidance of the Armed Forces Epidemiological Board. The initial grant was $54,000, and over the next eight years the total went up to $500,000. The Cornell group began a nationwide data-collection system about the second collision. This was achieved largely through the cooperation of about twenty states and five cities, which arranged for the dispatch of special accident reports, photographs, and medical reports showing vehicular damage, the nature and extent of injuries, and the vehicle features or components that were believed to have caused the injuries.

Military foresight made one other great contribution to crash injury research. Colonel John Paul Stapp of the United States Air Force risked his life to prove how tough the human anatomy can be in tolerating tremendous forces. True to the best heritage of his two professions, medicine and physics, Stapp devised the experimental equipment and chose himself as the guinea pig. In 1954 he culminated a series of tests begun in the late forties. Strapping himself into a giant sled powered by four solid-fuel Jato-type rocket motors and capable of supersonic speeds, he shot forward to a speed of 632 miles per hour—and stopped in 1.4 sec. at decelerations in excess of 40 g. (This means that the force on his body was equivalent to forty times his weight.) No other human being in history had "pulled down" so many "g's" voluntarily for such a period. With this historic demonstration, Stapp proved that if the human body had such tremendous tolerance for abrupt deceleration, it could also survive even the most severe vehicle collisions with little or no injury if the vehicle environment was safely designed.

During this same seminal period of the early fifties, the third phase of crash protection research was launched at the University of California at Los Angeles under the leadership of J. H. Mathewson and D. M. Severy. This involved the experimental crashing of automobiles to determine deceleration rates, vehicle damage, and the effects on instrument-laden anthropomorphic dummies strapped in the seats. In 1954 the UCLA group concluded that "there has been no significant automotive engineering contribution to the safety of motorists since about the beginning of World War II . . ." On the basis of mounting accident-injury data flowing into it from areas throughout the country, the Cornell Automotive Crash Injury Research (ACIR) annual report in 1955 provided statistical confirmation: "The newer model automobiles (1950-1954) are increasing the rate of fatalities in injury-producing accidents."

Until Stapp, UCLA, and Cornell began their tests and collected data, the public had no choice but to rely upon the automobile manufacturers as its sole source of information about the second collision. The industry had the field to itself and chose to dispense no information whatever.

The opening of independent sources of information on automobile hazards and their relation to injuries inflicted by the second collision is giving this country its first detailed critical look at what happens when cars crash, and what is needed to make them crashworthy. The Cornell Aeronautical Laboratory, which became the heir to ACIR in 1961, lists three general requirements for collision protection in a vehicle: 1) a sound outer shell structure which will retain its structural integrity under impact—and absorb as much energy as possible—without allowing undue penetration of the striking object into the passenger compartment; 2) elimination from the interior surfaces of the shell of any hard, sharp projections or edges and the prevention of vehicle components (such as steering columns and engines) from penetrating into the compartment; also the application of energy-absorbing materials to reduce impact forces on the human body at all probable points of contact with these surfaces; and 3) provision of passenger restraint systems, *not necessarily restricted to seat belt devices,* to prevent or minimize relative body motion and abrupt contact with the interior of the automobile, at the same time inducing little or no physiological damage to the passenger due to the operation of these restraint systems.

These Cornell criteria might seem to be based simply on common sense, but they are formulated on the basis of over 70,000 accident cases from which the processed data (see Fig. 3) have produced a ranking of leading causes of injury—the cause in this study being whatever particular feature or component of the vehicle inflicts the injury when the car is stopped and the occupant keeps going.

The steering assembly

The most flagrant instrument of trauma in Cornell's automobile autopsy is the steering assembly. It caused approximately twenty per cent of the injuries in the data sample taken during the past decade. As would be expected, it is the driver who is most often injured by the steering assembly, either by being thrown forward into it or by being impaled on a ramming steering column. The

FIGURE 3

LEADING CAUSES OF INJURY
RANKED BY TWO METHODS

NUMBER OF INJURIES FOR LEADING CAUSES
OF INJURY DISTRIBUTED BY IMPACT TYPE
(DEGREE OF INJURY NOT WEIGHTED)

INJURY SCORE FOR LEADING CAUSES
OF INJURY WITH CONTRIBUTION BY IMPACT TYPE—
(WEIGHTED INJURY, SCALE)

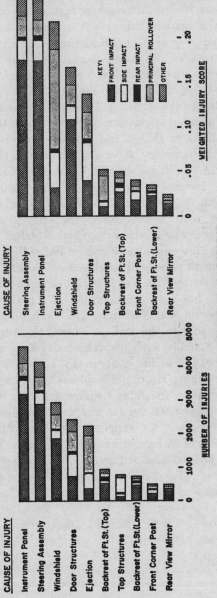

CAUSE OF INJURY

Instrument Panel
Steering Assembly
Windshield
Door Structures
Ejection
Backrest of Ft.St. (Top)
Top Structures
Backrest of Ft.St.(Lower)
Front Corner Post
Rear View Mirror

NUMBER OF INJURIES

CAUSE OF INJURY

Steering Assembly
Instrument Panel
Ejection
Windshield
Door Structures
Top Structures
Backrest of Ft.St.(Top)
Front Corner Post
Backrest of Ft.St.(Lower)
Rear View Mirror

WEIGHTED INJURY SCORE

KEY:
FRONT IMPACT
SIDE IMPACT
REAR IMPACT
PRINCIPAL ROLLOVER
OTHER

SEAT BELTS NOT PRESENT
(1956–1961 CARS)

latter kind of impact is the less common of the two but represents a disproportionate cause of serious injury.*

For years, the most common feature of crumpled automobiles has been a rearward displaced or arched steering column with broken spokes and bent wheel rims. Led by Ford, in 1956-1957 the auto makers introduced the recessed-hub steering wheel. The purpose of setting the hub below the plane of the wheel rim was to allow the rim to absorb the first force of impact before the driver struck the rigid and frequently sharp-edged hub. But Cornell follow-up data analysis, comparing the relative effectiveness of this new design and the old flat wheel type, has shown only a "weak tendency" toward a reduction in chest injury.

Robert A. Wolf, Director of Automotive Crash Injury Research, urges the automobile designers "to turn their talents toward developing an improved form of energy-absorbing steering wheel—something with several times the effectiveness of the present family of wheels." He has prepared sketches of various proposed wheels which would absorb energy and still protect the driver from the instrument panel and windshield. (See Fig. 4)

Wolf notes that the concept behind such shock-absorbing steering wheels has not been accepted in actual product development by automobile manufacturers. His evaluation of the reasons for this lag points to the lack of systematic search to find the best solutions. Actually, such a search needs only a management decision to go ahead. Patents that incorporated increasingly advanced energy-absorbing steering assemblies were issued to the manufacturers and other inventors beginning in the twenties. Automobile company representatives have a standard answer to the assertion that patents exist for various safety features. It was voiced by Ford president Arjay Miller when Senators Ribicoff and Robert Kennedy pressed him at the 1965 Senate hearings to explain why a number of his company's patents of such steering assemblies, or modifications of them, still had not been incorporated into the design of Ford cars. "We have got thousands of patents in the Ford Motor Company," he said, "that are not worthy of the light of day. You patent any idea you have." Clearly, as Mr. Miller

---

* There are many ways to design steering columns to prevent what engineers call their "rearward displacement relative to the firewall and instrument panel." The design alternatives are cheap, practical and long known to the manufacturers. (See Fig. 4)

should know, a company-held patent represents a stage of knowledge concerning a useful invention. The patents, along with their predecessors, define with some precision an *important safety problem* in motor vehicle crashes. It would be insulting to the suppressed creativity of auto industry engineers to suggest that such technology could not have been perfected for mass produced automobiles over a decade ago. This is an area where safer alternatives are "on the shelf."

The industry's shrugging off its patent holdings in crash safety technology as just "ideas" contrasts with what their engineers write in their professional journals. In 1953, George Willits, director of General Motors' patent section, emphasized that "GM patents are distinguished from the ordinary run in that almost all of them cover practical ideas. Our inventors know the practical possibilities in the fields in which they work."

Industry reaction to findings by Cornell and others about the hazards of steering columns is revealing. Cornell's data analysis showed great differences in the frequency of steering column penetration among different types of cars. ACIR reports that "in accidents of similar severity some classes of cars are about twice as likely as others to have steering column penetration. These findings emphasize the need for drastic corrective action by the automobile industry." At one point in 1963, Mr. Wolf showed rare exasperation when he told an audience of automobile safety specialists, "There is no point in endless descriptions of the possible spectrum of engineering solutions to the problem of steering column penetration. I have no doubt whatsoever that the ingenuity of the engineers will rise to the occasion if they are given a clear directive, by management, to solve the problem."

Dr. Horace Campbell, a Denver surgeon with many articles on auto design hazards to his credit, noticed during his investigations of automobile accidents that the Corvair steering shaft was routinely driven backward and upward in even minor left front-end collisions. He noted that the steering shaft extends from a point about two inches in front of the leading surface of the front tire—a design unique among American cars. He wrote to Harry Barr, now General Motors' vice-president for engineering, on October 26, 1962, inquiring about the apparent likelihood of impaling the driver on a steering shaft that takes all the impact not absorbed by the bumper and sheet metal. Barr replied that Chevrolet had conducted tests which showed to its satisfaction that there was no problem. What kinds of tests and with what results Barr did not mention. Campbell could find no one anywhere in the country, certainly not a governmental agency, who could provide an answer to his question. *Consumer Reports* in April 1965 took specific note of the danger of the Corvair's steering shaft position and indicated it was trying to set up tests with Automotive Crash Injury Research to find an answer. But nothing had materialized as of August 1965. ACIR has been reluctant to disclose the make and model names of vehicle performance in data analysis of steering shaft penetration.

Dr Campbell had a specific reason to pursue his quest for information about the Corvair shaft. On January 19, 1962, Milford Horn, a Denver engineer, driving at a slow speed, skidded in his Corvair on an icy road into the side of a slowly moving locomotive. Dr. Campbell investigated the accident and gave the following report to the Seventh Stapp Car Crash Conference in November 1963: "Horn had died instantly at the scene with a completely broken neck. The state patrolman told me to go and see the car and I would then understand why. The man's character [Horn's] was revealed on my inspection of the car. There were four seat belts; his widow told me later that every belt had to be fastened before he would start the engine. There were four electric flashing signal lights, to be placed on the road in case a tire change became necessary.

"His car, a 1961 Corvair, was extensively damaged at the left front corner. The hub of the steering wheel was displaced, by actual measurement against another car of the same make, two feet upward and backward. It broke his neck. He had no other injuries of consequence.

"The man who towed his car in told me that in every car of this make which he brought in with left front deformation, the steering shaft is driven backward, often more than a foot."

In a final attempt at communication, in March 1965, Dr. Campbell wrote an acquaintance, Kenneth A. Stonex of General Motors, asking him to provide crash data on a question that literally was one of life and death. Mr. Stonex, General Motors' leading automotive safety engineer, wrote back that "as a long-standing policy, engineering details of General Motors' developments have a degree of confidence equivalent to that between you and your patients."

Then he added, as if suddenly aware of the inverted engineering ethic he had voiced, "The best I can do is refer your request to people responsible for policy for their consideration." Dr. Campbell never heard further.

In recent years the data coming to Cornell has continued to show the pre-eminent danger of the steering assembly in collisions. Since the introduction of the recessed-hub steering concept by the industry in 1956-1957, the only changes in the steering wheel's configuration appear to have been drawn from the stylist's inspiration. (See Fig. 4) Industry engineers did claim minor improvements but could not reveal even experimentally in what way these changes were safer. Certainly the Cornell data showed no supporting evidence. The most generous comment about the so-called "safety steering wheel" which a Harvard collision investigator, Murray Burnstine, could make was: "In many cases, they function only well enough to allow the motorist to die in the hospital instead of on the road."

Some car models have two spokes on the steering wheel, others three, and while William Sherman of the Automobile Manufacturers Association, in a rare expression of his safety judgment, says that "the two spoke is *per se* safer than the three spoke wheel," there is no evaluation available regarding the respective designs. In addition, an alleged safety improvement frequently obscures an increased hazard—in this case the horn ring. Mr. Burnstine's crash studies in Massachusetts led him to conclude that the horn ring is a definite injury-producing structure. "It is not capable of energy absorption," he reports, "and shatters upon impact. The resultant exposed sharp edges serve only to identify the driver." He says, "Drivers wishing to remain anonymous usually purchase the minimum-trim body style which features the less lethal horn button of thirty years ago."

In the last five years a new kind of evidence has substantiated Cornell's conclusions drawn from accident injury reports: evidence collected in the on-the-scene investigations of collisions (supported financially by the U.S. Public Health Service) by groups at Harvard Medical School and the University of Michigan Medical School. These investigative teams arranged for the police to notify them of fatal accidents in their area immediately, so that they could arrive promptly at the accident scene. The Michigan investigators, Dr. Paul Gikas and Dr. Donald Huelke, reported on their investi-

FIGURE 4

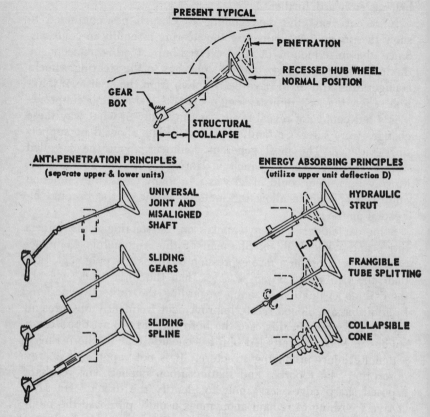

PRESENT TYPICAL

PENETRATION

RECESSED HUB WHEEL
NORMAL POSITION

GEAR
BOX

STRUCTURAL
COLLAPSE

|←C→|

ANTI-PENETRATION PRINCIPLES
(separate upper & lower units)

UNIVERSAL
JOINT AND
MISALIGNED
SHAFT

SLIDING
GEARS

SLIDING
SPLINE

ENERGY ABSORBING PRINCIPLES
(utilize upper unit deflection D)

HYDRAULIC
STRUT

FRANGIBLE
TUBE SPLITTING

COLLAPSIBLE
CONE

STEERING ASSEMBLY

gation of 104 accidents involving fatal injuries to 136 victims, in January 1965, before a Society of Automotive Engineers convention.

Twenty-five of the victims died from injuries sustained on the steering assembly. The report, confirming fully a finding by the Harvard team a few years earlier, concluded: "Invasion of the driver occupant area by the steering assembly is seen very often. The ramrod effect produced the majority of steering assembly deaths. Even if the driver had been restrained with a lap belt and upper torso restraint, so as not to be able to move forward and contact the steering assembly, he would have been killed anyway by the marked backward displacement of the steering column."

With such unanimous agreement over steering assembly hazards, both within and without the industry, it might have been expected that the automobile makers would have developed engineering solutions for effective energy-absorbing steering wheels and non-penetrating steering columns either separately or, even better, in combination. One reason they give for not doing so is the difficulty of designing a collapsible steering assembly that will suit both the ninety-pound woman and the two hundred-pound man. This alleged difficulty, said to have been puzzling industry engineers for years, is never mentioned to technical audiences, which would know that solutions have been available for this difficulty over the better part of a generation.

Another excuse for inaction was given by Ford's Arjay Miller before the 1965 Senate hearings: "Common sense seems to indicate that rearward displacement of the steering column in a crash is a serious hazard to the driver. However, preliminary data suggest that there are fewer injuries when some rearward displacement occurs, because the steering wheel then serves as an additional restraining device. At present, we do not know how much rearward displacement is best."

Mr. Miller could scarcely have given a more succinct example of the industry's endless diversionary tactics when pressed for greater vehicle safety. It is not "common sense" but thousands of cases processed by Cornell and accidents investigated and documented by university teams and state troopers that identify the steering column as a serious hazard. Mr. Miller neglected to specify what the "preliminary data" were, and when Senator Ribicoff gave him an opportunity to elaborate, Mr. Miller remained silent.

Finally, Mr. Miller's statement that not enough is known about rearward displacement seems inconsistent with his proud exposition of Ford's pioneering and intensive collision research and development over the past fifteen years. "Preliminary data" in 1965 suggests that Ford's highly advertised collision tests at company proving grounds produced more advertising copy than data.

If Ford and the other car makers perpetuate the traditional steering wheel assembly, that assembly should be made more energy-absorptive so as to deflect under impact forces but not to allow direct body contact with the instrument panel or windshield by "giving" all the way. Mr. Miller's testimony suggested that he believed the problem to be beyond the capabilities of the world's second largest automobile manufacturer.

A significant complaint against the Ford president's position was made by Senator Robert Kennedy, who ended an exchange on steering assemblies with Mr. Miller and Ford's vice-president for engineering, Herbert Misch, by saying, "Really the automobile industry has been derelict in this area. You come up here and say what we need is this kind of equipment and I ask you if you have the equipment, and you say, 'No, we do not.' You know, it does make one think that perhaps you could do better."

Miller answered simply, "Yes, sir."

Shortly afterward, Kennedy said, "It is difficult for me to understand why, after we have been talking about a collapsible steering column for ten years knowing what the problem is, that the Ford Motor Company and the rest of the automotive industry cannot come up with the answer. If everybody wanted to come up with an answer to this problem, they could find the answer to it. Do you not agree?" Misch admitted, "Yes, sir, if the right talents are applied to it, we can get these answers."

Senator Kennedy hardly overstated it when he said, "I think that progress has been slow; it has been very, very slow, really. That is, I think, the problem."

The instrument panel

On the Cornell list of leading causes of injury, the instrument panel stands first in frequency and second, behind the steering assembly, in seriousness of injury. This comes as no surprise to policemen and other accident investigators. The stylist who has been given great leeway to determine panel shape has devised a great variety of designs that have managed to provide spectacular dangers. Hugh De Haven told a House of Representatives subcommittee in 1959, "It has been my opinion for many years that we are putting into automobiles an instrument panel that has the characteristics that are not too different, so far as the head and face are concerned, from a steel beam or an anvil." De Haven's point was amply illustrated by Dr. William Haddon of the New York Department of Health in an address before the Society of Automotive Engineers: "A friend of mine, a prominent physician who has long served on one of the committees concerned with this area, saw not many months ago a case of a young child which lost one of its eyes because the vehicle in which it was riding decelerated unexpectedly, with the result that the child was thrown forward, as one knows happens with children riding in cars when cars, as is common, decelerate. The reason why this child lost its eye was that there was placed in the target area—an anticipated target area well known to all of us—a knob. Now the eye, through evolution, or nature, or creation, as each of you will have it, has been very nicely recessed, so that in hitting flat surfaces no damage, unless the impact is overwhelming, results. It has little chance, however, in landing on a protrusion. There *was* a protrusion, placed, by design, literally at the impact point at which children often hit."

What is wrong with instrument panels in a collision can be understood readily by considering what could be right with them. A reasonably safe instrument panel would not have sharp, unyielding edges, would have more and better application of padding materials or alternative absorptive surfaces, would recess knobs and controls or otherwise make them yield on impact, and would not have a protruding panel before the right front passenger area.

Beginning in 1956 the automobile makers, confronted with Cornell's statistical proof on instrument panel hazards, began to offer padding on an optional basis at extra cost. Some of this padding was no more than one-eighth of an inch thick. A Cornell study of padding effectiveness, based on accident data for model-year cars between 1956 and 1962, showed padding to be beneficial in reducing or preventing minor injuries, but making little difference in the class of accidents that resulted in fatal or serious injury. The study concluded that "More improvement will be necessary before the instrument panel will be changed from its prominent position [on the charts] associated with deaths and severe injury in automobile accidents."

Existing padding offers no protection from knobs, glove compartment doors, and sharp metal hoods projecting above various groups of instruments. Fatal injuries ranging from simple fracture of the pelvis to a crushed chest are found in the Cornell data to be the result of glove compartment doors opening on collision. Striking this compartment door even when it remains closed has resulted in serious injuries, but the protrusion of the open door is obviously a more serious hazard, and one remediable by any number of safer door or latch designs.

Even less engineering ingenuity would be required to eliminate dangerous protrusions *above* the instrument panel. Dr. Haddon recounts a case which he observed: "In a head-on off-center collision at relatively low speed, a practical nurse who had been driving in one of the cars was thrown diagonally across to the right and caught the front of her scalp on a small screw which was projecting perhaps only an eighth of an inch from the bracket which in that make and model holds on the sun visor. She left a piece of her scalp and her gray hair on it as it ripped her scalp almost from her hairline back to the back of her head. I think it is reasonable to say that someone placed that screw there by design not with injury production in mind, but that nevertheless its placement there undoubtedly in this case, as in probably many others, resulted in unnecessary injury."

In the other car involved in this accident, the woman riding in the right front seat was thrown diagonally across to the left behind the steering wheel and into the very sharply hooded projections above several of the instruments. She suffered serious injuries because of this impact and the localization of the forces produced by the projections. Dr. Haddon says, "These injuries were undoubtedly much more severe than they needed to be, and they were produced in substantial part by inadequate attention to crash design."

Instrument panel design varies with manufacturers, and the variation, however influenced by annual stylistic considerations, has been found to be significant for safety. There are indications that the safety factor has been involved in some Chrysler and Studebaker designs. But at General Motors the stylist luxuriates. The Corvair instrument panel hood, for example, in the model-years

1960 to 1964, extends to the right front section solely for symmetry with the pattern in front of the driver. Dr. Horace Campbell says flatly, "The General Motors' instrument panels are the most dangerous in the world."

ACIR director Robert Wolf has offered a basic approach to instrument panel hazards. "I would like to suggest," he has said, "that the automobile designers re-examine this traditional form of configuration and ask, 'Is the instrument panel a truly functional component of the car, or is it just an accepted hangover from the good old days? What can be done to redesign it or remove it entirely in order to improve crashworthiness?' "

The challenge laid down by Mr. Wolf would be a modest undertaking for a giant industry. Eliminating the center and right sections of the panel and shelf presents no engineering difficulty. The radio and glove compartment could be placed elsewhere conveniently. Mr. Wolf adds, "We're ready for a breakthrough and it would be a tragedy if the industry failed to recognize its opportunity."

But such a basic redesign is not appealing to company management, which sees little reason to eliminate a structure solely for safety purposes. Automobile industry engineers prefer to discuss the instrument panel problem on the assumption that the panel must keep its traditional configuration; on this assumption, they will gladly talk about safety—and at needless, time-consuming length.

A recent industry position on instrument panel hazards and what to do about them provides a fine example of how sophisticated delaying and diversionary tactics can become. This position was made clear at the first specification development conference held by the General Services Administration in Washington on November 12th and 13th 1964, to consider what safety standards the agency should establish for passenger vehicles purchased for the federal government.

GSA officials expressed their concern about several dangers of present instrument panel design. William Sherman of the Automobile Manufacturers Association raised the issue that it is necessary to determine how and where the vehicle occupant strikes the instrument panel. Ford's Robert Fredericks noted a general tendency for the body to strike downward on the top surface of the panel. Mr. Fredericks said that though the panel can be designed so that the occupant would not strike the top surface, style dictated that the "cluster hood" on the driver's side, which was necessary "to prevent reflections into the windshield from instruments and lighted controls," must be "carried in general across the car in the same general shape." Mr. Sherman broadened the dimensions of the problem. "The question here is the combination of surface structure under the surface and padding or whatever is on top of the surface and contours." In reply to an assertion by Colonel Stapp that enough is known now about the impact forces the human skull can safely absorb to give designers a basis for providing greater padding protection and diminished projections, Fredericks added to the industry's case for no action by explaining, "We know these sort of ball-park figures as to what will cause fracture, minimal concussion and things of that nature. But primarily when hitting flat surfaces. We do not know, for example, as a function of radius of curvature of a piece of sheet metal and padding combination what radii are tolerable and not tolerable. We know if it is a flat plate that naturally this is the best you can get."

While Fredericks and his industry colleagues were talking, a Federal Aviation Agency researcher in Oklahoma City was nearing the final phase of a project to determine the tolerances of the human face and skull of impact forces against a deforming surface. John Swearingen, a physiologist and chief of the protection and survival laboratory at the Civil Aeromedical Research Institute, concentrated on injuries to car occupants from dozens of different automobile instrument panel designs stretching back over a decade. With the rigor that has made him one of the most brilliant safety researchers in the aviation field, Swearingen studied over one hundred cases to correlate the injuries received with the forces necessary to duplicate the dents made in the particular dashboard panel. This was done in a variety of ways, but principally by the use of a small catapult with a speed capability of one hundred miles per hour. Dummies bearing instruments were shot down the track in aircraft seats with head and torso swinging forward freely to determine the force and time elements in deformation of the dashboard metal. By a meticulous process of comparing indentations with those on the panels struck by the victims, he was able to determine how much force produced how much head and facial injury. He further checked his data by using cadavers and measuring the results of forty-five head impacts against panels.

Swearingen's conclusions showed that under conditions easily within engineering accomplishment, the human head could take much greater impacts than previously thought possible. These conditions are two: proper padding to distribute the load over the facial area and the proper resilience in the metal underneath to dissipate the impact energy. With such a "transportation environment," as Swearingen terms it, "we should be able to eliminate hundreds of thousands of facial injuries." But with contemporary panel design, even forces generated by five-mile-an-hour impacts can be fatal, says Swearingen. With proper design, a person could hit his head on a panel at forty feet per second with no injuries at all, while presently people are dying from impacts at fifteen feet per second. Even a two-"g" impact on a sharp knob or metal projection such as the corner of a glove compartment door or the compartment latch could be fatal. Such pressure points can concentrate force into thousands of pounds per square inch.

Swearingen believes that the importance of the dashboard panel will increase as lap-type seat belts come into greater use. Passengers who would ordinarily have been hurled through the windshield would, when belted, be more likely to strike the panel. His tests indicate that the auto makers remain indifferent. Despite all the notice of panel hazard and despite explicit recognition of the problem by their safety engineers, the corporate decision-makers chose instrument panels for the 1965 models that were the most hazardous investigated by Swearingen. His instruments showed the highest "g" forces generated were those by impacts on several 1965 instrument panels.

Swearingen says the padding that has gone on autos in this decade has made very little difference in the safety the motorist gets. He concurs with Cornell's finding that the protection is primarily in the very low impacts; but he adds to it a more ominous finding: that "adding a padded lip to some panels has actually about doubled the hazard by using heavy reinforced channel iron to attach the pad." Other panels have a heavy brace beneath the metal which raises the "g" force to as much as one hundred. The so-called padded dash—provided only at extra cost—was offering, in some ways, pressure points far exceeding the unpadded dashboard designs.

The outcome of Swearingen's study was a specific list of design standards for the dashboard panel that will protect the knees and legs as well as the head:

1. No portion of the dashboard panel should be less than ten inches in radius of curvature. (A flat surface would be the best.)
2. The dashboard panel must be entirely covered with at least one-inch-thick, firm, slow-return padding.
3. The thickness of the metal in the dashboard panel should not exceed .030 inches.
4. There should be no metal bracing within three inches of the inside surface of the panel.
5. The glove compartment door along with its rigid frame should be eliminated.
6. All knobs, controls, etc., should be eliminated from the middle and right dashboard sections.
7. Heavy instruments such as the radio, speedometer and clock must be recessed at least three inches with light-weight yokes connecting them to the instrument panel.

Swearingen has systematic data on the maximum tolerable impact forces which the various portions of the face and head can absorb when striking a padded deformable surface. His is the first published study on the subject. Though later research may refine his recommendations, they answer a good many questions for industry engineers. The automobile makers have shown no reaction publicly to Swearingen's data, which they had told the General Services Administration were so badly needed, and which they had supposedly been working so long to obtain. Their position concerning the GSA deliberation over instrument panel standards remained the same after the Swearingen data were released in March, 1965, as it was at the November 1964 meeting. (See Fig. 5)

Swearingen's project—including salaries, materials, and equipment—cost an estimated $25,000. It was the first of its kind, and it was instituted and supported by a governmental aviation safety research facility—not by the twenty-five-billion-dollar automobile industry.

The windshield

The windshield ranks third in frequency and fourth in severity as a cause of injuries in automobile accidents. The Cornell study shows that 11.3 per cent of all people injured in automobile ac-

FIGURE 5

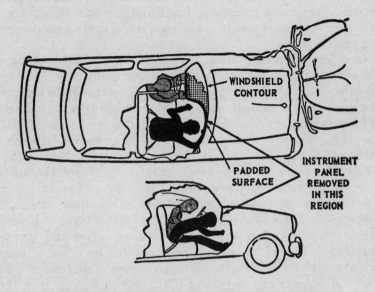

ELIMINATION OF INSTRUMENT PANEL AT RIGHT FRONT POSITION

cidents were hurt by windshield glass. Of this class of injuries, almost ninety per cent are injuries to the head, with neck injuries being rarer but usually more severe. Less severe windshield glass injuries often cause permanent facial disfigurement with psychological consequences that have not been coded in the data-processing machines.

In order to minimize injury, a windshield that is struck by a vehicle occupant must have two important qualities: it must not be so hard that the head snaps back with a concussion or fracture, nor must it yield so easily that the blow breaks it, with resultant hideous lacerations. All American automobiles use laminated glass (a plastic core with glass bonded to it) in contrast to tempered glass (solid glass, heat treated) employed on some European vehicles. The principal experimental research on windshield safety is being conducted at Wayne State University in Detroit and at the University of California at Los Angeles's Institute of Transportation and Traffic Engineering. The conflict over laminated versus tempered glass that rages between commercial groups here and in Europe has not yet been resolved by either of these projects, and a Cornell data analysis released in December 1964 does not indicate any significant differences in injuries from the two types of glass. Since all American cars use laminated glass, the bulk of the injury experience and consequently research attention has been with that type. Dr. Allan Nahum of UCLA points out that the laminated windshield hinges open to let the head through but closes like a razor-sharp jaw on the driver's head and face when his own weight pulls him back inside the car when the vehicle has come to a stop. It is this kind of injury that produces the severe and often fatal neck injuries. Evidence from dozens of crash tests using cadavers at Wayne State's department of engineering mechanics has shown the need for increased resistence to penetration, while at the same time retaining or increasing the yielding characteristics of the glass that are associated with a reduction in concussions.

According to the Cornell study, in cases where the windshield was struck, the severity of the injuries increased sharply with the severity of the damage to the glass. When the glass remains intact, injuries are generally mild. Injuries are twice as severe when the glass is "web-cracked," and twice as severe again when the glass is "web-broken"—using a rough index of progression.

Before the Senate traffic safety hearings in July 1965, General Motors took the occasion to announce that "an intensive research and development program" in this area, launched in 1962 with the cooperation of other automobile companies, had proved that a thicker layer of laminate between the glass would reduce the severity of head lacerations. (Actually, the major research and development work was done by the glass suppliers.) The Cornell data pointing to windshield hazards, alluded to by General Motors in the testimony as a motivating factor for developing safer glass, was first released in 1955. General Motors' representatives told the Senators that "the result of this work is a new windshield glass which nearly doubles occupant-penetration protection." All companies introduced this windshield for their 1966 models.

There was one gap, however, in General Motors' testimony about safety and windshields; namely, that numerous Wayne State laboratory crash tests showed penetration to have occurred in the standard windshields at vehicle speeds down to approximately 12.5 miles per hour. The new windshields, according to this finding, would prevent penetration up to 24 mph. It is not likely that many motorists were aware that the "safety glass" they have been looking through for years could take no more than a 12.5-miles-per-hour impact without threatening the victim with a jagged glass collar. This is not the sort of finding about its automobiles that the industry reveals to the public; nor have car buyers a legally protected right to obtain such critical information.

There is one point on which all specialists concur. The best way to avoid windshield injury is to avoid striking the windshield. At the present time the only available means of passenger restraint is the seat belt. In its way the history of this device tells the engineering and political story of the second collision better than any other vehicle feature.

Passenger restraint

Early in his search for greater automobile safety, Hugh De Haven asked, "Can people be packaged for transport in a manner assuring a better degree of protection against injury and death than is provided by our present vehicles of transportation?" One of the cardinal principles in "packaging" the passenger is that he be firmly but comfortably anchored, so as not to be thrown against the inside of the vehicle or ejected through it.

Seatbelts were adopted for airplanes in the early years of aviation just before World War I, when staying in his craft was one of the pilot's biggest challenges. Turbulent air currents or acrobatic maneuvers could easily throw the pilot from an open-cockpit plane; in one instance a pilot named Lieutenant Towers, later to be a Navy admiral, lost control of his airplane and was hurled from his seat. With luck and agility, he managed to grab hold of part of the plane as he plummeted downward, and he hung on until it crashed.

By the late twenties federal regulations required seat belts installed and worn on all civilian passenger aircraft. With advancing airplane design, it was recognized that such restraints protected occupants from injury in the event of a crash, a sudden stop on land, or a sudden drop in the air.

The transfer of safety knowledge and attitudes from airplanes to automobiles lagged greatly then, as it has ever since. In the thirties and early forties racing drivers rarely used seat belts; the man who did was considered to lack courage. But the work of De Haven at Cornell and the work of Colonel Stapp and his associates changed that attitude: racing associations began to require racing drivers to wear seat belts in the late forties and early fifties. A growing number of physicians, sickened at the sight of highway victims, began writing detailed descriptions for medical journals of injuries that were related to the lack of seat belts.

In 1954 and 1955 Cornell released data showing that ejection from the vehicle accounted for about twenty-five per cent of serious and fatal injuries. The risk of fatal injury was increased fivefold if the occupant was thrown from the car in car crashes. In addition, automobile crash testing done in 1951 by the Cornell Aeronautical Laboratory's collision researcher, Edward Dye, (with the support of the Liberty Mutual Insurance Company) recorded the extraordinary path of motion the human body took even at low impact speeds. One set of slides showed a dummy the size and weight of a six-year-old child in the back seat of a vehicle that was crashed at twenty miles an hour. At .30 seconds, the dummy hit the back of the seat, and at .53 seconds it struck the windshield and again bounced back into the rear seat.

The industry finally showed a reaction to these findings. Chrysler and Ford announced in the late summer of 1955 that they would make seat belts available to car buyers as an optional extra—at extra cost. It was not until January 1964 that the auto industry, prodded by legislation and overwhelming public pressure, accepted the proposition that seat belts should be standard equipment with all new cars.

General Motors played the central role in this delay. The company's chief spokesmen on the issue were engineering vice-president Charles Chayne and vehicle safety engineer Howard Gandelot. Mr. Chayne publicly stated that he thought seat belts offered little promise, and that General Motors did not plan to provide them. Mr. Gandelot constructed his opposition around two themes: (1) "There is not sufficient factual information on the protective value of seat belts in automobiles to form any definite conclusions" and, (2) "There is little interest on the part of the motoring public in actual use of seat belts."

He was particularly resourceful in giving what he thought were valid illustrations. One of his favorites was the experience of Nash Motors which offered a "seat belt" with its optional reclining seat for the Statesman and Ambassador models. Nash provided about fifty thousand of these reclining seats and found customers—as the story goes—so little interested in this so-called seat belt that it was dropped before the end of the 1950-model run. The Nash experience has been cited in one context or another by every automobile manufacturer up to the present day as proof of how little public interest there is in seat belts. The present president of American Motors, Roy Abernethy, remarked in July 1965, "We were the first company—in 1949—to attempt to make seat belts standard. We ran into so much apathy—and actual resistance—that we were forced to drop the feature."

Some facts seem continually to be obscured in the industry's interpretation. Nash provided a belt to hold a reclining passenger in place against the shifting and stopping that would ordinarily be experienced in a moving car. Billboards showed a grandmother sleeping peacefully, held snugly by the belt. It was not constructed, offered or advertised as a belt for collision protection. What are now known as seat belts were not offered by American Motors until the mid-fifties. This reclining-seat "seat belt" was not emphasized in Nash's promotion of the reclining seat option; in fact the belt was completely hidden underneath the seat, and many customers did not even know it was there. There was nothing in the owner's manual about the belt. Nash dropped the feature because it considered it a needless expense. Ralph Isbrandt, vice-president of American Motors, told the Roberts' House subcommittee on Traffic Safety in a 1957 hearing on seat belts, "As we gained experience with the reclining seat, it appeared that this feature actually did not create an increased need for a restraining device."

Gandelot gave further "evidence" of "public apathy" in the small number of letters which General Motors had received from the public about seat belts. He recounted how the seat belts and shoulder harnesses he had tested restricted his ability to reach some of the vehicle controls, rumpled his suit, and gave him aches. He denounced those who were pushing for seat belts as people motivated by "the profit angle."

The arguments General Motors adduced in its opposition to seat belts are less important than the reason for such arguments. The reason is simple: the seat belt is a constant reminder to the motorist of the risk of accident. The seat belt is an emphatic reminder of the second collision, an item that alerts people to expect more safety in the cars they buy. General Motors has never viewed these as desirable expectations to elicit from its customers.

Gandelot and his superior at General Motors, Chayne, watched with skepticism Ford's advertising campaign promoting seat belts as an option of its 1956 models. The public's response to the campaign brought a demand for more seat belts than the company could provide at first. Between September 1955 and January 1956, many Ford purchasers who wanted seat belts could not get them and had to accept delivery of their cars without the belts. Robert McNamara, then vice-president of the Ford division, reported in February 1957 that "more than 400,000 seat belts have been sold by Ford since we introduced them," and that no other optional feature "ever caught on so fast."

General Motors was not impressed. About this time, GM's president, Harlow Curtice, had a sharp exchange with Charles Shuman, president of the American Farm Bureau Federation, at a meeting of the President's Committee for Traffic Safety. Shuman wanted to know why the automobile industry as a whole was not offering seat belts as standard equipment. Curtice told him that the idea was impractical and inadvisable.

The Roberts' hearings in 1957 brought together expert testimony about the desirability of seat belts as shown in experimental work and accident experience. On the basis of the hearings record, Roberts' special subcommittee on traffic safety concluded that "seat belts, properly manufactured and properly installed, are a valuable safety device, and careful consideration for their use should be given by the motoring public." Charles Chayne appeared at these hearings to repeat the circular argument about the lack of public acceptance or demand for seat belts as a reason for not promoting them.

Gandelot, who was continually called upon to express the General Motors' view on the seat belt issue, once told an inquirer, "I delight in living my life each day, realizing that the information I give out is extremely factual." Such a sentiment cannot be faulted; the only difficulty was that GM's chief safety engineer never had any information to give out. While demanding more proof about the value of seat belts, he responded to requests for substantiating his skepticism with answers like this one, made in 1955: "While we certainly have a lot of engineering record films of barrier impact crashes, both normal and high speed, and quite a few simulated impact tests made with a new and very controllable apparatus which we designed and built some time ago, this is all under the classification of engineering data and not for public distribution." He chided his critics in the medical profession by contrasting their lack of knowledge about the seat belt issue with his own "factual view of things," which took into account "only those opinions which have been established on a basis of facts." Yet Gandelot never felt the need to justify the safety of existing vehicle design, however stringent were his standards for those who suggested improvements. In 1954, he offered this astonishing judgment to a physician who was pressing him on the seat belt matter: "Until we have substantially more information I find it difficult to believe that the seat belt can afford the driver any great amount of protection over and above that which is available to him through the medium of the safety-type steering wheel if he has his hands on the wheel and grips the rim sufficiently tight to take advantage of its energy absorption properties and also takes advantage of the shock absorbing action which can be achieved by correct positioning of the feet and legs." A few weeks later he wrote to the same physician, saying that there was very little data available about the effect of seat belts at higher deceleration rates and force values. "This makes me wonder," he wrote, "if, in the public interest, the industry should undertake a fact-finding program. Considering the quantity and type of instrumentation, the anthropomorphic dummies, vehicles and technical personnel required, it would be my guess that such a program would cost upward of 100 thousand dollars." Gandelot appeared to be turning a long overdue duty of the industry into an act of charity.

General Motors was understandably concerned about the consequences of overt emphasis on safety features as a competitive practice in selling cars. Such an emphasis could only serve to focus public attention on the role of vehicle design in causing injuries during the second collision. Claims by one company that its cars are safer would quicken the interest of federal officials in asking, "How safe is 'safe?'" They might propose that automobiles meet federal safety standards just as trains, ships, and aircraft have been required to do for decades.

It seemed particularly significant that less than a year after Ford began an unprecedented campaign advertising its "Life Guard Design" ("safety door locks," "safety steering wheels," "safety rear view mirror" as standard equipment, and "crash pads" for instrument panels and seat belts as options) the Roberts' committee opened on July 16, 1956, the first hearings on traffic safety in the history of the United States Congress.

Ford terminated its safety campaign in the spring of 1956 after an internal policy struggle won by those who agreed with the General Motors' analysis of the probable unsettling consequences of a vehicle safety campaign. The 1956 Ford finished second to Chevrolet in sales, but its failure to be number one had nothing to do with the Ford safety campaign.* Even so, it has since been cited to prove that "safety doesn't sell." Working through the Auto-

---

* That was not the only year that Ford failed to exceed Chevrolet in sales. Moreover, the 1956 Ford, in contrast to the Chevrolet and the Plymouth, was barely changed from the previous year. Ford's Robert McNamara released publicly in early 1957 detailed figures on safety option sales and market surveys showing the marked success of the safety features in attracting purchasers. But to the delight of the industry the saying that in 1956 "Ford sold safety and Chevy sold cars" caught hold and became a standard response to critics of the automobile companies. It is interesting to note that Ford officials never went out of their way to deny this erroneous impression unless they were specifically requested to do so.

mobile Manufacturers Association and other industry-constituted committees, General Motors found its views accepted by other domestic automobile makers. Vehicle safety became an industry-wide policy matter rather than an individual company matter.

After 1956, industry seat belt policy entered a period where belts were offered as an extra-cost option but were not widely promoted. While saturation advertising and continual repetition of the sales message are deemed necessary to sell automobiles, seat belts were left to win customers without such communication. The manufacturers then seemed mystified because more car buyers did not demand this option. Chevrolet general manager Edward Cole said in 1959, "One of the startling problems so far as crash injury is concerned is the utter refusal on the part of the American motorists to be strapped into a seat by a safety belt or a shoulder harness. We have made provision in our cars to attach seat belts properly and we have made seat belts and shoulder harnesses available to our dealers. The fact of the matter is that the sale of these safety features is practically nil, indicating a real disinterest on the part of the public in their own safety."

Before Mr. Cole wrote these words, he might have found that Chevrolets, along with other General Motors' cars, presented great obstacles to "attaching seat belts properly." In 1961, C. M. Olson of the American Society of Safety Engineers commented on the unique problems of installing seat belts on General Motors' models of the late fifties: "All four-door GM cars are exceedingly difficult in which to make front seat installations. Removing the sharp wire clips deep down in the front seat construction is a strenuous task—and somewhat like gynecological surgery in the dark—but has to be done to insure that the belt is not abraded or cut where the user cannot see the damage being done." Mr. Cole had not explained how shoulder harnesses could be installed in the "hard-top" models featuring doors without a pillar to anchor the harness on, and Olson offered an obvious insight: "I feel that people will otherwise [in cars without pillars] be reluctant to attempt such a difficult do-it-yourself job, or to slit new car upholstery to get the belts through, or pay the price of having it done properly so the belts will not be damaged in use."

Although they had a long record of success in creating a public demand for even the most superficial automotive features, the manufacturers lamented the absence of demand for seat belts while they made it difficult for such a demand ever to materialize. Paul Ackerman, engineering vice-president of Chrysler Corporation, said to the Roberts' subcommittee in a 1959 hearing, "In considering the question as to whether or not we should provide fixed and permanent attachments for safety belts, I intended to explain that many people have very definite objections to the installation of belts in their cars." John Moore, former director of the Cornell project, provided the answer. "No safety device can be used by the public unless it is first made available to the public."

The first step in the drive for availability was to make seat belts standard equipment on all automobiles. The initiative was taken by the New York State joint legislative committee on motor vehicles and traffic safety under the chairmanship of Senator Edward Speno. The committee decided in 1959 that seat belts must come as "standard factory-installed equipment, just as hydraulic brakes and sealed beam headlights." The following year the committee said, "It is the Committee's opinion that the auto manufacturers will not—now or in the foreseeable future—install seat belts as standard equipment in all cars unless forced to do so." The Speno committee then gave the automobile makers an opportunity to disprove its prediction. During the 1960 legislative sessions, automobile industry lobbyists defeated a bill requiring seat belts on all new cars sold in New York.

The following year, Senator Speno decided upon a strategy that would show the absurdity of the industry's position. He filed a bill to require new cars to have anchorage units for belts to facilitate and reduce the cost of installation. These anchorage units were merely threaded holes through the car floor, supported by steel plates which could be punched out during fabrication at no added cost to the car buyer. (At that time, a pair of seat belts cost between thirty and thirty-five dollars, plus about fifteen dollars for the mechanic's work in installing them.) The automobile manufacturers resisted. Speno and a group of legislators and administrators went to Detroit to confront company officials directly. The industry must have thought this was a routine visit by a legislative committee; the visitors got the routine tour of company plants in a special bus equipped with a loudspeaker and were given a show of crashing a few castoff vehicles with dummies. The usual points were made by the car makers: if New York passed one statute and other states passed conflicting ones, it would make it impossible for the manufacturers to comply; it is sometimes safer to be ejected from a vehicle than to remain inside; it would cost the consumer more; seat belts would hurt automobile sales. General Motors' Charles Chayne told Senator Speno that car safety is best decided by car makers. "A lot of people come here with ideas," he said. "Roberts came here. Ribicoff came here. They went away."

Speno was not impressed. At a dinner for the visiting committee in the Detroit Athletic Club, he told a group of industry vice-presidents that the "comfortable delusion of safety the public gets in your cars is in sharp contrast to the broken bodies these cars cause. You've been showing me the ballpark, gentlemen, but you're not talking to me. I hope you will put in the anchorage units. It will cost you almost nothing. But whether you do or not, we're going to legislate it." He asked for a meeting at four P.M. the following day and indicated that he expected a formal reply. The next morning Mark Bauer of the Automobile Manufacturers Association informed Speno that the industry would provide anchorage units in all 1962 models, but they would like to restrict them to the front seat since such a small proportion of people killed are back seat riders. Speno reluctantly made the concession. It was agreed explicitly that following the afternoon meeting there would be a joint announcement. Bauer told Speno that the industry wanted no public release before the meeting. But early that afternoon, four of the automobile companies sent out press releases announcing that they would provide anchorage units in the coming model year. The industry had avoided the joint announcement and preserved the carefully nurtured fiction that all safety advances are made voluntarily.

Speno went back to Albany and sponsored legislation requiring anchorage units on cars to make sure that there would be no reversal by the automobile manufacturers in the future. The manufacturers opposed the bill, but it was passed. Other states followed New York's example. In 1963 New York, impressed by a Wisconsin law enacted in 1961, passed legislation requiring front seat belts beginning with all 1965 model cars sold in New York. By this time, the automobile companies, prodded by legislation, were cooperating with the U.S. Public Health Service and voluntary agencies in promoting seat belts. Many government agencies and commercial fleets had installed belts. But the automobile makers were still opposed to standard installation.

The first break in this opposition came from a smaller manufacturer. Early in 1963, Sherwood Egbert, president of Studebaker, announced that his company would install front seat belts on all cars manufactured after February 15, 1963, and contributed this heretical statement: "It is our feeling—a strong feeling—that safety measures in motor cars should not come by petition from motorists but that automobile manufacturers should lead in safety equipment."

Under pressure from Speno to begin standard installation before the New York law's effective date of June 30, 1964, the automobile companies finally agreed. In August 1963, they announced that, effective January 1, 1964, they would make front seat belts standard on 1964 passenger cars with list prices adjusted to include the additional cost. Each company alluded to its long-standing interest in safety and seat belts and its gratification for the increasing public acceptance which made such an announcement possible.

Thus the industry rounded out a decade of strenuous opposition before its cars were equipped with a primitive passenger restraint device as standard equipment. The seat belt should have been introduced in the twenties and rendered obsolete by the early fifties, for it is only the first step toward a more rational passenger restraint system which modern technology could develop and perfect for mass production. Such a system ideally would not rely on the active participation of the passenger to take effect; it would be the superior *passive* safety design which would come into use only when needed, and without active participation of the occupant. It would eliminate the "acceleration overshoot" characteristic of conventional seat belts, which do not prevent the passenger from striking his head or his upper body or both on the corner post, instrument panel, windshield, or header strip. It would also eliminate the "bottoming effect" or the passenger's sliding under, and the backlash or rebound effects.

Protection like this could be achieved by a kind of inflatable air bag restraint which would be actuated to envelop a passenger before a crash. Such a system has been recently experimented with for airplane passenger protection. Both General Motors and Ford did work on a system like this about 1958 but dropped the inquiry and now refuse even to communicate with outside scientists and engineers interested in this approach to injury prevention. There are a number of general energy-absorption systems that engineering ingenuity could devise to operate either inside or outside the vehicle.

It has long been recognized that a combination lap belt and shoulder harness—called the three-point belt—is more effective than the simple lap belt. It prevents forward jack-knifing and provides lateral restraint against side impacts. Cornell analyzed data from California accident reports and found that simple lap seat belts were quite effective in controlling passenger ejection, reducing dangerous and fatal injury by thirty-five per cent or more. But later data on front seat-belted passengers, released in a 1963 Cornell report, found that in head-on collisions, when passengers stay in the car, there seems to be little difference in injury between those who wore seat belts and unbelted occupants. Cornell added that "the problem is not that the seat belt is a failure but that the front compartment—the dash panel and steering assembly—is not providing forward clearance for the head, knees, and torso, so that the body can jack-knife without interference."

The installation of the three-point belt is now being pressed by crash research specialists outside the industry as the second stage in passenger restraint development. This belt presents complications that the automobile makers would like to avoid. Cornell's Robert Wolf told the annual convention of the American Automobile Association in September 1964 what the difficulty is: "Installing a shoulder harness, however, in one's own car is an extremely discouraging project, much like that of trying to fit a homemade seat belt installation ten years ago. The problem is first to find a structurally sound anchor point for the shoulder strap and in a position where the strap doesn't slip off of the shoulder. To make a good anchor point usually requires a good mechanic with a good engineering sense. The chances of early large-scale adaptation to all types of American cars by the simple expedient of the industry's providing standard shoulder strap anchor points, as was the case for seat belts, seems remote to me because of the difficulty of providing a structurally sound attachment point on hardtops and convertibles, which have no center post to the roof."

Hardtops and convertibles have been gaining rapidly in the percentage of total car sales, reaching almost fifty per cent in 1964. Even the recent sedan models with center posts present formidable difficulties in attaching the upper anchor of the harness and, when installed, give no assurance that they are strong enough to take the pull. Because the manufacturers are on the defensive they take the hard line. Once again, their rationale is based on unspecified tests of only one of the several kinds of possible shoulder harnesses. General Motors' president James Roche delivered a statement to the Ribicoff Senate subcommittee in July 1965. He said, "At this time, our plans do not include the installation of anchorages for shoulder harnesses. We have conducted extensive tests and studies of this device. Some of these tests have indicated that in a severe impact situation, shoulder harnesses can do more harm than good. While the harness does restrain the car occupant's forward motion, it also can deflect the impact force into a downward motion, forcing the occupant farther under the seat belt. This downward force can result in highly injurious pressures on the abdominal area. A shoulder harness also can exert dangerous pressure on the occupant's neck, particularly in the case of a relatively high-speed side impact."

It is obvious that poorly designed shoulder harnesses, inappropriately anchored, might result in some injuries at the same time that others were prevented. But it is just as obvious that good design and installation at proper anchorage points can avoid these small risks. Crash studies and accident analysis of the effect of these harnesses in England and Sweden, where they are in more widespread use, have shown results highly in their favor.

At the Eighth Stapp Car Crash Conference, held in Detroit in October 1964, all the automobile companies had representatives present. None denied the superiority of shoulder harnesses over lap belts. Several, especially Chrysler's Roy Haeusler, actively advocated the use of harnesses. Dr. Paul Joliet, chief of the U.S. Public Health Service's division of accident prevention, has urged that shoulder harnesses be made standard equipment on new cars.

But the lack of an adequate center post, or any center post at all, on most models remains a problem. The search for making the seat belt more effective leads, as General Motors accurately foresaw years ago, to probes of other design inadequacies. In this case, the focus is on the seat structure. Seats that tear away from their moorings and add unbearable "g" forces to a passenger already hurtling forward are one of the most common design failures recorded by crash investigators. The General Motors' *Engineering Journal* May-June 1955 reported that for a GM seat to be considered satisfactory, it had to withstand a load of one thousand pounds. This means that two 150-pound persons sitting in the rear seats and striking the back of the front seat at only a 3½ "g" force (or any combination thereof) would dislodge the seat from its moorings. In recent years, seats have been a little more firmly anchored, but the problem remains. Medical investigators reported a case in which a 195-pound football player, seated in the back seat of a car involved in an accident, was thrown against the back of the front seat, pushing it forward and crushing to death a front-seat passenger.

In March 1965, *Product Engineering* reported the development of an integrated seat by an automobile company supplier: "Current seat belt anchoring hooks the belt to bolts in the car floor; the new system anchors the seat, then attaches the belts to the seat. And that's the safety feature; positive seat anchoring should prevent the seat from being torn loose during a crash. The seat is designed to accommodate a retractable harness system and headrests (to prevent the head from snapping back on rear end collisions). It can be added to existing cars or incorporated as original equipment at little or no extra cost, according to the manufacturer, which presented prototypes to all the domestic car producers."

What is important in this example, as in other examples of automobile safety features, is not the particular design, but the performance function which is ignored by contemporary automobiles. UCLA's Derwyn Severy has pointedly criticized the industry at technical meetings for not designing a seat that will prevent the neck or spinal injury of the common rear-end collision. "It is the one most easily corrected by design and the one given least attention after perhaps the steering wheel and shaft," he said in 1964. Yet university crash injury researchers have not succeeded in getting industry specialists to discuss this problem in open forum on a high technical level. It is the most neglected aspect of passenger restraint.

Seat belts are now standard equipment and their installed cost to the car buyer is about one third of what they cost five years ago. Nearly thirty per cent of all automobiles on the road are equipped with seat belts, and the number of motorists using them is steadily increasing. The growth of habitual seat belt usage will accelerate now that the seat belt has been removed from its place as the ugly duckling of the automobile world's vast array of optional equipment and gingerbread.

The passenger compartment

In a collision, an automobile passenger can be adequately restrained and still be injured or killed if another vehicle, a tree, an abutment, or any other striking object invades the passenger compartment. Nearly a third of all injury-producing accidents involve either roof impact caused by a car rolling over or penetration of the side wall of the vehicle cabin.

The two elements of the car's structure most directly involved in such accidents are the chassis frame and the body frame. The purpose of the chassis frame is to give proper support for the body and chassis components. The body frame, which has been welded or joined with bolts to the chassis frame, is the other load-bearing structure in the car.

It is also a function of the car's body structure and frame to absorb collision energy and maintain what collision specialists call the "structural integrity of the outer shell which surrounds the restrained passenger." But when it comes to design and manufacture for such performance in collisions, the automobile industry has either ignored the statistical evidence of the problem or is deliberately withholding knowledge about it. Despite the reports of Cornell's Automotive Crash Injury Research project and other crash injury research groups on the significant role of car frames and bodies in side-impact crashes, there is not a single discussion of the subject to be found in the technical literature produced by the industry's engineers and stylists. There is neither published evidence nor claims by the companies to any proving-ground tests of direct side-impact crashes involving the passenger compartment. Nor is there in the technical literature any attempt to establish load criteria, to evaluate existing frame types, or to study the relative adequacy of proposed alternatives. In this critical area of automotive engineering there is instead almost total confusion—leaving the consumer helpless to make any meaningful distinctions about the relative safety of the various types of body structures and frames employed.

A case in point is the "X" or "cruciform" type chassis frame. This frame was introduced in 1957, primarily to reduce the problem of restricted headroom and difficult entry into the "low-profile" automobiles that were becoming popular after the mid-fifties. The X frame construction does not have side rails along the passenger compartment, as did most previous conventional frame designs. From the time the cruciform type frame was introduced, it was widely used by General Motors on Chevrolet, Buick, and Cadillac. The Ford Motor Company continued to use frames with side rails, and it was evident that the two companies held strongly different opinions about the two designs.

In the fall of 1959, a photograph of a Chevrolet Impala that was broken in half after striking a tree broadside was widely circulated in newspapers throughout the country. The frame had severed at the intersection of the X. The report of the General Motors' investigators who rushed to the scene attributed the severance of the frame to the semi-airborne position of the car as it struck the tree. This had apparently allowed the engine mass to act as the head of a sledge hammer. At the General Motors' engineering center in Michigan the conclusion was that "automobiles are not designed to withstand such tremendous lateral forces —this would be extremely uneconomical."

General Motors' spokesmen continued to defend the cruciform type frame as offering substantial resistance to side impacts because of the rocker panel and floor pan under-bracing members— even though by 1965 all General Motors' models except the Buick Riviera had abandoned the design in favor of the perimeter type. In 1960 the General Motors' technical center offered proof that a unitized structure with side rails can also split into two pieces. A picture of a Ford Thunderbird, torn in half after slamming against a telephone pole and tree, was offered as evidence to critics of the X type frame.

This comparison enraged Ford engineers. Fletcher N. Platt, a highly talented research engineer at Ford, retorted that the Thunderbird case involved a telephone guy-wire that had "acted as a knife on the entire body structure." In contrast, he said, "the Chevrolet that broke in half failed at the center of the X frame after hitting a tree." Platt said, "The X frame has no advantages from the standpoint of passenger protection. It requires less material to support the four corners of the car, but it is obviously less rigid and provides little lateral [side] protection to the passenger compartment." He suggests consulting any "'unbiased' structural engineer regarding these two designs." Mr. Platt might not consider Mr. Harry Barr, vice-president for engineering of General Motors, qualified for the designation "unbiased," but Mr. Barr did admit grudgingly, under questioning, that the Oldsmobile perimeter type frame had some advantages over the Chevrolet X type frame in side-impact crashes at speeds of about fifteen miles per hour. Further proof that some General Motors' engineers agreed with Ford's Platt came in the form of an internal memorandum prepared by the Oldsmobile division in 1963 in which the Oldsmobile "guard-beam" frame was described as offering an "extra margin of protection" over the X type frames of Chevrolet, Buick, and Cadillac.

The manufacturers may disagree about the relative effectiveness of different kinds of body frames, but they say little or nothing about the comparative safety of the conventional sedan and the so-called hard-top models.

In the hard-top models there is no center door pillar from the window sill upward and no upper half of the door frame. The same is true of convertible models, but at least the customer is on obvious notice when he buys a convertible, while the hard-top resembles the conventional sedan in the apparent security of the enclosure.

One danger in the hard-top model was cited by Robert Wolf of ACIR, who said, "It is quite common in a side impact of a four-door hard-top car for the center post to tear out at the floor attachment joint, where the post is loaded severely in bending. These posts are probably not designed to withstand a severe crash load—they are there for other purposes."

Still another hazard is the dangerous consequence of a "roll-over" in a hard-top model. Without the upper center post to support the roof structure, the hard-top offers less protection to its occupants than does the conventional sedan. In many accidents involving roll-overs, the hard-top has been described as having "crumpled like a Japanese lantern." One official of the Fisher Body Corporation said of General Motors' hard-tops that they were "on the borderline." But who knows what the borderline is?

If the companies insist on pillarless construction, there are various engineering approaches that can strengthen the crash resistance of their cars. The manufacturers themselves have patented practical kinds of latch and reinforcing member arrangements which lock the side of the vehicle into an integral unity by the use of multiple latch locations. Nothing has been done to apply these patents to current automobile production.

Likewise, the provision of roll bars to protect against the impact of a roll-over is another possible improvement that is viewed negatively by the industry. Many physicians with an interest in automobile races have been impressed with the protection given drivers by roll bars or equivalent reinforcement when their vehicles go through spectacular accidents, sometimes flipping over and over for hundreds of feet. Dr. John States, president of the American Association for Automotive Medicine, has urged the automobile makers to incorporate roll bars in their designs. But such a safety feature would apparently inconvenience the designers of hard-tops and, even in sedans with upper center posts, would involve changes which are abhorrent to the cost analysts and stylists.

In the whole area of reinforced and strengthened body and chassis structures, the industry has steadfastly avoided testing, research, and change for safety. While gearing its public relations to stories of vehicles crashing at proving grounds, it continues to ignore the work of the men who have done the necessary studies. One such man, James J. Ryan, a recently retired professor of engineering at the University of Minnesota, has done extensive car collision experiments. Just one of his findings suggests the direction the car makers could follow. Mr. Ryan said recently, "From our tests we have determined means of strengthening the structure of the vehicle to prevent displacement of the walls, the door, and the posts and the penetration of the driver's compartment. The forces of impact could be reduced four times by the proper construction of any vehicle without increasing its cost or weight."

It has become evident that the Cornell data play a central role in any discussion of the second collision. After half a century of automobile usage, a staff of only nine people began, with federal support, the first statistical reporting system on how interior car designs injure and kill motorists. The time for analyzing the design of automobiles had come, and the crucial distinction between the causes of accidents and the causes of injury was shown with unmistakable clarity. The driver could no longer be the scapegoat for industry negligence in the design of their vehicles. From the day De Haven's group began work in 1952, segments of the automobile industry suspected that things might never be the same again if they remained aloof from Cornell's probings.

Two events in 1955 moved the industry to act. The U.S. Public Health Service joined the Department of the Army in support of Cornell's Automotive Crash Injury Research (ACIR), thus assuring continuity and growth to the project. Early in the year ACIR released a comparative study of automobiles manufactured from 1940 to 1949 and those manufactured from 1950 to 1954 on the question of whether the newer group produced more or less injury than the older group in similar accidents. The study concluded that "on the most conservative basis, 'new' (1950-54) car designs have not demonstrated any improvements in the injury effects produced by accidents. When injury-producing accidents occur, occupants of 1950-54 cars are injured more often than occupants of 1940-49 cars. Further, there is a statistically significant increase in the frequency of fatality among the occupants of 'newer' cars. The contention that present day automobiles are 'safer' in injury-producing accidents is not borne out by the facts."

For its part, General Motors shrugged off the findings. Some Ford and Chrysler officials, however, were more sensitive to the possible consequences of this kind of information. An independent project, solidly financed, was acquiring the statistical capability to evaluate on a comparative basis the safety of automobiles based on their actual accident injury experience. The officials realized that it would be to the industry's advantage to establish their presence in ACIR's work. Before the end of 1955 Ford and Chrysler each announced a two-year grant to ACIR of $100,000 per year. In 1957 General Motors finally joined them in providing financial support through the Automobile Manufacturers Association. During the past several years, ACIR has relied on annual grants of $175,000 from the Automobile Manufacturers Association and $300,000 from the U. S. Public Health Service.

From the standpoint of protecting its interests, the industry has never received so much for so little. The result has been an impressive perpetuation of the status quo in vehicle safety design, in spite of the potentially devastating impact of the collected data. Right from the beginning a close liaison was established between ACIR and the automobile industry. ACIR's director, Robert Wolf, said recently that interim studies and preliminary findings are often reviewed with the Automobile Manufacturers Association. The AMA is consistently asked for guidance and usually reviews drafts of reports before they are released to the public. Prior to a major announcement, such as the one made in November 1964, called "Automobile Crash Injury in Relation to Car Size," it has been common practice for ACIR to meet with industry representatives and go over the wording in the release.

Why Cornell finds it necessary to seek the advice and approval of the AMA concerning statistical analysis and reporting of data dealing with past accidents is not explained. Certainly ACIR has an adequate statistical staff and all the necessary data-processing equipment. The answer, in large part, lies in the AMA's desire to exercise a reviewing function which assures that ACIR does not name makes and models. To say, for instance, that the steering assembly is a major instrument of injury is a finding that can be tolerated by the automobile companies, but to have ACIR reports say that Make A's steering column is twice as likely to injure the driver as those in Make B, C, and D, would be damaging; it would tell consumers, insurance companies, and interested public agencies that some cars are not as safe as other cars.

The manufacturers have been almost entirely successful in making ACIR see matters their way. On only two occasions has Cornell named the brands of cars involved in ACIR reports. In 1964, ACIR's B. J. Campbell reported that an analysis of door latch effectiveness on very late model cars showed little difference between General Motors, Ford and Chrysler. Three years earlier, when a Cornell report found significant differences in door latch failure among the "Big Three," it deleted the car names and replaced them with Brand X designations. Another instance came in November of 1964. The Cornell report, called "The Safety Performance of 1962-1963 Automobile Door Latches and Comparison with Earlier Latch Designs," was based on data from 24,342 cars in which at least one occupant was injured during an accident. Among its more interesting conclusions was: "The doors of General Motors' cars were torn off more frequently than those of Ford or Chrysler and the type of hinge damage appeared to be different, too: the General Motors' hinge appeared to snap off cleanly with little or none of the deformation or twisting observed for other cars." ACIR was specific with its figures:

PERCENTAGE OF CARS WITH DOORS TORN OFF

	Chrysler	Ford	General Motors
pre-1956	1.9	2.8	2.5
1956	0.6	3.7	2.5
1957	2.2	1.6	2.0
1958	2.4	2.2	1.3
1959	2.1	0.6	3.3
1960	0.7	1.3	2.6
1961	0.7	1.0	4.2
1962	0.9	1.0	5.9
1963	0.8	0.6	5.1

In the past two years there have been indications that ACIR is not entirely satisfied with the constraints placed upon it as a result of its "understanding" with the Automobile Manufacturers Association, but the chafing has not yet resulted in any blossoming of scientific independence.

However cautious ACIR has been in seeing that its internal workings and projected studies be kept from the public view, it made a mistake with the formally announced and suddenly suppressed Shoemaker and Narragon report. This was an analysis of steering column penetration scheduled for release in November 1963. ACIR director Robert Wolf gave a preview of the findings in an address he delivered that month at a Liberty Mutual Life Insurance Company conference on the automobile and public health. Wolf said, "This study, which examines accidents involving standard American cars, compacts and European cars, shows clearly that injury to drivers is strongly increased when column penetration occurs." He noted that in accidents of similar severity, the column on some makes of cars held up much less effectively than on others. Wolf then cited the report as "Narragon, Eugene A., and Shoemaker, Norris E., Steering Column Penetration in Automobile Accidents. Automotive Crash Injury Research, Cornell Aeronautical Laboratory, Inc., Report No. VJ-1823-R4, November 1963." Several months earlier in a laboratory pamphlet entitled "Transportation Research," the same reference appeared. The month of November ended, and there was no report. There has still been no such report released. In ACIR's annual report for 1964, it was disclosed that the Shoemaker study was released to the AMA for the "purpose of securing technical guidance for use in a final report." The report also said, "the ACIR staff is still not satisfied that the best approach to the study has been formulated." Since the study pertained to what Robert Wolf called "important comparisons between car makes," caution indeed had been the order of the day.

The general explanation about statistical difficulties given by ACIR is not persuasive for two reasons. First, the ACIR seven-man statistical staff, headed by Dr. Jaakko Kihlberg, is acknowledged to have a high order of technical skill. Second, statistical difficulties of such seriousness would seem to have been discoverable well before the announcement that the report would be issued on a specific date.

As the Cornell data have accumulated to levels permitting more refined analysis of makes and models, private criticism by certain crash injury research specialists and observers of ACIR's tabu against naming manufacturers and models has mounted as well. Yet future plans for topics and studies to be undertaken by ACIR give no indication that analyses by manufacturer or make will be published.

Aversion to naming the manufacturer or make of car is not the only way that ACIR pays interest on the funds supplied by the Automobile Manufacturers Association. For almost a decade, ACIR has been providing each sponsoring automobile company with microfilm copies of accident photographs and police and medical reports of cases involving that company's products. For example, General Motors receives case reports relating to GM automobiles. These cases are provided only to the manufacturers. Furthermore, when an unusual occurrence of structural collapse or an injury relating to a particular make is observed, even if it is just one clinical investigation, notification is given to the producer of that automobile.

The exclusive funneling of specific case materials to the automobile makers by ACIR raises serious questions of public policy. ACIR's work is largely financed and supported by public agencies and funds. Over sixty per cent of its annual funds come from the U.S. Public Health Service, but the public contribution is much greater than indicated by the percentage. ACIR receives data for only a small fraction of its true cost since police and public health personnel freely contribute their time in preparing the specially designed report form that ACIR supplies them. This information should be considered a national data bank to be used for the benefit of the public generally.

In the present situation an injured person cannot obtain even the reports pertaining to the accident in which he was involved. Yet victims of marine or air disasters or their legal representatives have the explicit legal right to the detailed accident investigation data gathered by the Coast Guard or Civil Aeronautics Board. The Cornell data should be freely available to the public. In his final report on four years of investigation of fatal automobile accidents in the Boston area under a U.S. Public Health Service grant similar to that given Cornell, Alfred L. Moseley urged, "The findings should be public records so that justice and fair play in criminal and liability proceedings would be assured."

ACIR has rebuffed requests from public agencies to release to them even a small portion of the data which ACIR has given to the manufacturers. The New York State Joint Legislative Committee on Motor Vehicles and Traffic Safety (the Speno Committee) got in touch with Mr. Wolf in May 1963, taking note of an ACIR study released in 1961 that showed significant variations in door opening frequency among cars made by the "Big Three" manufacturers. The committee requested identification of the manufacturers and photographs of door latch and hinge failures in order to give it a basis on which to determine what design differences in the various door latches and hinges were associated with a higher frequency of door openings. The committee was in the middle of its pioneering investigation into vehicle safety and the need for safety design standards. ACIR turned down the committee's request, but a year and a half later decided it was wiser to publish the fact, with accompanying photographs, that General Motors had the worst door-opening record, followed in order by Ford and Chrysler.

On March 27, 1965, the Speno Committee wrote to Dr. Paul Joliet, chief of the Division of Accident Prevention in the U.S. Public Health Service, the organization that administers the federal grant to ACIR. The Speno Committee said that since the basic case data that ACIR supplies to the manufacturers is available to the Public Health Service, the committee would like to review these records in order to make its own analysis. The committee further pointed out that it considered the Cornell data to be publicly owned and therefore accessible to public agencies—local, state, or federal.

Dr. Joliet called in the principals of the ACIR project to review the Public Health Service's policy concerning the issues raised by the Speno Committee. The result was a blanket endorsement of the status quo. Dr. Joliet stated flatly that ACIR was "free to determine with whom they wish to discuss the nature of any preliminary analyses they have performed, to whom they wish to make available any of their raw data material, and also to determine whether they wish to consult with their sponsors regarding publication of particular preliminary or final analyses. Further, the release of case data material to other investigators or other interested parties is at the discretion of the principal investigator and the institution."

Not only has Dr. Joliet's division endorsed ACIR's policy of sharing its data only with the car manufacturers, but also it has denied *itself* the use of the data. Though the Division of Accident Prevention has the right to receive the same case material given to the manufacturers, it has deliberately chosen not to do so. When asked the reason for this policy, one employee of the division answered, "Who wants hot potatoes?"

Dr. Joliet and his associates seem to believe that their responsibility ends after they determine the value of the research proposal they are financing. In view of the Public Health Service's legal mandate, this is a remarkably limited role. The Division of Accident Prevention's key purpose is to plan and conduct "a nationwide accident prevention program aimed at encouraging and assisting state and local health and other agencies in the development, operation and improvement of local accident prevention programs." Dr. Joliet has told many Congressional committees that his division's interest is in preventing deaths and injuries. Presumably empirical data would help in this work.

To permit public funds to be mixed with industry money in such a project as ACIR and to give researchers full discretion to give data to manufacturers while denying it to all others is nothing short of an abdication of the public trust. By this action, the Division of Accident Prevention of the U.S. Public Health Service is sanctioning what amounts to a subsidy of the automobile industry, since the industry is the exclusive recipient of data that is paid for mainly through taxpayer contributions. This is a real bargain for the automobile manufacturers, whose contribution to ACIR amounts to the equivalent of only 2¢ for every car they sell.

There is no evidence that the industry has improved the safety of its vehicles as a result of the case reports it obtains from ACIR. In an article generally sympathetic to the automobile makers, *Automotive News* in May, 1965 commented, "Regrettably, the companies are making little use of these reports."

In addition to disseminating its case data exclusively to the automobile industry, ACIR appears to have an unreal vision of how its studies would find ultimate application to the design of safer vehicles. According to the Cornell scientists, their dreamed-of progress would proceed this way: 1) "Statistical studies discover a problem, define the problem area, and point toward a solution; 2) laboratory and engineering work result in a solution which is then incorporated into the vehicle; and 3) statistical studies evaluate effectiveness of the solution and indicate the need for further refinement."

The fallacy of this reasoning is illustrated by the history of just one item. So far, the door latch is the only vehicle feature that has gone through this sequence. First, Cornell found that the risk of serious injury or death was markedly greater when occupants were ejected than when they remained in the car. In the pre-1956 cars, ACIR data revealed that at least one door opened in nearly half of the injury-producing accidents. Then, in its 1956 models, the industry introduced so-called safety door latches, which involved a simple design change that was at least thirty years overdue. Finally, in 1961, Cornell released a study showing that door opening frequency in the 1956-1959 models, compared with the pre-1956 models, was reduced by about thirty per cent. The next door latch improvements came in 1962 from Ford, in 1963 from General Motors, and in 1964 from Chrysler. In other words, for ten years motorists were used as guinea pigs while the car makers were awaiting statistics on how many of them were being thrown from cars during collision before deciding to inch forward with the next improvement.

Statistical evidence is, after all, only *one* basis on which to decide the need for safer design. Clinical studies of a single, or a small number of cases can define a safety problem that demands a design change. Even before waiting for blood to be shed or a mangled vehicle to be investigated, as in the General Motors' door hinge failure, advance design analysis and testing under collision conditions could detect a large majority of hazards before the final mass-production specifications are completed.

To move a manufacturer to action should not—as it did—require statistical confirmation by Cornell that the rear-view mirror is one of the ten top instruments of injury in automobile collisions. It is enough to know, as the Ford Motor Company knew in 1964, according to their consultant Dr. Donald Huelke, of twenty fatal cases which occurred when the victims struck the rear-view mirror in Ford Falcons. If the possibility of this particular hazard did not occur to the automobile designers before the vehicle was built, these fatal cases are proof of the need for redesigning the rear-view mirror.

ACIR has been subjected to some unfounded criticism. Certain foreign-car manufacturers, for example, intimated that the Cornell group made its "Big Car-Little Car" study—which found, under similar accident conditions, a considerably higher incidence of serious injuries and deaths occurring in small-car accidents—under pressure from American car manufacturers. In fact, the study was done on Cornell's initiative. But some fundamental criticisms of ACIR are justified. ACIR scientists have not displayed much commitment to giving a broader significance to their work. Like their colleagues at the Harvard School of Public Health, UCLA, and Wayne State University (all working with federal funds and industry assistance), they have been in possession of information that is relevant to the elimination of millions of casualties, and the expertise to utilize that information. Like their colleagues, they have shown only a slight appreciation that their special roles should require them to state forcefully in public forums the issues for discussion and resolution. As nuclear physicists and medical scientists learned years ago, public discussion is of great importance to their research undertakings. Ultimately, the successful implementation of research findings provides the public support for additional research. The absence of scientific statesmanship among these independent accident-injury researchers working under federal grants explains to a great degree why their funds have not increased noticeably for a decade. These scientists who do not make known to the public the importance of their work and the practical possibility of a vastly safer vehicle cannot, of course, enjoy public support.

The ACIR staff might well refer back to the testimony before the Roberts' subcommittee in 1959 of Dr. T. P. Wright, vice-president for research at Cornell University. As an engineer with wide experience in problems of transportation safety, Dr. Wright addressed himself to the question of whether engineered safety design of vehicles can result in dramatic reductions in the annual highway injury and fatality toll. His answer was, "Most decidedly, yes," with these provisos: "If a concerted effort is made toward fuller utilization of the information which scientific research has already provided; if appropriate support for present and future investigation and research can be assured; if present and future findings can be channelized to individuals and organizations willing and able to act on their implications by applying them at the practical level; if appropriate public educational measures are assured and maintained." Then, in words which should have weighed heavily on the minds of the university accident-injury researchers, Dr. Wright added, "Furthermore, as a matter of personal ethics, I should consider myself guilty of a crime against humanity if, for whatever reason, I were responsible for prolonging the ravages of a disease which is the unnecessary and shameful byproduct of the greatest transportation system the world has ever known. . . . Delay will be measured in inexorable terms of human life, suffering, and permanent disability."

John Moore, the director of ACIR between 1955 and 1960, did lend his assistance to the Roberts' committee in its attempt to establish a public record on vehicle safety problems. The present director, Robert Wolf, delivered two addresses in 1963 and 1964 when he recommended corrective measures that were available and effective for improving automobile crashworthiness. Small as these efforts have been, they are improvements on the timidity of other university scientists and engineers working in the area of vehicle safety. Perhaps with the accumulated record of industry intransigence and the opening up of diversified sources of financial support from public agencies (recent contracts from General Services Administration and the Department of Commerce fund for special projects are the first indications), ACIR will rise to its public responsibility.

ACIR should make publc its general and specific findings on design hazards. It should explain the deeper issues of why such hazards persist year after year, and the engineering feasibility of producing much safer automobiles. The sooner ACIR performs these missions of scientific statesmanship, the sooner the scientific-engineering community and the major institutions which form public policy will be awakened to their long-neglected responsibilities to save lives.

4
The power to pollute:
The smog that wasn't there

In 1950 a prominent California biochemist made the discovery which was to establish as a definite fact the link between automobile exhausts and smog conditions in Los Angeles.

Dr. Arlie Haagen-Smit stated that hydrocarbon compounds produced by automobile exhaust react with oxides of nitrogen under sunlight to produce photochemical smog—the hazy eye-irritating blanket so familiar to residents of Los Angeles and other cities.

This discovery, coupled with extensive studies made by the Los Angeles Air Pollution Control District, showed that more than half of the Los Angeles air pollution problem is caused by automotive exhausts. The situation is not limited to Los Angeles; cars, buses, and trucks contribute half the air pollution in the United States. This pollution contains the most serious toxic contaminants which are associated with a significantly higher incidence of morbidity and mortality from emphysema, chronic bronchitis, lung cancer, and heart disease. In property damage due to air pollution, the United States Public Health Service estimates a loss of roughly sixty-five dollars per capita each year, or over eleven billion dollars altogether. Pollution corrodes metals, deteriorates rubber products, erodes concrete and building stone, soils a great variety of materials, and deposits dust and soot on highly sensitive machinery and instruments. The total quantity of pollutants belched forth by motor vehicles in this country last year included over fourteen million tons of hydrocarbons, seventy-five million tons of carbon monoxide, and four million tons of oxides of nitrogen.

It is significant that the major role the automobile plays in the creation of smog was discovered by someone outside the automobile industry. For years the automobile manufacturers felt no obligation either to engage in research themselves or to support outside inquiry into the nature and effect of automotive pollutants.

Paul Ackerman, then chairman of the engineering advisory committee of the Automobile Manufacturers Association (AMA), admitted before the California legislature in 1959 that the "unique characteristics of the California atmosphere came to our attention during the 1920's, when we noticed that tires and other rubber products cracked and deteriorated in the Los Angeles area." (Ozone, which results from the chemical interaction of automobile exhaust elements, is the chief attacker of tire and rubber products. The industry knew of the high concentration of ozone in Los Angeles.) During the early forties, official reports on the Los Angeles air pollution problem showed heightening concern over vehicle exhausts. Although the signs of the future pollution epidemic were unmistakable, the industry did no research to develop the preventive mechanisms that would forestall the increasing severity of photochemical smog. Even after Dr. Haagen-Smit's conclusive experiments were reported in 1950, the industry refused to admit that motor vehicles played any more than a minor role in producing photochemical smog.

Automotive exhaust gases have long been recognized as a direct hazard to driving safety. As a major contributor to smog, these emissions frequently have curtailed highway visibility to the point where freeways have been temporarily cleared of traffic in order to avoid chain accidents. Also, this hazard is great enough to cause air crashes. Civil Aeronautics Board investigations have attributed numerous air accidents every year to poor visibility due to smog.

The health hazard posed by various combustive byproducts is of a far more serious nature than the problem of reduced visibility. In 1962 Professor McFarland of Harvard summarized the studies on carbon monoxide as follows:

Carbon monoxide poisoning is an ever-present possibility in the operation of motor vehicles. The problem is becoming increasingly serious because of the increased density of smog and the concentration of idling vehicles in the metropolitan areas. Small amounts of carbon monoxide are absorbed rapidly by the blood stream, resulting in an oxygen deficiency that may at first be unnoticed by the individual. The initial reaction to carbon monoxide poisoning consists primarily in lowered attention, difficulty in concentration and retention, slight muscular incoordination, sleepiness, and mental and physical lethargy.

In other words, you drive as you breathe.

Carbon monoxide kills at a concentration of approximately 1000 parts per million (ppm). At the level of 100 ppm, it produces headaches, nausea, and dizziness. The California State Health Department has determined that 30 ppm is an "adverse" level, and that 30 ppm for eight hours, or 120 ppm for one hour is a "serious level of pollution." Bumper-to-bumper freeway traffic pours forth a stream of deadly gas for motorists to absorb. In the Los Angeles area, Dr. Haagen-Smit has recorded highway concentrations of carbon monoxide of up to 120 ppm; in Detroit, levels have exceeded 100 ppm. Many urban roads routinely experience such concentrations in heavy traffic.

In July 1965, spokesmen for the automobile companies told Senator Abraham Ribicoff's subcommittee on executive reorganization, which was investigating the traffic safety situation, that the control of vehicle emissions has no relation to driver safety. This is the industry's official position taken before the General Services Administration and state legislatures.

Carbon monoxide has the additional effect of reducing body tolerance to alcohol and certain drugs. Through replacing normal carbon dioxide in the blood, carbon monoxide sets up a situation where either drugs or alcohol, both taken within moderate or prescribed limits, become dangerous to the driver.

A 1959 Department of Commerce research report warned about the consequences of rapid deterioration of poor exhaust systems: "This type of failure, which can be presented or delayed by use of better materials in the muffler and other parts of the exhaust system, brings carbon monoxide concentrations in the vicinity of the passenger compartment, and under certain conditions can cause car occupants to become drowsy, experience eye irritation, headaches and nausea, or actually endanger their lives, depending on the length of exposure and, of course, the concentrations."

When Senator Ribicoff asked why the automobile industry did not adopt nationally the California requirements (mandatory exhaust controls on all new vehicles sold in that state beginning with the 1966 models), he was told that automobile exhaust conditions did not warrant such action. The senator displayed unusual irritation at such replies during the hearings and, judging by the evidence he had in hand, his displeasure was well founded. Two years ago, Professor John Middleton of the University of California reported that "manifestations of photochemical air pollution, including oxidant index, plant damage, and rubber cracking, have now been seen and reported in urban and adjacent rural areas in twenty-seven states and the District of Columbia." The 1963 *Yearbook of Agriculture,* an authoritative and cautious source, stated: "Los Angeles no longer has, if it ever had, a monopoly on photochemical smog. The characteristic symptoms in plants have been found in almost every metropolitan area in the country . . . the entire coastal area roughly from Washington, D. C., to Boston has come to rival southern California." Since 1950 independent researchers have been accumulating increasingly specific evidence that the tens of millions of little pollution factories on wheels do serious harm to the health and safety of the American people. In May 1965 Senator Muskie submitted a report compiled from expert testimony which his special subcommittee on air and water pollution heard during sessions conducted throughout the nation. The report stated: "In all of the hearings held since the adoption of the Clean Air Act of 1963, automotive exhaust from some 84 million automobiles, trucks and buses was cited as responsible for about 50 per cent of the national air pollution problem. Photochemical air pollution, or smog, is a problem of growing national importance and is attributable largely to the operation of the motor vehicle. This type of air pollution is appearing with increasing frequency and severity in metropolitan areas throughout the nation."

In a study released in June 1965, based on data from the federal government's continuous air monitoring program, U.S. Public Health Service scientists reported: "The data show that although Los Angeles experiences photochemical smog incidents more frequently, smog incidents in other cities are severe and are not infrequent."*

The automobile industry seems to have ignored the increasing problem of air pollution because of its own economic interests. From their own point of view, automobile makers see no reason to spend money to produce a device which allows them neither to increase profits nor to effect any economies.

Or to put it another way, the manufacturers have two basic criteria for judging a potential design change: 1) will it reduce costs? and 2) will it increase sales? The automobile makers seem to have decided that cleaning up exhausts will do neither.

The struggle beween air pollution authorities and officials of the major automobile companies has been long and frustrating. Los Angeles, which has done the pioneering work in the field of air pollution, has spent fifteen years trying to get some action out of Detroit. The industry's almost purely defensive attitude is illustrated by an exchange of correspondence between Los Angeles County Supervisor Kenneth Hahn and the Ford Motor Company in February and March of 1953. Mr. Hahn wrote to Henry Ford II to express his concern about vehicle exhausts and to ask a number of specific questions. His letter was referred to Dan J. Chabek of the engineering staff for reply. Mr. Chabek wrote: "Dear Mr. Hahn: The Ford engineering staff, although mindful that automobile engines produce exhaust gases, feels these waste vapors are dissipated in the atmosphere quickly and do not present an air pollution problem. Therefore, our research department has not conducted any experimental work aimed at totally eliminating these gases.

"The fine automotive power plants which modern-day engineers design do not 'smoke.' Only aging engines subjected to improper care and maintenance burn oil.

* Los Angeles does have a particular combination of topography and sluggish air currents conducive to frequent smog formations. Other cities, however, have a greater density of automobiles per square mile than Los Angeles. In 1962 Los Angeles had 1,350 automobiles per square mile; the corresponding figures for other major cities were: Chicago, 1,541; Detroit, 1,580; New York City, 2,220; Philadelphia, 3,730 and Washington, D.C., 4,100.

"To date, the need for a device which will more effectively reduce exhaust vapors has not been established."

Mr. Chabek's letter revealed a basic operating principle of the automobile industry whenever it is confronted with pressures to curb the harmful effects of its products: "We *feel;* therefore, we do not research."

When Mr. Hahn went to Detroit to get some direct answers about adoption of exhaust controls, a senior official of one of the companies asked: "Well, Mr. Hahn, will that device sell more cars?" "No," said Mr. Hahn. "Will it look prettier, will it give us more horsepower? If not, we are not interested."

The industry saw no need to defend its continued production of polluting vehicles. On the contrary, it was up to the Los Angeles authorities to establish the data and shoulder the burden of proof, with the industry being judge and jury over whether the burden was met. It took the expenditure of several millions of dollars of public funds for the Los Angeles Air Pollution Control District (APCD) to conduct the research into automobile operation, local driving conditions and the composition of gasolines in order to determine the specific contributions of various pollutants to smog. By 1953 the APCD had established beyond any doubt that motor vehicles were the largest source of air pollutants and the chief source of hydrocarbons in the area. The automobile companies were unable to fault this finding. In response to the increasing public pressure the industry decided to close ranks. In December 1953 through their trade body, the Automobile Manufacturers Association, the companies formed the Vehicle Combustion Products Committee to initiate a cooperative program of research and development on an industry-wide basis. To facilitate the exchange of information so that no company would have any advantage over another, member companies entered into a royalty-free, cross-licensing agreement for devices or systems primarily designed to reduce emissions.

Both company executives and spokesmen for the Automobile Manufacturers Association made it clear from the outset that reduction of vehicle emissions was a highly complex technical undertaking. General Motors' Charles Chayne compared it to the problems involved in trying to find a cure for cancer. (Subsequent data strongly pointed to vehicle contaminants as a cause of cancer.) First, the automobile makers said they wanted to determine the composition of exhaust gases, a phase of the automobile's operation about which they claimed almost total ignorance. For one thing, they said they lacked the proper instruments with which to begin a research program on auto emissions. For another, they said that before they could begin they would need to compile a profile of the driving habits of the average motorist. To achieve these objectives, the automobile industry as a whole spent a million dollars a year, a figure which seems rather inadequate to the magnitude of the problem.

In January 1954 automobile representatives assured the Los Angeles County Board of Supervisors that controls would be developed and ready for the 1958 models. As late as April 1956, high company executives declared that the 1958 model-year was still the target date. Company engineers began cranking out technical papers on the automotive emissions problem which were read before engineering meetings to show the pace of progress. But the 1958 models went into the showrooms without any controls.

By November 1957 the Los Angeles County air pollution control officer, S. Smith Griswold, publicly declared before the National Advisory Committee to the United States Surgeon General his despair about community air pollution. "We have done everything that it is within our power to do," he said. "We have cleaned up industries that other sections of the country have deemed impossible to control—steel mills, petroleum refineries, smelters, railroads, shipping. We have helped our electrical utilities obtain more gas for their steam plants. We have issued 5000 citations in the last three years, and levied half a million dollars in fines. Despite this, we still have smog.

"There remains one source of air pollution beyond our power to control. Every day in Los Angeles County, 2,700,000 automobiles are burning 5½ million gallons of gasoline, and fouling our air with 8,000 tons of contaminants. These emissions include: 6,400 tons of carbon monoxide, 300 tons of oxides of nitrogen and 1,050 tons of hydrocarbons."

Mr. Griswold went on to describe the financial burdens entailed by the massive abatement program in just one urban area. Local industry spent fifty million dollars for control equipment and five million dollars a year to operate it. Back-yard incinerators worth forty-eight million dollars were junked. Yet the automobile industry, which has seen a single manufacturer spend about $250 million to develop a new car (as Ford did for the Edsel), was devoting only a million dollars a year to its cooperative vehicle emissions control program.

Around the same time, Harry Williams, managing director of the Automobile Manufacturers Association, revealed in another way how the industry saw its responsibility. Before the first National Conference on Air Pollution in Washington, D. C., he made this remarkable introduction: "What I want to discuss today is something which, so far as I know, no other industry has ever been called upon to do: namely, to concern itself with how the consumer uses or misuses the product long after its sale to the public."

He followed with an account of the conditions that prevailed before the time of the automobile: "It must have been impossible for our elders to imagine life in this land without the polluted air in which they lived—before people were liberated from the congested cities by the motor vehicle. There were reeking livery stables in every neighborhood. Cowbarns were the customary auxiliaries to dairies. There were malodorous privies in every backyard. The dirt in the unpaved streets was, therefore, a fetid compound of filth, laid down by successive generations of people and animals. There were few screens on doors or windows to bar marauding disease-bearing insects."

Mr. Williams reminded his audience that the unsavoriness he described had vanished with the advent of the motor vehicle. He stated further that the industry was making a serious study of the question of air pollution: a "million dollars a year spent on one problem by one industry is still a substantial outlay."

Many delegates to the conference were aghast. But politeness prevailed. In summing up the proceedings at the end of the conference, NBC's Martin Agronsky told the assemblage what he thought of the one million dollars a year: "Well, with all due respect to a twenty billion dollar industry, I am not impressed."

Los Angeles County authorities questioned the real difficulty of solving the emission control problem if the companies were content to devote such a pittance to its solution. They were given comfort that the breakthrough was imminent. An Automobile Manufacturers Association spokesman in late 1958 said emphatically,

"The program now is at a point where the technical feasibility of exhaust control has been established. Prototype devices are being tested and are near the point where they will pass from research to product development."

Then in 1959 the automobile industry announced a discovery: auto crankcase emissions were found to be a major source of hydrocarbons. At the end of the year, all the U. S. auto makers announced together that 1961 model automobiles sold in California would be equipped with crankcase ventilation systems (popularly called blowby devices) to eliminate most of the hydrocarbons from that source. Their action, according to the press releases, was voluntary: a California law requiring such installation by that date was, they said, simply coincidental.

The Federal Government, conscious of the spread of air pollution, began to take action. In December 1961, Abraham Ribicoff, then Secretary of Health, Education, and Welfare, warned that if blowby devices were not placed on all cars by the industry, he would recommend that mandatory legislation be passed by Congress. Promptly thereafter, the industry announced voluntarily that all 1963 model automobiles would be so equipped. The secretary relented. The 1963 model-year came and all new domestic automobiles had blowby devices on them. But a report on automotive air pollution submitted to Congress in January 1965 by the Department of Health, Education, and Welfare confirmed the tenuous foundation on which the "voluntary approach," so popular in some government circles can rest: "During the 1964 model-year one of the domestic manufacturers ceased the routine installation of crankcase emission control devices on its various product lines except on vehicles for sale in the regulated states of California and New York. Model-year 1965 automobiles from the same manufacturer are also not routinely equipped with crankcase emission controls."

The report continued a government tradition of not referring to the culpable car manufacturer by name, even at the risk of tainting all of them as suspect. In fact, the company involved was Ford. In a letter replying to Assistant Secretary James Quigley's inquiry about the elimination of the blowby device, H. Misch, Ford's engineering vice-president, said that the action was taken because of operational and maintenance difficulties. He promised that Ford would resume use of the device on cars produced after

March 1, 1965. Mr. Misch did not explain why Ford neglected to inform their customers or the Federal Government of the elimination, although the government had withheld action on the basis of company compliance.

Previously, the Los Angeles Air Pollution Control District had gone outside the automobile industry for other solutions to the pollution exhaust problem. It had encouraged companies in the chemical and automobile accessory industries to develop catalytic or other types of acceptable exhaust controls. The APCD had also established an automotive combustion laboratory and constructed environmental test chambers to evaluate proposals submitted to it as well as to research independently various engineering alternatives for control of auto exhaust and test them on the highway. The idea behind these initiatives was to encourage other sources of scientific data and engineering development which would help break the near-monopoly of information and technical capability held by the automobile industry.

By 1963 several groups of companies with no previous experience in the field came up with workable exhaust control devices. There were still some maintenance problems to be ironed out but the engineering performance in a short period of development time was impressive. These companies were aiming at the California market because of a state law providing for compulsory exhaust controls on all new cars one year after the State Motor Vehicle Pollution Control Board approved two or more devices. To win approval, the system or device had to keep hydrocarbons below 275 parts per million and carbon monoxide to 1.5 per cent of exhaust fumes coming from the tail pipe. Realizing that board approval of two or more devices was imminent, the automobile industry tried to head it off. On March 10, 1964, the automobile companies announced with one voice that they expected to be able to meet the California standard in time for the 1967 models. What the automobile companies could not tolerate was to be compelled to attach some other firm's device to their engine complex. They claimed there would be all kinds of technical difficulties, but the blow to their pride seemed to be the most weighty factor.

As late as June 1964 an industry smog specialist, George A. Delaney, speaking for the Automobile Manufacturers Association, described the industry's March tenth announcement as one "based on a careful and realistic determination that this time schedule is needed to engineer and test specific applications of control measures for each engine-transmission combination. . . ." On June 17, 1964, the California Board approved the four exhaust control devices submitted by four groups of companies: Norris-Thermidor Corp. and W. R. Grace & Co.; American Machine and Foundry and Chromalloy Corp.; Arvin Industries and Universal Oil Products Co.; and American Cyanamid and Walker Manufacturing Co. According to the California law, the board's action meant the requiring of controls on 1966 model-year gasoline-powered vehicles. It also moved the top management of the four domestic automobile companies. Their representatives rushed out to San Francisco in August and declared in unison that they had accelerated their program, and, in time for the 1966 models, emission control systems meeting California's standards would be produced by the car makers themselves. They had cut a year off their schedule; two months earlier that schedule had been described by them as "a careful and realistic determination." Competition and the law had finally moved a monolithic industry.

Competition within the industry could have commenced in 1962 when Chrysler developed a "Cleaner Air Package" involving modification of fuel mixture, timing and other engine combustion variables. The "package" was made available to the other car companies and to the Los Angeles APCD. Predictably, there was no reaction in public from the other companies, but the APCD found the Chrysler system the most encouraging development to come out of Detroit in a decade. Compared to an average emission of nearly nine hundred parts per million of hydrocarbons from Los Angeles County vehicles, the Chrysler cars equipped with the "package" operated at emission rates of less than three hundred parts of hydrocarbons per million parts of exhaust. The following year, the APCD established air pollution control specifications for the purchase of new motor vehicles by the Los Angeles County government. The County proceeded to buy only Chrysler automobiles even though other automobile companies frequently bid lower. These other companies could not meet the pollution control specifications.

This break in the industry's united front, in light of the cooperative research program and cross-licensing agreement, must have enraged General Motors and Ford management. Charles Heinen—Chrysler's leading automotive pollution expert and chief mover within his company for a little more sincerity and speed—began to get the cool treatment from his industry colleagues after Chrysler captured the Los Angeles County business. His superiors promptly played down this competitive success. While automotive makers will advertise a victory in one phase of an economy run or auto endurance race, Chrysler banned any advertising of the fact that only its vehicles could meet the emissions standards of Los Angeles County.

Under increasing pressure from California authorities, federal agencies, and outside producers of exhaust control devices, the industry closed ranks with impressive determination, presenting a more closely united front than they had before Chrysler's unilateral initiative. When Senator Muskie's Senate subcommittee began questioning the automobile manufacturers in 1964, the manufacturers made their presentation as a chorus. Not a single disagreement, however small, pervaded the many pages of testimony given in the June 1964 and April 1965 hearings. Even the bibliography of articles reporting industry research on automotive emissions that was supplied the Senate subcommittee was entitled "From the U. S. Automobile Industry Laboratories." No company affiliations were given the various authors, although their affiliations had appeared on the original technical papers.

Such unanimity and conformity began right at the beginning of the industry cooperative research program in 1953. Only once in all these years had any company adhering to this arrangement and cross-licensing agreement made a single unilateral move in announcing or implementing a more effective emissions control system. While the Chrysler episode might be considered a temporary deviation, the initiative for it came from the aggressiveness of Los Angeles pollution control authorities.

Drawing on the work of Los Angeles air pollution specialists and on dozens of meetings with auto company representatives during his ten years as that city's chief pollution control officer, S. Smith Griswold said to the annual meeting of the Air Pollution Control Association in June 1964, "What has the industry accomplished during these ten years? Until recently, very little. In 1953, a pooling of efforts was announced. Through an agreement to cross-license, progress by one would be progress by all. How has this worked out? Apparently it has served to guarantee that no manufacturer would break ranks and bring into the field of air pollution control the same kind of competitive stimulus that spokesmen for the industry frequently pay homage to as the force that has made them what they are today.

"I term it a great delaying action, because that is what I believe the auto industry has been engaged in for a decade. Everything that the industry has disclosed it is able to do today to control auto exhaust was possible technically ten years ago. No new principle had to be developed,* no technological advance was needed, no scientific breakthrough was required. Crankcase emissions have been controlled by a method in use for at least half a century. Hydrocarbons and carbon monoxide are being controlled by relatively simple adjustments of those most basic engine components—the carburetor and ignition systems."

There is emphatic agreement with this estimate by both government and non-industry specialists in automotive pollution problems. But few of these specialists will express their concurrence outright as did Ulric Bray, a California chemist and air pollution authority. He told the American Institute of Chemists at a meeting in September 1964: "Except for the recent installation of crankcase devices and a tune-up accessory kit offered by Chrysler, almost everything Detroit has done with automobiles since World War II has been wrong from the standpoint of smog."

The basic issue of air pollution transcends the simple argument over how long a particular solution was really known and how difficult it is to apply in practice. It is that the industry left it to others to discover the harmful side-effects of the product it manufactures, refused to recognize the need for prompt and effective remedy, and moved in the direction of emissions control only under the compulsion of law and imminent competition. When pollution authorities implored the industry to do something, the automobile manufacturers' reaction, as a recent critical editorial in

---

* Auto emissions specialists outside the industry were amused when they learned that for the 1966 models sold in California three auto companies had chosen a system which uses an air pump to inject air directly into the exhaust port. The principle is to mix the air with hot exhaust gases as they are discharged and oxidize unburned hydrocarbon and carbon monoxide into carbon dioxide and water vapor. This principle has been known for decades (one engineer pointed to U.S. Patent number 908,527, January 5, 1909), and translating it into engineering practice for contemporary automobile engines is no more difficult than applying suspension principles to actual bridge building.

Chemical Week put it, "consisted of setting up a committee." Even with this industry-wide program, the most elemental canons of scientific-engineering research for an announced public welfare goal were violated. Contrary to its alleged purpose of facilitating a free flow of data and innovation, the industry established a ring of secrecy which no outside companies or public agencies could penetrate.

Members of the industry committee, speaking before serious legislative and administrative forums, behaved more like lobbyists and public relations men than the scientists and engineers that they purported to be. One can share the astonishment of Mr. Griswold who recently noted that "the greatest achievement in air pollution control proffered by General Motors to account for its years of effort is the construction of an environmental study chamber, in which they have been duplicating much of the work that has led to the conclusion that auto exhaust is the basic ingredient of photo-chemical smog."

Most people are not aware of the strength of the legal position of the auto industry. The burden of proof rests on the local, state, and federal officials and legislators concerned. Before these officials could move to act against the auto industry to compel them to do anything about smog, they first had to put together a painstakingly researched case which proved beyond a doubt both the fact that automotive emissions cause the damages attributed to them and that auto manufacturers are in a position to do something about it. The time that all this took gave the auto industry a long breathing period during which the car makers could sit on its hands and tell the investigative bodies, "show me." Inaction carries no penalties.

A good example of this attitude is the industry's attitude toward efforts to curb the emission of oxides of nitrogen. This ingredient, which is as dangerous to the public as carbon monoxide or any of the hydrocarbon series, has been largely ignored, and the industry has refused to offer any cooperation with people interested in the problem.

There are neither standards nor laws to deal with what will become the more serious of the vehicle pollutants in coming years, as hydrocarbons come under control. In 1960, some preliminary but promising research into the control of oxides of nitrogen was announced by the Los Angeles Air Pollution Control District based on work done by the department of engineering at UCLA. A functioning device incorporating this principle was successfully tested on an automobile for a period of five months, showing a reduction of eighty to ninety per cent in oxides of nitrogen. There were some unresolved minor problems which the vastly greater resources and experience of an automobile producer could have overcome. But the reaction from Detroit eliminated the possibility of any objective interchange. In May 1964 the California State Department of Public Health held a hearing to consider the adoption of an air quality standard for oxides of nitrogen. General Motors and Ford air pollution engineers challenged the need for any control of this contaminant; once more, they demanded to be shown. No research was offered by these two companies as to the harmlessness of oxides of nitrogen, which would seem reasonable to expect as substantiation of their mulish stance. It is apparent from the Muskie subcommittee hearings and reports that research to develop controls for oxides of nitrogen will be up to the federal government to undertake.

As in the case of nitrogen oxides, the car makers claim inability to prevent hydrocarbon losses from the carburetor and fuel tank —estimated at fifteen per cent of total hydrocarbon emission from motor vehicles. Again it will be up to federally financed research to suggest answers to the industry which will then proceed to modify them to suit its corporate *Gestalt*. The process could not be more calculated to consume the calendar.

But the representatives of the Automobile Manufacturers Association have more demanding tests which they still require of the body politic. They told Senator Muskie's subcommittee in the summer of 1964 that there is much more information to be obtained before action on vehicle exhausts is taken on a national basis. Once more they wished to be shown that a serious problem existed outside of Los Angeles before they chose to act. Their emphasis on being shown a substantial smog phenemenon—a presence determined for several years beyond any reasonable doubt —implies a disregard for the fatal effects of even a little smog on those victims of chronic respiratory diseases whose hold on life is so fragile. In mid-1965 the Automobile Manufacturers Association began to highlight another approach—whether the costs of controlling automobile exhausts would be justified by the benefits. This strategy is calculated to keep computers whirring away indefinitely in every urban area which the Automobile Manufacturers Association insists is a separate and distinct one.

Increasingly, the industry points to the bill the consumer must pay for having a cleaner automobile. The auto makers see no anomaly in spending over a billion dollars a year for the annual changeover, consisting mainly of styling changes, without raising the price to the car buyer, while demanding that a specific price increase will follow the incorporation of exhaust controls through engine modification. The annual changeover is seen as overall product improvement and absorbed by the company as expected annual investment, but exhaust controls for health and safety are not part of the annual changeover.

There is one obvious reason for this policy. By saying that control systems "will require substantial investment by every motorist in the nation," as Harry Williams of the Automobile Manufacturers Association put it recently, then the issue shifts from the industry's obligation to the arena of consumer acceptance.

The industry is still playing for time as far as a national policy on air pollution caused by automobiles is concerned. It forced a year's delay—until the 1968 model-year—in the federal legislation requiring the same kinds of exhaust controls as will be on the 1966 model cars sold in California. The original Muskie bill had provided for controls by the 1967 model-year.

The chief gambit for buying time is the insistence that more research is needed before action is taken. Back in 1958 at the National Conference on Air Pollution, the United States Surgeon General, Dr. Leroy E. Burney, met head-on the industry's incessant demand for absolute proof that smog is harmful to health. "When it comes to human health," Dr. Burney told the audience, "such absolute proof is often thousands of lives late in coming. To wait for it is to invite disaster." He pointed out that years before causative agents were identified, community leaders observed the association between epidemics and filth. "Cleaning up the city filth resulted in better health. Years later they found out why." Dr. Burney made these remarks seven years ago. Since then much more proof of the harm to health and safety from man-made contaminants of the air has been published. Yet the auto industry is unmoved. The question they should be required to answer is: "What is the purpose of automobile pollution?" This shifts the burden of proof to where it belongs.

The case of Los Angeles does offer some hope. There pollution control officials, with the strong support of local citizenry, have challenged, prodded, and negotiated with the automobile companies for fifteen years. The agony inflicted on the people of Los Angeles by automobile industry intransigence has had one redeeming result: it has given this country a history of how the car makers react to public efforts at curbing harmful effects of their products. In this history, there are lessons that should not be forgotten. Los Angeles officials have made a strong case that the absence of competition within the industry has been a major obstacle to adoption of exhaust control systems. (See Appendix B for the Resolution of the Board of Supervisors.) In 1965 the antitrust division of the U. S. Department of Justice began an investigation of the automobile industry's cooperative research program and cross-licensing agreement. Specifically, the division wants to determine whether there has been concerted action by the automobile companies, in violation of the antitrust laws, to restrain competition in the development and marketing of automobile exhaust control systems and devices. This probe of possible "product fixing" represents an important new phase of antitrust enforcement that explicitly recognizes safety as a value to be protected from collusive practices.

5
The engineers

Nearly one-half of all the automobiles on the road today will eventually be involved in an injury-producing accident. In 1964, automobiles killed 47,700 people and injured over four million. At present rates, one of every two Americans will be injured or killed in an automobile accident. The number of deaths by automobile is twenty-five per cent greater than it was in 1961; the increase from 1951 to 1961 was only three per cent. In accidents involving all modes of transportation—motor vehicles, trains, ships, and planes—the motor vehicle accounts for over ninety-two per cent of the deaths, and ninety-eight per cent of the injuries. This mass trauma represents a breakdown in the relation between the highway transport system and the people who use and control it. From an engineering standpoint, when an accident injury occurs, it is a result of the failure of the technological components of the vehicle and the highway to adapt adequately to the driver's capacities and limitations. This failure is, above all, a challenge to professional engineering, which in its finest work has not hesitated to aim for total safety.

Automatic elevators are the safest transportation system known to man; anyone can use them with the assurance that accidents will be at an absolute minimum. In automobile manufacturing plants, engineers responsible for worker safety have "zero frequency" of accidents as their objective. In the aviation and space fields, the meticulous anticipation of possible breakdowns in man-machine interactions and the development of fail-safe mechanisms are the fundamental orientations. In the space field, waiting to learn from accident reports is an unthinkable procedure; in aviation it is a last resort.

In car manufacturing plants, the production engineers analyze machine design, operation, and work practices so they can anticipate and eliminate accident-injury risks to men working on the production of automobiles. The stated goal of General Motors of "no injury-producing accidents" is attained in a number of their plants each year. This plant safety has produced dividends in the form of greater quantity and consistency in production, less worker training, fewer breakdowns in the production process, and lower insurance costs.

But the dead and injured consumers of automobiles do not interfere with production and sales. They are outside the self-disciplining systems of plant safety, and when it comes to passenger safety the hard-headed empiricism of the production engineer does not apply. Rather, the so-called automotive safety engineer devotes himself to the defense of the automobile created by his colleagues in the styling and marketing departments.

For example, in 1954 a banker in New York who owned a Buick wrote to General Motors suggesting that the dashboards were dangerous in accident conditions. "The other day I had to step quickly on the brake to avoid hitting a little kitten, and in so doing, my son, eight, was thrown against the dash and broke off a front second tooth. If some padding can be applied it will help save faces and maybe lives. This is just a suggestion for safer motoring for all." The letter was given to Mr. Howard Gandelot for reply. As the company's vehicle safety engineer, Mr. Gandelot displayed sympathy with his correspondent's predicament. "Driving with young children in an automobile always presents some problems," he wrote. "As soon as the youngsters get large enough to be able to see out when standing up, that's what they want to do—and I don't blame them. When this time arrived with both our boys I made it a practice to train them so that at the command 'Hands!' they would immediately place their hands on the instrument panel if standing in the front compartment, or on the back of the front seat if in the rear, to protect themselves against sudden stops. This took a little effort and on a couple of occasions I purposely pumped them a trifle when they didn't respond immediately to the command, so that they learned quickly. Even now when either one of them is on the front seat, at the command of 'Hands!' they brace themselves. I frequently give these commands even when there is no occasion to do so, just so we all keep in practice."

Another attitude toward passenger safety was reflected in the observation in 1958 of Dr. Lawrence Hafstad, director of the General Motors' research laboratories, who said "More progress can be made in traffic safety by emphasizing the relation between the driver, the signaling system, and the road, than by undue emphasis on a crash-proof car, which could lead us to a progressive stalemate analagous to the classic conflict between projectile and armor plate."

Dr. Hafstad is a physicist, the former head of the Atomic Energy Commission's reactor development division. In making his political defense of corporate policy, Dr. Hafstad was not speaking as a scientist. Nor was Mr. Gandelot advising as a professional engineer. Both men were behaving as employees, and for them General Motors is more than an employer, it is a faith to which they have committed their occupational, if not their professional efforts. This sort of commitment has been most clearly reflected in the careers of the automotive safety engineers, who have been assigned the task of being the company spokesmen whenever the issue of safe vehicle design is raised at technical meetings or in public forums.

One of these men is Kenneth A. Stonex of General Motors, who has in recent years been the major spokesman and chief researcher for his company on the subject of safety. Mr. Stonex's approach has been obtuse and ingenious—and has consistently avoided confronting the problem of the unsafe vehicle. Although he is a mathematician and engineer, Stonex has shown greater interest in history. Only with a perspective over the years, he believes, can people appreciate how fortunate they are in having their present-day automobiles. For his point of reference, Stonex borrowed a 1910 Oldsmobile Limited from the museum of the Oldsmobile division and prepared several technical papers comparing it with the 1955, 1960, and 1964 models.

The 1910 model was half a story high, which made getting into it something of a climb and getting out of it a hazard of some significance to elderly people. By contrast, he showed that current automobiles are about two and one-half feet lower and much more difficult to overturn. The 1910 Oldsmobile had a large, flat plate-glass windshield which shattered into sharp pieces when it broke. It had a wooden steering wheel with a cast-aluminum hub and spokes which would break into piercing stubs on light impact. It had acetylene headlamps with no provision for dimming or aiming except by bending the suppports. Heavy brass rails for lap-robes were attached to the seat back and presented a collision hazard. The car had rear-wheel, external mechanical brakes with linings exposed to water, dust, and dirt. The rear door latch of the 1910 Oldsmobile moved forward to open the door, and the car had a manual crank and elementary suspension system.

Stonex then compared these features with contemporary designs and concluded that "there has been a great deal of improvement in design over the fifty-four-year period." His basic conclusion cannot be denied, but he might have added that the demands of greatly increased speed and power requirements show that the *relative* increase in operational safety was far from as large as the absolute increase.

It is true that since the turn of the century the automobile companies have adopted better brakes, the electric self-starter, "safety glass," all steel bodies and roofs, independent front suspension, the automatic transmission, and directional signals, and have attached longer-lasting tires. Manufacturers are producing a car that is more reliable operationally than the vehicle which launched the motor age at the turn of the century. The same luminous comparison can, of course, be made between modern turnpikes and the muddy roads that existed before World War I, or between jet aircraft and a 1910 monoplane. The difference is that the builders of roads and planes do not make a practice of referring to their primitive predecessors as evidence of present progress. The question regularly begged by Stonex as he makes his rounds with his 1910 analogy is, "Why has General Motors not come up with the answers to make the modern car as safe as technology can make it?"

This line of inquiry is a probe against which Stonex has prepared an elaborate defense. The most concise expression of his theory appeared in an article he wrote for the General Motors' *Engineering Journal* in 1963. The journal is aimed at the engineering faculty and students at technical institutes and universities. Stonex set these limits on engineering imagination: "Early post-war impact tests were performed at the [General Motors] Proving Ground by letting a remotely controlled test car coast down a steep grade and collide with a massive concrete barrier. In these tests the impact speeds were approximately 30 mph and deceleration rates on the underformed part of a car frame were about 30 g. The catastrophic nature of these tests resulted in the belief that the threshold of serious and probably fatal injury is far below normal highway speeds. These tests led to the conclusion that it is impossible to provide secure protection during impacts of this nature by any amount of design modification, or by any restraining devices that the average driver would be willing to use."

In numbers of other technical articles, Stonex has repeated in one form or another this early post-war discovery as though it were an immutable law of nature. Vehicle design for crashworthiness, he told an automobile safety meeting in 1963, is effective protection against injury and death for no more than the "range of present suburban traffic speeds." Five seconds later in the same report he admitted that "little energy-absorption engineering has been done" by the industry; he did concede that this work was the industry's responsibility. Doggedly adhering to his position, Stonex ignored a technical paper presented at the Fifth Stapp Car Crash Conference by two General Motors' engineers whose report said that "even in car-to-car collision impacts at 50 mph, cars can be designed so that the crash energy is absorbed and dissipated with little or no damage to, and reduced deceleration in the occupant compartments of, the colliding cars."

Stonex's viewpoint about the limits of vehicle design safety puts him in the class of the engineer at the turn of the century who saw no further need for the patent office because every conceivable useful idea had already been patented. He also avoids the fact that the large majority of accidents that produce serious injuries and fatalities occur at impact speeds under forty miles per hour and that even within his arbitrary "low ceiling," a tremendous number of accidents could be prevented with the design of safer vehicle features, such as braking and control systems and adequate tires.

Stonex displays such engineering eccentricity about car safety because of the realities he has learned as a thirty-year employee of General Motors. His adjustment has taken the form of convincing his superiors that, as the world's largest car manufacturer, it had nothing to lose and much to gain by devoting some attention to the problem of highway design. As Stonex told a friend, somewhat wistfully, "My interest in improved highway design will probably contribute more to highway safety than anything else I can do."

The case for General Motors taking an interest in highway design delighted the public relations office of the company. The research program was launched with the announcement that the safest highway system in the world was the sixty-five-mile private road system at the General Motors' proving grounds in Milford, Michigan. This was supported with accident injury figures which, up to 1958, showed that the proving grounds roads were twenty-five times safer than public highways.

At that point Stonex expanded his work. He reasoned that the impressive safety record was due primarily to the control of access, one-way traffic, and fewer roadside obstacles. This led him to propose the general elimination of roadside obstructions—stones, boulders, trees, culvert head-walls, sharp ditches and severe slopes, lamps and utility poles, bridge abutments, present types of guard rails, road signs, and other vehicles, whether they were parked or moving in opposing directions or at intersections. This clearing out, Stonex held, would come close to preventing collisions characterized as "ran-off-the-road" and "opposite-direction" types. These kinds of collisions cause, on the average, twelve thousand and six thousand fatalities respectively every year.

One-way highways with controlled access can eliminate opposing traffic collisions; clearing the roadside of obstacles can allow the driver to recover control of his vehicle or simply come to a stop on a gently sloping roadside, instead of smashing into a tree or other impediment. According to Stonex, these ideal road conditions are possible with the "application of well-known engineering technology."

A three-year program ending in 1962 was undertaken at the General Motors' proving grounds to put Stonex's ideas into practice. Trees were uprooted, ditch bottoms rounded, slopes graded, dangerous guard-rail constructions replaced with designs made safe for collision. Stonex and his associates designed lamp poles, bridge parapets, and suspended traffic signs to meet the criteria of the no-obstacle highway. As a result of this work, the roadsides at the proving grounds are now clear of obstacles and are safely traversable for almost one hundred feet from the edge of the road pavement. "It would be pretty hard to commit suicide on proving ground roadsides," Stonex observes proudly.

When Stonex looks at the American highway system he is only partly satisfied with the 41,000-mile interstate system scheduled for completion by 1972. Although many of his suggestions were foreseen in 1956 when federal and state officials wrote the standards for this new highway system, Stonex describes the other three and a half million miles of American roads with fervid indignation: "I propose that our highway system design and operating practice is precisely that which we would have built if our objective had been to kill as many people as possible; we have made a game of it by some qualifications, such as 'Drive to the right,' 'Yield to the car on the right at an intersection,' 'Stop at stop signs,' 'Keep your car under control.' This is the real transportation problem that remains to be approached. What we must do is to operate the 90% or more of our surface streets just as we do our freeways . . . [converting] the surface highway and street network to freeway and Proving Ground road and roadside conditions."

Stonex has looked into the urban road problem even from the aerial perspective. On this subject he said, "The passenger who flies over any of our cities is struck by the tremendously large proportion of the surface area which is given over to roof tops; in many areas, the most conspicuous parts of the landscape below are the roof tops and the street surfaces. To conserve this valuable area, there does not seem to be any practical reason why long-term planning cannot arrange that new roads be built over the buildings in commercial districts and heavily congested residential districts so that the road pavement serves as the roof deck. In central business districts, we might even have to think of horizontal tunnels through the buildings to carry automotive traffic, just as we have vertical tunnels to carry elevator traffic."

This summary of General Motors' highway deşign work comprises the major published output of its crash research during the past ten years. Mr. Stonex blithely ignores that fact. In April 1963 the *American Engineer,* journal of the National Society of Professional Engineers, opened a critical analysis of the automobile with these words: "It would be hard to imagine anything on such a large scale that seems quite as badly engineered as the American automobile. It is, in fact, probably a classic example of what engineering should *not* be." Stonex wrote a long rebuttal to the editors in which he cited six technical papers to show the crash research going on at General Motors. Insofar as any technical contributions were concerned, every one of these papers dealt with highway safety design.

Concentrating on highway design rather than vehicle design serves two important purposes of General Motors' management. First, it is extraordinarily cheap. The work keeps three or four engineers busy at the proving ground crashing a few cars against some guard rails and bridge parapets for the benefit of visiting delegations and provides the company with the material for endlessly repetitive papers at technical meetings. Second, there are no tooling costs implicit in highway design suggestions. Safer highways, obviously, are paid for by the public, not by General Motors.

Stonex's work is a useful contribution to the standards already employed in building the new interstate system. But raising the other ninety-nine per cent of the highway system to New York Thruway standards would amount to the largest public works' project in history. Changing over a nation's three and a half million miles of highways in this way would take thirty to thirty-five years and would cost hundreds of billions of dollars.

But the cars on the road today—their average age is six years —can be changed over in a much shorter time and at an immeasurably lower cost. It hardly seems the most logical route to traffic safety for the largest producer of automobiles in the country to devote the bulk of its staff and resources in crash safety research to the area where it has no implementing power, rather than to put its talents to work on vehicle design, where it has full power and control.

The work of Stonex as chief "automotive safety engineer" for General Motors has been devoted almost exclusively to an ambitious project to remake the road system of America, a proposal that only diverts attention and concern away from the vehicles that must negotiate those roads.

Alex Haynes is the Ford Motor Company's executive engineer in charge of safety. In this capacity he has represented his company before the Roberts' House subcommittee on traffic safety, and in 1964 and 1965 he was Ford's representative at the industry conferences with the General Services Administration, the agency charged with establishing safety standards for federally purchased passenger vehicles.

Haynes pursues company directives with a persistence that subdues any critical capacity he may have as a professional automotive safety engineer. As the Ford spokesman, Haynes has been the most intransigent participant in the discussions leading to the preparation of GSA standards. At formal conferences, in personal meetings with GSA officials, and in frantic last-minute telephone calls from Detroit, he waged a battle to narrow the number of safety features for GSA consideration and, later, to water down the proposed standards prior to their final revision in June 1965. His fervor surprised even his counterparts at Chrysler, General Motors, and American Motors. One of them explained Haynes's behavior as being the result of the pressure he was under from top management at Ford because of problems of certain Ford models in meeting the originally proposed standards.

Whatever the reason, Ford, represented by Haynes, was the only vehicle manufacturer which advised GSA not to consider any standards dealing with bumpers, rearward displacement of the steering column, and exhaust emission controls.

At the first meeting with GSA, in November 1964, Haynes was particularly adamant about bumpers. He did not see what was so essential about them "from a safety standpoint." Dr. Floyd Van Atta, of the Department of Labor, asked which of the two functions, decoration or energy-absorption, the current automobile bumper was intended to perform. Haynes seemed incapable of separating the two points, finally conceding only that "our business includes styling" as a "very necessary thing." It was left for Chrysler's Roy Haeusler to put an end to the fencing: "I think today's bumpers serve primarily as a parking guard. . . . The bumper is not playing a major role in the total job of absorbing collision energy when these collisions are of greater magnitude than simply rough parking."

Other manufacturers agreed to an innocuous bumper height standard, but Haynes fought until the end against even the principle of including the bumper under any safety standard. Haynes's engineering background must have taught him the great potential in safer bumpers for the significant energy-absorption of impact forces. Prior to 1958, his engineering associates at Ford had worked on such safety bumpers. But this background obviously receded before Ford management's desire to defend the unfettered flexibility of company stylists. For their part, the stylists seem dedicated to the proposition that the function of the bumper is to look nice—and to protect the bumper. (Ford's engineering skills labored under no such inhibitions in its work on energy-absorptive mechanisms for the aerospace field. Its aeronutronic division developed in 1962 and 1963 an "impact limiter" for the Ranger project, designed to modify the tremendous landing forces to levels that protect the most delicate instruments in the lunar-landing spacecraft.)

Another position which Haynes presented to GSA was the highly exaggerated claim that three to four years' advance notice must be given to his company before it could adopt the standards in its vehicles. In May 1965 he told GSA that it was too late to change the location of the ignition key (for safety purposes) in the 1967 models. He favored talking about 1969 models when considering safety features for instrument panels.

It has long been routine practice for the automobile companies to talk about the "three year lead-time" needed for planning a particular model-year's automobile. This put off any legislation from going into effect before three years' time and discouraged a number of administrators and legislators from doing anything in the safety field.

Depending on the vehicle component or feature, "lead-time" is a relative concept that can be shortened or lengthened according to the importance attached to prompt change by company management. New manufacturing operations are cutting down necessary "lead-time." The so-called "lead-time" for design, tooling, and manufacturing of an entirely new car, like the Corvair or the Mustang, was only two years.

V. D. Kaptur of General Motors has said, "An engineering breakthrough by one of the divisions, or the announcement of new competitive cars, may change the entire concept of a program already under way. As an example, the wedge-roof four-door hardtop on the '59 and '60 cars was a last-minute addition to the line, and turned out to be one of our best sellers." Chevrolet's Godfrey Burrows described the development of a new frame for the 1955 Chevrolet—no minor change—as taking only fourteen months from preliminary design to mass production. In reply to a question in late 1964 about whether the 1967 models were "frozen," a Fisher Body engineer replied, "Nonsense; even the 1965's aren't frozen," and he cited a case where a grill was changed in the middle of the model year. In 1963, Ford stylist Joseph Oros said, "Today it takes two years to get a car out and into production. Technology will soon be cutting six to eight months off that time. It means we will be able to swing better with public whimsy and give cheaper, better products to people."

Alex Haynes was not unaware of these facts of automobile production. But his job was to disguise management reluctance as technological impossibility. In performing that task he served his superiors with unquestioning loyalty and single-mindedness.

Roy Haeusler, Chrysler's leading automotive safety engineer, is the most articulate spokesman on safety in the industry. At times his candor in public forums and safety meetings, though more analytical than blunt, has embarrassed his colleagues. After hearing Haeusler say publicly that there are many ways to make a vehicle safer without increasing costs if only the engineering is done right in the first place, one company engineer said, "There goes honest Roy again; he's the kind of person of whom you don't ask a question unless you can stand the answer."

Haeusler has labored since 1934 with singular ineffectiveness insofar as persuading Chrysler management to produce safer cars. Perhaps a high point in his career occurred at the Eighth Stapp Car Crash Conference. George Gibson, Chrysler's Director of Product Planning, delivered an address (prepared substantially by Haeusler) in which he told an audience composed of hard-boiled, independent collision researchers, some of whom had risked personal danger in order to advance the frontiers of collision protection: "Safe car design is one way to keep a customer . . . We hope that the public will use the safety features that we do have available. There is nothing that will accelerate progress in safety design more than public demand for the safety features and safety equipment which are available. Public acceptance of available safety features will come only if those in a position to exercise leadership do exercise it. We ourselves are taking the lead in urging all our executives to order available safety options on their own cars."

Haeusler thanked Gibson by saying, "You can be sure that no one appreciated those words more than I." He was not being polite. For Gibson's words represent Haeusler's adjustments to the constraints of corporate reality, while at the same time salvaging some achievements from a frustrating career in automotive safety. Like the good soldier who disagrees with his superior, Haeusler has maintained a strong loyalty to company policy, but has tried to bring about a change through normal channels.

He has chosen to emphasize the element of consumer demand, which, because it votes with dollars, is more likely to catch the ear of the company policy makers who then might be persuaded to "give them more of what they want."

Haeusler has even gone so far as to state that what is needed is "arousing of the public to a greater sense of personal responsibility for making decisions in favor of safety equipment in buying a car, rather than confining attention to wheel covers and whitewall tires. If the motorist were willing to give up these two frills alone, he would then have the money to pay for at least four and maybe six seat belts for his car." To suggest that consumers divert money from style to safety is revolutionary talk in Detroit, and Haeusler is not prone to say it often or publicly. The consequences of following through would be disagreeable to corporate management. For example, Haeusler has said that the consumer's welfare requires that the automobile companies inform them of the difference between function and appearance on an entirely objective basis. This would mean, for example, that Chrysler should inform consumers of the differences in side-impact and roll-over strength between the hard-top convertibles and conventional four-door sedans with upper center posts. But Chrysler does not inform the public of these differences, and neither do any of the other manufacturers.

The difficulty with Haeusler's approach is that it shifts the responsibility from the automobile maker—where it belongs and can be most completely exercised—to the consumer whose exercise of initiative can only be trivial and agonizingly slow. Fundamental automobile safety is not a matter of attachable devices and features offered as optional extra-cost equipment. It is a matter of building safer designs into the car.

The industry has not recognized the immorality of selling style as part of the basic cost of cars while requiring the buyer to pay extra for safety. For example padded dashboard panels have been offered as optional equipment for ten years; the consumer purchase of this extra-cost option has been high, yet not until the GSA regulations were imminent did the industry decide to make such padding standard equipment on all 1966 models.

This is consistent with the industry's long practice of not introducing safety features as standard equipment unless there is compulsion or threat of legislation or regulation. Haeusler wants the compulsion of the marketplace instead of the compulsion of the law. The consumer, who is expected to buy more and more products each day, is also expected to exercise a purchasing sophistication that is wholly unrealistic. In 1850, the consumer's day was twenty-four hours long and a purchase was a major event. Today the day is still twenty-four hours long, but purchases come in rapid succession—purchases of much more complex products. To provide controlling guidelines, Haeusler wants the consumer to demand not just "safety," but those limited safety features which the companies decide to reveal to the market. This approach would keep consumer safety expectations within bounds and avoid public participation (through government) in corporate safety policies. Then the car makers would determine whether to provide them as options or standard equipment, and at what price.

As a strategy to get his company moving, Haeusler's approach is understandable. But as a belief it is detrimental to the emergence of manufacturing integrity. That Haeusler does, indeed, believe in it is illustrated by his comparison of compelling the customer to take safety as being similar to compelling people to take polio shots. This is analogy by desperation.

The issue is not, as Haeusler would have it, a matter of compulsion, but simply one of value not received. Every year American car buyers are paying, according to a study by Massachusetts

Institute of Technology economists, about seven hundred dollars per car for the costs of the annual model change. With such a gigantic billing, it would not be unreasonable to anticipate an annual product improvement that afforded a substantial safety advance.

The positions taken by Stonex, Haynes, and Haeusler on automotive safety reflect their secondary status in the hierarchy of corporate priorities and budgeting. In the absence of company figures, federal highway safety researchers estimate that the automobile manufacturers allot a total of two million dollars a year to the design and evaluation of crash safety improvements. This amounts to about twenty-three cents for every car sold. This is an estimate that gives a generous benefit of the doubt to the companies. For the research output disclosed by them to the world of engineering and science is so insignificant that it constitutes a mockery. The few technical papers describing their crash tests are heavily repetitive and offer little insight into the development of safer designs. The major studies in collision protection have been done by a handful of university and military researchers—and even company safety engineers have recognized this fact.

Although the collision safety testing and development programs of the automobile manufacturers have been woefully deficient, there is strong evidence in the form of company-held patents and certain public statements that more is known than is admitted at meetings such as the ones the industry held with GSA officials. For example, in describing a new impact sled, Stonex told a group of specialists, "This laboratory instrument makes it possible to simulate dynamic tests of complete cars in up to 30 mph head-on crashes, and of components to much higher severity. Test results are confidential, naturally." Statements like this shock physicians who are working with safety problems. Such policies, wrote Dr. C. Hunter Shelden in 1955, if "translated into medicine would be comparable to withholding known methods of life-saving value."

Secrecy in safety data and developments is part of the environment which forces men like Stonex, Haynes, and Haeusler to subordinate whatever initiatives might flow from professional dictates in favor of preserving their passive roles as engineer-employees. The 1965 graduating class of Lawrence Institute of

Technology heard the message that has shaped the working lives of the automotive safety engineers. Sumner B. Twiss of Chrysler advised the new engineers at commencement exercises that "a prime requisite for getting ahead in industry is identification of your personal objectives with the objectives of the company." Twiss declared that leadership in industry goes to those who believe in the company and what it is doing and feel that its grand schemes reflect their own personal schemes. This attitude, he said, can be more important for advancement than depth of technical knowledge.

Engineer-employees serve their companies in other important activities intended to reduce the scope of conflict between automobile makers and to control the content of government action wherever it cannot be avoided altogether. The principal institution for the industry coordination of decisions concerning the technical issues in vehicle safety is the Society of Automotive Engineers (SAE), a tax-exempt organization founded in 1905, which describes itself as follows: "The object of the Society is to promote the Arts, Sciences, Standards and Engineering Practices connected with the design, construction and utilization of self-propelled mechanisms, prime movers, components thereof, and related equipment." The society holds meetings to discuss technical papers and develops engineering standards and recommended practices. SAE reported a gross income in 1963 of $1,549,808, composed mainly of individual membership dues and industry contributions.

The control by the automobile industry of SAE's motor vehicle standards work is so complete that the engineering community does not consider the society as anything more than a ratifier of industry policies and decisions. The Automobile Manufacturers Association is SAE's traffic light.

In the structure and operation of SAE's working committees is seen the impressive connections between SAE and the automobile industry. The automotive council of the SAE technical board is composed of numerous committees and subcommittees dealing with automobile safety. Membership on these committees is held mostly by engineer-employees of the motor vehicle manufacturers. Although membership in SAE is on an individual basis, the corporate employer is always identified alongside the member's name on the committee rosters. The automotive safety committee is composed of eight members—all employees of motor vehicle producers. The same is true of the bumper height technical committee, and over four-fifths of the membership of the body engineering committee is similarly constituted. Other committees, such as the brake committee, include a few representatives from universities, government agencies, and companies who supply the automobile industry.

Apart from numerical dominance, the automobile manufacturers have a practical veto power. SAE Technical Board Rule 8.1 states: "Reports submitted to the Council for approval, in general, should have the unanimous approval of the committee making such a submittal. Where unanimous approval cannot be achieved, reports shall have the approval of at least three-quarters of the members." Rule 8.6 reads: "Councils will strive for unanimous approval, and in no case will they approve a report which has not been approved by three-quarters of their members."

The automobile industry also finances the work leading to the development of standards or recommended practices. It does this by contributing to SAE staff support and by absorbing the time and expenses of its employees who, as SAE members, attend committee meetings and use company testing facilities in the writing of standards. SAE does not undertake work on a new standard or recommended practice unless requested to do so by the industry-dominated SAE technical boards—which must reflect a consensus of their members. This intricate network of participation and control is a basic reason why no SAE standard, recommended practice, or information report in the motor vehicle field has ever been promulgated without industry endorsement.

SAE's entry into the automobile crash protection area was a late one. The first SAE recommended practice was in 1955, and dealt with specifying a minimum loop strength of three thousand pounds for a two-inch-wide seat belt. Since that year, SAE's work in vehicle safety has dealt either with specifying test procedures or with establishing minimum performance levels for those safety features which had become the subject of legislation or threatened legislation. These include seat belt assemblies and anchorages, passenger car side-door latches, and rear vision in passenger cars. Generally, however, SAE technical positions on vehicle safety are grossly incomplete or nonexistent. Bumper standards are apparently taken care of by SAE Standard J681, concerning bumper heights, which defines heights only for front bumper "dip" and rear bumper "lift" when the vehicle experiences a maximum brake stop at five to ten miles per hour. Another standard, SAE J903, deals with performance requirements of the windshield wiper, but not the area of the windshield to be wiped. SAE J839, the standard for passenger car side-door latches, was written by a subcommittee composed entirely of automobile industry employees. The standard calls for the latch to have a load resistance of 1500 pounds—an unusually weak level that some automobile manufacturers have recently felt necessary to exceed. The requirements in Standard J839 for testing the latches are even more limited, failing to provide for several kinds of crash stresses.

SAE has never developed, for example, standards or recommended practices for tires, impact criteria for the steering assembly, glare levels, dashboard panel instruments and controls, sun visors, handles, knobs or other load-concentrating projections and passenger compartment crashworthiness. It was not until 1951 that industry representatives allowed the establishment of the Automotive Safety Committee.

The only other private standardizing organization that has dealt with aspects of the automobile is the major standards group in the United States—the American Standards Association (ASA). (It has approved standards for automobile safety glass, glare and reflection levels, and vehicle inspection criteria.) ASA is a national federation of 140 technical societies and trade organizations, and has some 2200 company members. ASA does not initiate or write standards; it considers standards for approval only on the request of a responsible organization or group.*

As a result, ASA has reflected the desire of the automotive industry to have SAE standards dominate the motor vehicle field. This important domination is made possible by the consensus principle that is crucial to the way ASA works. An ASA standard can be approved only if there is a consensus among all groups

* ASA estimates its own prestige in this way: "There is general understanding that ASA operates in the public interest. An example will illustrate the significance of this impartiality. Years ago, an association had difficulty in getting its safety standard accepted by a number of states as the basis for state safety regulations. The standard was technically sound. But apparently it was considered a special-interest group pursuing its own commercial motives. The standard was then submitted to ASA and was subsequently approved without changes as an American Standard. As such, it was accepted by the states without objection."

which are substantially concerned with its subject matter. This gives the automobile industry another veto on all proposals dealing with automobiles for, as an ASA statement reads, "Votes are weighed rather than counted." An objection by the automobile industry, or even a major automobile company, would be enough to outweigh all opposing votes.

Both SAE and ASA standards are advisory only. Their use by anyone engaged in industry or trade is voluntary, but since they are approved by the majority, they are used by the majority. In the motor vehicle safety field, these standards form the substance of a unified industry policy on particular technical issues. And the consensus principle makes almost certain that the lowest common denominator of performance requirements is adopted.

The typical pattern followed in SAE automotive safety standards or recommended practices is to state only a single minimum performance value—such as the load to be withstood by door latch and striker assemblies—without any accompanying technical reasoning or explanation. The committees work in secret, and there is no release of proposed standards or recommended practices for technical comment or criticism by SAE membership or the scientific and engineering community at large. The first time an SAE member sees the standard is after it has been formally promulgated. Once a standard is announced, the automobile industry can then say to the outside world that its products meet the standards set by the Society of Automotive Engineers—which, in the words of a former SAE president, James Zeder, "serves no selfish interest."

The industry has found more ambitious objectives for SAE standards when it comes to translating those standards into public law. Their policy runs in this pattern: since standards inform the buyer of what he has a right to expect from the seller, the industry, as seller, recognizes the importance of getting SAE standards incorporated into laws and regulations which define the level of safety that must be assured to the consumer. As public pressure for safety legislation increases, activity of SAE committees will also increase to make sure that lawmakers will have industry-approved criteria to put into the new laws.

There is ample precedent for this approach. Automobile Manufacturers Association "field representatives" routinely advocate—with success—that state legislation employ an SAE standard as its yardstick. Seat belt laws in many states explicitly include SAE standards, for example. Brake fluid legislation in over twenty-five states is written on the basis of SAE standards. AMA lobbyists usually have little difficulty. Since state lawmakers have no alternative recognized source of technical standards, whatever is available is adopted. Should there be any skeptics, the prestige and standing of SAE is emphasized by citing its formal participation in the work of the ASA, the Highway Research Board of the National Academy of Sciences, the Interstate Commerce Commission's advisory committees, the National Committee on Uniform Traffic Laws and Ordinances, the National Highway Users' Conference and the National Safety Council. Such prestige and power make almost irresistible the casting of SAE into the role of *ad hoc* legislator.

The Automobile Manufacturers Association is also alert to any threat of an independent standards-setting capability being set up in government. In 1960, the AMA suggested an amendment to H.R. 1341 (the original House bill directing the General Services Administration to set safety standards for government-procured vehicles). The proposed amendment read: "Such standards shall conform to nationally recognized standards such as those published by the American Standards Association and the Society of Automotive Engineers [and shall] be revised from time to time to revisions in said nationally recognized standards." This language was not adopted in the bill which finally became law (called the Roberts' law) on August 30, 1964. The automobile makers simply shifted gears and tried to achieve the same objective through their industry advisory committee to the GSA officials who were administering the Roberts' law. At the specification development conferences, the duet of William Sherman of the AMA and George Gaudaen of the SAE (who was formerly Sherman's assistant at AMA) sang a similar tune: if we don't already have the standards and test procedures for you, we'll have them soon.

Gaudaen's position was so blatantly attuned to the special interests of the industry that it became embarrassing to his colleagues from the AMA. SAE, after all, is supposed to be a professional association with a suite separate from that of the AMA in the New Center Building in Detroit. But Gaudaen advised GSA, with a mixture of the arbitrariness and authority that is so characteristic of the SAE, that it should dismiss from its proposed lists of safety features a number of items not considered to be of safety significance. Included in the list were seats to prevent neck injuries, bumper performance and heights, rear window defogger and wiper, and exhaust controls. He then insisted that consideration of five other features on GSA's proposed list be deferred until long-run studies by the SAE and the industry were completed. This group included safer instruments and knobs, handles and window controls, padded roof lining, driver signaling, and the design of instrument panel controls. The remaining items on the list Gaudaen tied to SAE standards and test procedures that were either already established or imminent under the SAE's speeded-up program to serve GSA in its mission.

SAE is no less diligent in protecting the commercial interests of the industry than it has been in defending the political interests of its sponsor. SAE's role as minion is shown in the story of the industry's long-standing practice of rigging odometers—the devices that record the number of miles traveled.

In 1963 the National Bureau of Standards (Department of Commerce) released the MacKay report, which showed with irrefutable exactness that for American automobiles, a mile is not necessarily a mile. For years, as some alert motorists know, Americans have been driving less than they think they have. The MacKay study showed that automobile odometers over-registered mileage on an average of 3.21 per cent, with some cars registering an error of over 5 per cent.

Complaints about odometers have been registered for years with state agencies and the Federal Trade Commission. But state regulations defining the permissible margin of error were ignored by the industry and not enforced by the state administrators.

Few practices can be more deceptive than tampering with the integrity of a measurement, whether it be miles, pounds, or inches. Few deceptions could serve such a variety of purposes. Car and tire warranties based on mileage run out sooner when odometers are over-set. Gas-mileage-per-gallon claims of manufacturers are overestimated or inflated, making easier the task described by Ford's Ray Pittman: "We fight for fractions of one per cent for fuel economy." A car owner could receive a lower trade-in value because depreciation is estimated partly on total mileage traveled. Over-set odometers tend to make the car owner think his vehicle is ready to trade in sooner, which helps feed the new car turnover.

Finally, customers who rent cars pay for miles they did not drive. Based on the estimate of 1.25 billion miles traveled in 1964 by rented passenger cars, a 3.31 per cent overcharge, at the rate of ten cents a mile, would amount to an overcharge of almost four million dollars. An average 3.21 per cent premium on gross sales is a healthy fillip for the large, car-buying rental companies.

The automobile industry learned of the National Bureau of Standards study of odometer performance in 1962. An Automobile Manufacturers Association odometer committee was formed to represent the industry in meetings with bureau officials who were working out new standards for the states so that odometers would have to register an average error nearer to zero. (Because a variety of conditions such as tire size, inflation pressure, weight, and road pavement affect odometer readings, it has been customary to provide for a plus-or-minus error tolerance range around zero.)

The AMA odometer committee did not dispute the National Bureau of Standards findings. It stated that member companies ordered odometers from suppliers according to SAE specifications. SAE recommended practice J678b permits a five per cent over-registration error.

But the AMA knew that the game was over, at least to the extent that it was played, and in December 1964 the Automobile Manufacturers Association informed the National Bureau of Standards that in 1965 manufacturers would install odometers that were set to the new bureau specifications.

The AMA position, so long unquestioned by the public guardians of weights and measures, was wholly untenable from both an engineering and a moral viewpoint. It was technically simple to produce more accurate odometers. Yet inquiries about the role of SAE as a ratifying participant in a fraud on consumers still elicit only the stock reply from SAE's New York headquarters that "the speedometer and odometer are designed and manufactured to be as accurate as possible."

Despite all the facts, SAE apparently does not consider its position any more incongruous than the fact that it held shares in Hertz Corporation during the period of the odometer investigation.*

---

* SAE also owns shares in several petroleum and tire manufacturing companies whose products are obviously integral to the automobile over which the society exercises its standardizing functions.

Another service performed by SAE for the automobile industry is public relations. For example, since a company brochure on the safety of its automobiles cannot avoid a partisanship that would call its objectivity into question, it is far more effective to have the "message" relayed to the public under the auspices of SAE. Indeed, anyone who writes to one of the "big three" automobile companies for printed matter on safety is likely to receive a thirty-seven-page paper entitled "The Safety the Motorist Gets," with the SAE emblem prominently displayed in the upper left hand corner. This booklet is a detailed attempt to show that the automobile manufacturers give the motorist "all the safety that can be built in without destroying the utility of his vehicle." The pamphlet has five sections, including contributions by all the domestic automobile makers; it ends with a section of full-page maps of all the companies' proving grounds and the assurance that safer automobiles have probably been the greatest contribution toward keeping the casualty rate down.

"The Safety the Motorist Gets" was published as SAE paper SP-165 in June 1959 and is still being circulated, suggesting that vehicle safety developments since that year have not diminished its enduring currency. It is an argumentative brief for the industry's commercial practices and policies in automotive safety. One of the instances in which the pamphlet was used occurred when the House subcommittee on health and safety began its hearings in 1959. One of the issues it was considering was whether new safety devices should be standard equipment or extra-cost options. The SAE paper, a copy of which had been dispatched to the committee by SAE General Manager John Warner, explained that proven safety devices fall into two categories: those devices whose "immediate application on all cars is considered virtually imperative, such as sealed-beam head lamps," and those which are "clearly an aid to safe driving, but something less than a vital necessity." The pamphlet went on to explain that safety equipment in the second category is first introduced as an option and only adopted as standard equipment "when public demand becomes substantial enough." As examples of items that had passed this test of the marketplace, the pamphlet cited windshield wipers and directional signals. As current examples of devices which the industry felt should first be put through this test, the paper listed power windows, power seats, reclining seats, head rests—and *seat belts!*

"The Safety the Motorist Gets" discusses and defends controversial issues of design and industry policy which have no connection whatever with the stated purpose of SAE to advance the state of the art of automotive engineering. The SAE constitution said, "Matters relating to politics or purely to trade shall not be discussed at a meeting of this Society or be included in its publications." But "The Safety the Motorist Gets" is sprinkled with dozens of references to "industry" or "manufacturers" in the general context of praising the high industry standards, the rigorous testing and inspection, and the millions of miles of durability runs on the industry proving grounds.

Three months before SP-165 was released, Lloyd Withrow, head of the General Motors' fuels and lubricants department, expressed his concern that SAE ought to publish better technical papers. He wrote: "I have talked with people who believe that SAE performs more like a trade association than a professional engineering society. These people say that the society appears to be more concerned with the production, sale and distribution of automotive products than either the development of new engineering knowledge or the application of sound engineering principles to the design of new automotive equipment." Few of SAE's 25,000 members would be surprised at Withrow's observations.

Only one member formally challenged the propriety of "The Safety the Motorist Gets" before the SAE's National Council. The council unanimously rejected the challenge, but SAE president Leonard Raymond wrote in the March 1960 issue of the SAE journal that "there may have been departures from best practice in connection with the paper in question . . . and we intend to see to it that they are not repeated in the future." But Mr. Raymond did not request the automobile makers' public relations offices to cease distributing the paper.

The SAE automotive council and its committees are rarely called on to confront challenges or dissent. By planning the subject matter for the technical meetings, and by arranging for the papers to be delivered, SAE leaders have made certain that not a single paper devoted to engineering criticism of contemporary vehicle safety design has found its way into the SAE program. This is quite a record, since almost five hundred technical papers and articles on motor vehicle subjects are delivered each year at SAE gatherings.

On only one occasion—the summer meeting of 1961—was the curtain parted briefly to permit the reading of a paper by Dr. William Haddon, a leading accident researcher who is associated with the New York State Department of Health. Dr. Haddon, whose background is in medicine and engineering, made an incisive analysis of the ways the medical and public health professions were approaching the problem of motor vehicle accident injuries, aided by techniques originally developed for the investigation and control of communicable diseases. He characterized both goals—disease prevention and accident prevention—as being fundamentally "engineering" problems. That is, concentration on the hostile environment—the malaria swamp or the interior of a vehicle—is almost invariably more productive than trying to manipulate the behavior of people. He described to his engineering audience the path he saw ahead. "Our two professions," Dr. Haddon said, "have an objective in common which will continue to confront us probably for the remainder of our professional lives. This objective is the prevention, partial or complete, of some forty thousand deaths per year, and the reduction, amelioration or elimination of an additional four million injuries. . . . The greatest challenge which you as a profession now face and may ever have faced, is the challenge of designing a vehicle which, under the normal conditions of its daily use, does not, in the accidents which inevitably happen, result in injury and death of substantial numbers of its users. . . . the success of your profession in the present decade will largely be weighed in terms of its success in handling this overwhelming problem."

Dr. Haddon's powerful appeal to automotive engineers to apply their professional dedication to the safety of their products was received with polite lack of interest. Later, even the politeness vanished. No SAE publication list contains a reference to his address. The heads of SAE did not consider it worthy of publication, and no reason had to be given for the omission, just as no reason had to be given for the inclusion of such items as remote from engineering as *The Feminine Mystique in Design*.

Actually Dr. Haddon's effort was doomed from the beginning. He was addressing a body that does not exist: the automotive engineering *profession*. The Society of Automotive Engineers has no code of ethics, and it subscribes to no code of ethics in the engineering world. This is a serious lapse; ethics are more than slogans meant to fill a plaque to be hung on office walls. Ethics define important social interests which a profession assumes the responsibility to serve, and they require an independence from the erosive or destructive effects of commercial pressures.

For example, the code of ethics of the National Society of Professional Engineers makes clear what the duty of the individual engineer is in regard to safety. Section Two says, "The Engineer will have proper regard for the safety, health and welfare of the public in the performance of his professional duties. If his engineering judgment is overruled by non-technical authority, he will clearly point out the consequences. He will notify the proper authority of any observed conditions which endanger public safety and health. . . . He will not complete, sign or seal plans and/or specifications that are not of a design safe to the public health and welfare. . . . If the client or employer insists on such unprofessional conduct, he shall notify the proper authorities and withdraw from further service on the project."

In order concretely to develop the meaning of its code, the National Society of Professional Engineers' board of ethical review comments on actual cases that are brought to its attention. One case involved a company which manufactured a defective automated mass transportation system. The engineer responsible for the project reported to his superiors that the system failed the final tests and, as it was, presented a danger to the public. He was told that to meet contract commitments, the equipment would be shipped to the client-purchaser without notification of failure of the final tests. Over the objection of the engineer, the shipment was made. Did the engineer have any further ethical duty? The board concluded that he did, stating that he should have brought the danger to the attention of the client and the responsible authorities.

In medicine, law, architecture, and other professions, academic institutions provide nourishment for the perpetuation of professional standards. But only a shadow of a professional discipline in the automotive engineering field exists at universities. It is decidedly the poorest segment of the engineering curricula. Research on vehicle mechanics, for instance, involves only a half-dozen small projects. Automobile collision testing and measurement is limited to UCLA's Institute of Transportation and Traffic Engineering—and there on only a sporadic basis. Automotive engineering courses —indeed, even engineering professors specializing in automotive mechanics—are a rarity, as are graduate students who follow such a course of study. The amount of technical literature flowing from the universities is pitifully small. As the new engineering specialities expand and absorb the better engineering students, the situation in automotive studies and facilities at universities is not likely to improve. It is a condition that goes back many years and has had most unfortunate consequences which Leonard Segel of the Cornell Aeronautical Laboratory has described thus: "Instead of a student and faculty focus on automotive engineering that would generate a 'free' and an 'all-divulging' automotive literature, we have had an *industry focus* which . . . does not develop a professional attitude among most engineers employed within the automotive industry. Both business management and engineering management are willing to take undergraduates, give them test-and-process engineering assignments, and gradually teach them the 'industry way.' It is argued that unless an atmosphere of professionalism surrounds the research worker, his efforts, whether good, bad, or mediocre, will come to no avail."

Professor Wolfgang Meyer of Pennsylvania State University is concerned with how the automotive engineering curriculum has neglected engineering problems with immense human welfare implications—such as vehicle emissions and vehicle safety. Meyer points out that the development of automobile engineering has been overwhelmingly a proving ground, cut-and-try process.

For example, the theoretical study of engines or vehicle handling and braking has lagged far behind the engineering applications. This deficiency makes empirical findings less complete, reduces their predictive value and limits the advance of automotive engineering.

The creative work published on the theoretical aspects of automotive technology—from tires to engines to vehicle dynamics—has for many years been far greater at European universities and technical institutes than that coming from American academic institutions or the American automobile industry. The European research has long been the vanguard of the automotive engineering discipline.

The automobile companies have been wary of the possible

implications of independent automotive research centers at universities. Such projects could become alternative sources of information about automobile technology, including the performance of contemporary cars, techniques for making them safer, and detailed data from which to prepare standards for government safety regulation. So far, the industry has had little to worry about; there are no such centers. So long as the professors remain "detached" in their pursuit of knowledge, the automobile companies have found that occasional retainers and educators' conferences at their manufacturing plants are enough to form their university relations policy.

Only one professor, James Ryan of the University of Minnesota, has squarely and persistently challenged the automobile manufacturers to build crashworthy vehicles. Ryan's credentials are impressive. They include creative achievements in industry and a thirty-year academic career during which he invented numerous devices, the most famous of which was the flight recorder that is now standard equipment for all jet transports. His distinction is not just one of intellect, but of courage, and a professional commitment to engineering responsibility. On many occasions, in spite of frail health, he strapped himself into special deceleration carts and had himself driven into a wall to test his designs for reducing the forces of collisions. For fourteen years, until his retirement in 1963 because of a rheumatic heart condition, Ryan investigated and tested automobiles designed to prevent injuries to occupants during collisions. With a total budget of about $140,000, he developed automatic seat belts, hydraulic shock-absorbing bumpers, a large padded steering post with a short-travel absorber, a retracting steering-wheel rim for the driver, and a dashboard recessed under the windshield in front of the passenger. He tested all these designs in dozens of collision impacts, carefully recording the data from each test. His chief contribution was the energy absorbing bumper. On November 13, 1957, accompanied by a graduate student, Ryan got into a 1956 Ford car, fitted with this bumper, at Holloman Air Force Base in New Mexico. The car was driven into a solid crash barricade at twenty miles per hour, with no injuries resulting to the passengers or the vehicle. In March 1961 a volunteer, Peter Schoeck, rode a cart into a wall at twenty-five miles per hour and suffered no injuries. Although a barrier crash at forty miles per hour generates four times more energy than a crash at twenty miles per hour, Ryan was set in his intention to prove that with refinements of his energy-absorbing designs, a collision at the forty-mile speed would result in no more than superficial injury. His funds and his health ran out before he could do so.

The response of automobile company engineers to Ryan's work was either to ignore it, or to scorn and ridicule him. In the classic pose of engineers reflecting corporate policies, they leveled criticisms about his bumper in a pejorative vein not at all characteristic of science. Every engineering authority outside of the automobile industry considers Ryan's work to be an important contribution to vehicle safety. A Cornell Aeronautical Laboratory document stated in 1965: "Among the various proposed devices for injury attenuation in automobile crashes, the concept of an energy-absorbing front bumper presents the most favorable opportunity for a direct application of analytical and experimental techniques. It is noteworthy that the majority of both verbal and written criticism [there was only one written reference, a one-hundred word memo without data by GM's Kenneth Stonex] of Professor Ryan's experimentation are leveled at faults in his design, rather than at the basic principle of a controlled rate of energy absorption. In fact, it is sometimes claimed, without substantiating proof or evidence, that the sheet metal on modern automobiles is 'equivalent' to Ryan's bumper for the energy absorption function. However, Ryan's experimental results indicate distinct benefits, when compared with the corresponding frontal-collision responses of a 'standard' automobile, in the forms of a reduced peak vehicle deceleration and reduced peak seat-belt loads on the occupants."

The reception the industry gave Ryan's work illustrates how futile it is to expect that engineering contributions to recognized problems in collision safety will affect the automobile makers' product policy. Ernest Cunningham, editor of *Design News*, made the relevant distinction in 1960: "I do not question the ability of automotive designers. They can improve design safety. I question the moral honesty of the executive management responsible for policy direction, which year after year ignores design safety."

The lesson of many years is plain. The liberation of the engineering imagination for automotive safety cannot take place within the automobile industry. Nor, apparently, can it be stimulated to overcome internal corporate resistance by such outside contributions as Professor Ryan's. The remaining alternative is the creation of an independent technical capability outside the industry which sees vehicle safety as an engineering problem to be solved by engineering solutions, unfettered by industry constraints, secrecy, and sophistry.

Because of the efforts of New York State Senator Edward Speno, and his automotive consultant, Henry Wakeland, the first positive step toward this objective has been taken. Their efforts resulted in an overwhelming vote by the New York legislature for the passage of a bill authorizing a feasibility study of a prototype safety car program. The bill with a $100,000 appropriation, was signed by Governor Rockefeller on July 15, 1965.

Should the feasibility study result in the launching of the safety car program in 1966, it will be the first attempt to bring automotive safety technology within the mainstream of the modern systems analysis that has been used with such success in attaining aerospace missions. It is this level of technological capability, which makes the disingenuous efforts of the automobile industry in safety appear so old-fashioned. As the achievements of space and defense technology reveal, missions today need only to be defined and financed in order to be performed. Now for the first time a state government is considering the purchase of such a performed mission in order to exercise its responsibility of applying the most effective measures to reduce casualties on the highway.

The Speno-Wakeland program will cost three to five million dollars—about the price of the latest jet fighter plane. For this modest expenditure three primary goals are anticipated: (1) the research, design, construction, and testing of several prototype cars embodying all feasible safety features and suitable for mass production, (2) a complete set of performance requirements and tests supported by full technical rationale on the basis of which the legislature can adopt safety standards and (3) complete public disclosure of design drawings, construction specifications, and knowledge, together with tooling requirements and cost analysis for limited mass production.

Two longer-range objectives of the program are the establishment of clear performance criteria that will enable motorists to judge the relative safety levels of the cars they purchase, and the provision of detailed data and designs for any manufacturer to utilize. It is hoped that competition for safety, so long avoided by the giant automobile companies acting jointly, will be stimulated in this manner.

The noble attainments which Wakeland, as director of the New York State Safety Car Project, has set for himself recall the comment of Dr. J. Douglas Brown, dean of the faculty at Princeton University: "The central attribute of a learned profession is responsibility, not for a segmented detail of a total problem, but for an effective solution of the total problem. This means for the profession of engineering that the days are past when each specialist can withdraw into his specialty and become a servant of someone else's grand design. . . . If engineers can design space ships to go to the moon, why can't they design a safer automobile?"

6
The stylists:
It's the curve that counts

The importance of the stylist's role in automobile design is frequently obscured by critics whose principal tools are adjectives. The words are familiar: stylists build "insolent chariots," they deal with tremendous trifles to place on "Detroit Iron." Or, in the moralist's language, the work of the stylists is "decadent, wasteful, and superficial."

The stylists' work cannot be dismissed so glibly. For however transitory or trivial their visible creations may be on the scale of human values, their function has been designated by automobile company top management as *the* prerequisite for maintaining the annual high volume of automobile sales—no small assignment in an industry that has a volume of at least twenty billion dollars every year.

It is the stylists who are responsible for most of the annual model change which promises the consumer "new" automobiles. It is not surprising, therefore, to find that this "newness" is almost entirely stylistic in content and that engineering innovation is restricted to a decidedly secondary role in product development.

In the matter of vehicle safety, this restriction has two main effects. First, of the dollar amount that the manufacturer is investing in a vehicle, whatever is spent for styling cannot be spent for engineering. Thus, the costs of styling divert money that might be devoted to safety. Second, stylistic suggestions often conflict with engineering ideas, and since the industry holds the view that "seeing is selling," style gets the priority.

Styling's precedence over engineering safety is well illustrated by this statement in a General Motors' engineering journal: "The choice of latching means and actuating means, or handles, is also dictated by styling requirements. Changes in body style will continue to force redesign of door locks and handles." Another feature of style's priority over safety shows up in the paint and chrome finishes of the vehicle, which, while they provide a shiny new automobile for the dealer's floor, also create dangerous glare. Stylists can even be credited with overall concepts that result in a whole new variety of hazard. The hard-top convertible and the pillarless models, for example, were clearly the products of General Motors' styling staff.

Engineering features that are crucial to the transportation function of the vehicle do exert some restraining influence on styling decisions. A car must have four tires, and though the stylists may succeed shortly in coloring them, it is unlikely that aromatic creampuffs will replace the rubber. But conflicts between style and traditional engineering features are not often resolved in the latter's favor. For example, rational design of the instrument panel does not call for yearly change or recurring variety. Yet the stylists have had their way and at the same time have met management's demands for the interchangeability of components between different car makes. In one instance the 1964 Oldsmobile used exactly the same heater control as the 1964 Buick. In one brand it was placed in a horizontal position; in the other it was used vertically. With this technique, four separate and "different" instrument panels were created for each division.

This differentiating more and more about less and less has reached staggering proportions. In 1957 the Fisher body division produced for the five General Motors' car divisions more than 75 different body styles with 450 interior soft trim combinations and a huge number of exterior paint combinations. By 1963 this output proliferated to 140 body styles and 843 trim combinations.

Different designs for what General Motors' styling chief Harley Earl called "dynamic obsolescence" must be created for many elements of the car: front ends, rear ends, hoods, ornaments, rear decks and rear quarter panels, tail lamps, bumper shades, rocker panels, and the latest items being offered in an outburst of infinite variation—wheel covers and lugs.

These styling features form the substance of sales promotion and advertising. The car makers' appeals are emotional; they seek to inspire excitement, aesthetic pleasure, and the association of the glistening model in its provocative setting with the prospect's most far-reaching personal visions and wish-fulfillment. This approach may seem flighty, but the industry had learned that the technique sells cars to people who have no other reason to buy them with such frequency.

In recent years, campaigns saturated with the "style sell" have moved on to bolder themes. A 1964 advertisement for the Chevrolet Chevelle said, "We didn't just make the Chevelle beautiful and hope for the best. . . . If you think all we had in mind was a good-looking car smaller than the Chevrolet and bigger than Chevy II, read on." Curved side windows, the ad continued, are not just for appearance, "they slant way in for easy entry and don't need bulky space-wasting doors to roll down into." In addition, Chevelle's "long wide hood looks nice, too," because of all that goes under it—"a wide choice of Six and V-8 engines."

A Buick advertisement listed a number of regular vehicle features and commented, "You don't really need these, but how can you resist them?"

In *Motor Trend* magazine, a publication not addressed to "hot rodders" but to well-informed car hobbyists, the headline of a Plymouth advertisement read, "This is a status symbol." Its final paragraph read, "Plymouth Satellite's a decidedly undemocratic machine. Power-hungry people are the ones it really goes for."

Such advertisements are anything but hidden and subliminal persuaders. To turn the promotion of a transportation machine into an appeal so far removed from the functional quality of that machine, and to do so with commercial success, is an impressive, if disturbing, achievement in applied social science. It is an achievement made possible in large part by the amazing rise of the stylist in the hierarchy of automobile company management.

The stylist did not carve out his own role: it was waiting for him in the late twenties, at the death of the Model T Ford. For years after introducing his Model T in 1909, Henry Ford did very well selling cars to Americans, giving them "any color so long as it was black." Going into the twenties, the Ford held a commanding lead over its numerous competitors. The twenties was the crucial decade for the kind of automobile the public was to be sold in future years and for the industry that was going to produce it. During the first half of that decade, the mechanical features of the automobile—the power plant, drive train, and running gear—achieved engineering maturity and became more reliable. A stronger chassis frame and a passenger cabin were developed, and the suspension system improved the security and comfort of travel. Important assembly line production problems were overcome, and this permitted more uniform and efficient output. In other words, car companies were no longer forced to appeal to their customers with the kind of fundamental assurance that an early ad carried: "It gets you there and it brings you back." In 1925, 3,735,171 passenger cars were sold, compared with 1,905,560 in 1920.

In 1927, for the first time since it introduced the Model T, Ford lost its sales lead to General Motors, never again to regain it. In that year the 1927 La Salle became the first car to be "styled" —by Harley Earl, who had joined General Motors a year earlier. In response, Henry Ford came out with his "re-styled" Model A. The era of styling began.

At first the stylist was little more than a decorator of the trim and color of the basic body, after its size, shape, and materials had been determined by the engineers and approved by management. The change in emphasis from mechanical to styling features was explained by a leading stylist, Charles Jordan: "For economic reasons the mechanical assemblies couldn't be frequently changed, since no sales appeal lay in changing them when the result had no dramatic effect on performance. This evolutionary engineering of the car's functional parts tended to promote nearsameness in the products of all major competitors. This, in turn, opened the eyes and ears of company management to the arguments of the men who could provide real visible change under these conditions—the stylists."

Another General Motors' stylist, Vincent Kaptur, Jr., described the cars of the late twenties as having become more than cars. They expressed "status, power, fun, glamor, and freedom. The comforts, desires, and whims of the human being took precedence over the machine."

Actually, the problem the automobile industry was grappling with was one of maintaining a sales pace every year for a product that lasts for nearly a decade. Up to a point, a new invention like the automobile can show rising sales by simply meeting the demand for transportation. At that saturation point, however, the demand becomes less and less responsive to price reduction (the Model T had gone as low as $290) and functional improvement. A satiety threshold sets in that is similar to the limits which govern the consumer demand for food. But an emotional demand can be exploited for a much higher curve on the sales chart. There has never been established a human quota for "status, power, fun, glamor, and freedom." Thus the second stage in the evolution of a consumer product is reached: the time for catering to buyers' wants instead of simply to their needs.

General Motors had been the most aggressive advocate of styling. The first distinct styling section was organized in 1927 under Harley Earl. It was called "The Art and Colour Section." At first, the stylists' position was not secure when it came to disagreements with engineers. Earl's first contributions, slanted windshields and thin corner-pillars, had to be justified as "improving visibility." But by the late thirties Earl's group became the "General Motors' styling section," and he was elevated to a vice-presidency, indicating that the stylist's function was equal in importance to the work of the engineering, legal, company public relations, and manufacturing departments. The styling departments went through similar developments in other automobile companies. The engineer's authority over the design of the automobile was finished. As Charles Jordan of General Motors said, "Previously, functional improvement or cost reduction was a good reason for component redesign, but [in the thirties] the engineer had to learn to appreciate new reasons for redesigns." In a paper delivered before the Society of Automotive Engineers in 1962, Jordan demonstrated how the importance of the stylist has continued to grow when he urged that the word "styling" be replaced by the word "designer." Jordan said that the "designer" (that is, the stylist) is "the architect of the car, the coordinator of all the elements that make up the complete car, and the artist who gives it form. He stands at the beginning, his approach to and responsibility for the design of the vehicle is parallel to that of an architect of a building." An observer might wonder what was left for the engineer to do but play the part of a technical minion. Jordan ended his address by looking into the future. He foresaw changes in the automobile industry that he described as "drastic and far-reaching." He listed eleven questions in advanced research inquiry for which the styling research and the advanced vehicle design sections were working to find answers. Not one concerned collision protection.

Other manufacturers have not stated such a dominant role for the stylist, though they agree that the automobile will continue to be the major industrial art form in our society. Gene Bordinat, vice president and director of styling for Ford Motor Company said, "Styling serves to make the public aware that here is a new product, with improvements in materials, components and mechanical design—features that might be hidden to anyone but a mechanic or an engineer. People want to know about these things. And if they buy the car, they don't want its best features to be concealed. They want identification where it is visible to one and all. It's the same sort of urge that causes some girls to wear tight sweaters."

That urge to make its assets visible was certainly the central motivation behind the development of the car that created the most dramatic success story in Mr. Bordinat's own company. The introduction, the promotion, and the success of Ford's Mustang was the climactic triumph in the advancement of the stylist to the level of pre-eminence in the industry. The stylist in this case was helped by another new tool: market research. For the mass psychological phenomenon of the Mustang began with a market analysis that discovered even such details as how many college students wanted bucket seats for "first dates" (42%). It moved on, after Ford's decision that the advance surveys had identified a "real market," to advance publicity. The Mustang was to be "a new breed of horse." Both *Time* and *Newsweek,* for the first time devoted simultaneous cover stories to a new automobile.

Even before the press coverage and massive advertising campaigns were under way, Ford began receiving thousands of orders from people who had never even seen the Mustang. On the day the car was introduced, almost four million people went to

Ford dealers to look at it. Ford soon found that it could not keep up with the huge and increasing demand.

There is little doubt that never before had there been such an intense, immediate identification by so many people with a vehicle. Their immediate involvement with the "wild Mustang" paralleled in some ways the animism in certain primitive tribes, which see inanimate objects like trees as possessing animate qualities. Letters from early buyers of the Mustang revealed even other connections. One woman wrote to the company to confide that the "Mustang is as exciting as sex." A woman from St. Louis maintained, "Yes, it is true that blondes have more fun; but now I'm convinced that blondes have more fun in a new Mustang." A massive "after-market" sprang up quickly, anxious to be part of the Mustang boom. The American Racing Equipment Company advertised its aluminum sport wheels with the headline: "Mustangs are meant to be wild. Don't tame them with ordinary wheels!"

Ford had an explanation of the overwhelmingly favorable verdict of the public. Lee Iacocca, the executive in charge of the Mustang project, cited his own pre-production analysis: "People would want this car because it offers them status at low cost . . . because it satisfied in one package their need for basic transportation and their desire for comfort, style, handling, and a choice in performance capabilities." Ford's marketing manager, Frank Zimmerman, Jr., added some comments that Iacocca, as "father of the Mustang," could not make with modesty. Ford had been convinced, Mr. Zimmerman said, that the Mustang would have a stable market and would not be just a fad. He said that the car had an emotional appeal, that people reacted to it personally—a kind of "Mustang spirit."

What Ford had produced, in fact, was the stylist's dream. The product planning committee, working closely with the stylists, had chosen the prototype and had approved the basic sheet metal and two body styles—*before* it informed the development engineers at Ford. Sheet metal, glass, bumpers and moldings of the vehicle were new, while the chassis, engine, suspension and drive-line components were copies of Ford's Falcon and the Fairlane models.

The goal of distinctiveness had been achieved in what Bordinat called "the battles of the inch." He gave as an example: "The close-fitting rear bumper was essential to the lithe and lovely look. Here the battle of dimensions was waged over fractions of an inch. If the gap between bumper and sheet metal had become an inch greater, the resultant effect would have detracted from the appearance of the entire vehicle." Other little differences that collectively made "all the difference" to Bordinat and his staff included simple lines with little ornamentation, single headlights, tail lights with a vertical pattern, pointed fenders, slimmer bumpers, a small, cropped grill and "roll-under" to expose the wheels and tires for a more "gutty" look. The overall profile was as recognizable as the 1946 Studebaker—long, low hood, close-coupled passenger cabin, and a short rear deck.

After such a stylistic triumph there was little left for the engineer to do to the Mustang. The independent automobile evaluation magazine, Road Test, described the car as "a hoked-up Falcon with inadequate brakes, poor handling, and marvelous promotion." Their report, based on careful road testing, also said, "Like most American cars, the Mustang abounds with new and startling engineering features carried over from 1910." The magazine cited the "very bad" glare from windshield wiper arms and blades, and warned that its soft shock control could be dangerous on high speed diagonal railroad crossings, where the vehicle moves onto the road abruptly as the springs reach the limit of their travel. The magazine further described the Mustang as having "rear-axle hop and instability." Road Test advised Mustang owners, "With heavy duty suspensions the car is safer, but a severe ride penalty is paid, which would be unnecessary if some advertising dollars were spent for advanced, independent rear suspension."

Steve Wilder, an automobile expert, wrote an article for Car Life entitled, "Taming the Wild Mustang." In it he described the Mustang chassis as "the quintessence of what's generally wrong with American cars. It's a heavy-nosed blunderbuss with a teen-age rear suspension." Among his dozen of indictments was this observation: "If you hit a bump heeled over, the suspension immediately bottoms out, the tire loses its already tenuous grip. and the Mustang jumps to the side like a frisky colt."

Neither the public appraisal, nor Ford's own explanation of its success, nor even the writings of automobile experts addressing the buffs take into account one piece of Mustang history. In January 1963, over a year before the Mustang made its public appearance, Mr. R. C. Lunn, a Ford engineer, delivered a technical paper to the Society of Automotive Engineers on the subject of an experimental model of the Mustang which was being displayed in various parts of the country. Mr. Lunn's comments were remarkably candid. They showed a glimpse of what the industry could do in the elementary stages of safety design. Lunn included references to the following features incorporated in the operational model: a "fail-safe" dual braking system, integrated headrests to prevent or minimize neck and spinal injuries, a rollbar to strengthen the roof structure in the event of roll-overs, a steering column preventing rearward displacement into the driver during a front-end collision, a collapsible steering shaft, provision for shoulder harness and lap belts, strongly anchored seats, and bucket seats with lateral holding power. In the production-model Mustang which was introduced in April, 1964 (and of which nearly half a million were sold in twelve months) *every one of these features had been eliminated.*

A vast corporate effort, keyed to stylistic features, had built a new vehicle. The result was impressive brand-name recognition and soaring sales. The compromise in this achievement was that new or improved automotive engineering for safety once again took a back seat.

The Mustang is a classic case of styling imperatives superceding engineering development in the total concept of car design. But long before the Mustang's pyrotechnical introduction to the public, the stylists' control over the design of front- and rear-end appearance and exterior sheet metal created serious pedestrian hazards that never were permitted to fall within the concern of the engineers.

Senator Ribicoff raised the issue directly with Arjay Miller, president of Ford, during the 1965 Senate hearings on automobile safety. "Mr. Miller," he said, "one of the problems we have is the pedestrian. Very little has been said of the pedestrian. There are about 500,000 pedestrians injured; 8,000 pedestrians are killed every year.* Much of the injury and death is caused by sharp

---

* Drs. James Goddard and William Haddon have estimated that as least four per cent of all vehicles, at some time during their use, strike and injure pedestrians.

edges on automobiles—hood ornaments, fins—all these sharp features you have on cars. Do you ever take the pedestrian into account when you design automobiles?"

Mr. Miller replied, "Very definitely, Senator. I am on the styling committee and this question never fails to be raised before any styling is approved, and furthermore, it is in the knowledge of the stylists and the engineers at the time the vehicle is designed and styled."

The most charitable estimate that can be made of this statement is that it is utterly lacking in candor. If Senator Ribicoff had pointed out that his own Mustang—even more than other Ford models—had a hood edge that was sharp enough to act as a chopper, Mr. Miller might have had to face specific charges. He would not have been able to refer for defense of the Ford design to Gene Bordinat, Ford's chief stylist. In the October 1964 issue of *Automotive Industries*, Mr. Bordinat had approvingly described the Lincoln Continental's flush-mounted parking lights in the "leading edges of the blade-like front fenders."

The callousness of the stylists about the effects of their creations on pedestrians is seen clearly in the case of William Mitchell, chief stylist at General Motors and the principal creator of the Cadillac tail fin. This sharp, rising fin was first introduced in the late forties, soaring in height and prominence each year until it reached a grotesque peak in 1959 and gradually declining thereafter until it was finally eliminated in the 1966 models. To understand how a man could devise and promote such a potentially lethal protuberance, it is necessary to understand the enthusiasm of Mr. Mitchell, who frequently confides to interviewers that he has "gasoline in his blood." His vibrancy in conversation revolves around the concepts of "movement," "excitement," and "flair." Samples of his recent statements are illustrative: "When you sat behind the wheel, you looked down that long hood, and then there were two headlight shapes, and then two fender curves—why, you felt excited just sitting there." A car "should be exciting." Or, "Cars will be more clearly masculine or feminine," and "For now we deal with aesthetics . . . that indefinable, intangible quality that makes *all* the difference." Mr. Mitchell's reported view of safety is that it is the driver's responsibility to avoid accidents, and that if cars were made crashworthy, the "nuts behind the wheel" would take even greater chances.

The world of Mr. Mitchell centers around the General Motors' technical center, where in surroundings of lavish extravagance he presides over a staff of more than 1,400 styling specialists. It is a world of motion, color, contour, trim, fabric. To illustrate the degree of specialization involved, one color selector holds 2,888 metal samples of colors; glass-enclosed studios, surrounding verdant roof gardens, are specially designed so that colors may be matched under varying lighting conditions. In such an environment, it is easy for Mr. Mitchell to believe that "Eighty-five per cent of all the information we receive is visual." His two favorite sayings are, "Seeing is selling," and "The shape of things shape man."

The matter of Cadillac tail fins, however, transcends the visual world of Mr. Mitchell. Fins have been felt as well as seen, and felt fatally when not seen. In ways that should have been anticipated by Mr. Mitchell, these fins have "shaped" man.

In the year of its greatest height, the Cadillac fin bore an uncanny resemblance to the tail of the stegosaurus, a dinosaur that had two sharp rearward-projecting horns on each side of the tail. In 1964 a California motorcycle driver learned the dangers of the Cadillac tail fin. The cyclist was following a heavy line of traffic on the freeway going toward Newport Harbor in Santa Ana. As the four-lane road narrowed to two lanes, the confusion of highway construction and the swerving of vehicles in the merging traffic led to the Cadillac's sudden stop. The motorcyclist was boxed in and was unable to turn aside. He hit the rear bumper of the car at a speed of about twenty miles per hour, and was hurled into the tail fin, which pierced his body below the heart and cut him all the way down to the thigh bone in a large circular gash. Both fin and man survived this encounter.

The same was not true in the case of nine-year-old Peggy Swan. On September 29, 1963, she was riding her bicycle near her home in Kensington, Maryland. Coming down Kensington Boulevard she bumped into a parked car in a typical childhood accident. But the car was a 1962 Cadillac, and she hit the tail fin, which ripped into her body below the throat. She died at Holy Cross Hospital a few hours later of thoracic hemorrhage.

Almost a year and a half earlier, Henry Wakeland, the independent automotive engineer, had sent by registered mail a formal advisory to General Motors and its chief safety engineer, Howard

Gandelot. The letter was sent in the spirit of the Canons of Ethics for Engineers, and began with these words: "This letter is to insure that you as an engineer and the General Motors Corporation are advised of the hazard to pedestrians which exists in the sharp-pointed tail fins of recent production 1962 Cadillac automobiles and other recent models of Cadillacs. The ability of the sharp and pointed tail fins to cause injury when they contact a pedestrian is visually apparent." Wakeland gave details of two recent fatal cases that had come to his attention. In one instance, an old woman in New York City had been struck by a Cadillac which was rolling slowly backward after its power brakes failed. The blow of the tail fin had killed her. In the other case, a thirteen-year-old Chicago boy, trying to catch a fly ball on a summer day in 1961, had run into a 1961 Cadillac fin, which pierced his heart.

Wakeland said, "An obviously apparent hazard should not be allowed to be included in an automobile because there are only a few circumstances under which the hazard would cause accident or injury. When any large number of automobiles which carry the hazard are in use, the circumstances which translate the hazard into accident or injury will eventually arise. Since it is technically possible to add [fins to automobiles] it is also technically possible to remove them, either before or after manufacture."

Howard Gandelot replied to Wakeland, saying that only a small number of pedestrian injuries due to fins or other ornamentation had come to the attention of General Motors, adding that there "always is a likelihood of the few unusual types of accidents."

The lack of complaints is a standard defense of the automobile companies when they are asked to explain hazardous design features. Certainly no company has urged the public to make complaints about such injuries as described by Wakeland. Nor has any company tried to find out about these injuries either consistently or through a pilot study. Moreover, the truth of the statement that "very few complaints" are received by the automobile companies is a self-serving one that is not verifiable by any objective source or agency outside the companies. Also, it must be remembered that since there is no statistical reporting system on this kind of accident—whether the system is sponsored by the government or the insurance industry—there is no publicly available objective source of data concerning such accidents.

As an insider, Gandelot knew that the trend of Cadillac tail fin design was to lower the height of the fin. He included in his reply to Wakeland this "confidential information" about the forthcoming 1963 Cadillac: "The fins were lowered to bring them closer to the bumper and positioned a little farther forward so that the bumper face now affords more protection."

Gandelot's comment touches on an important practice. The introduction, promotion, and finally the "phasing out" of external hazards is purely a result of stylistic fashions. For example, a few years ago sharp and pointed horizontal hood ornaments were the fad. Recent models avoid these particular ornament designs, not for pedestrian safety but to conform to the new "clean look" that is the trademark of current styling. The deadly Cadillac tail fin has disappeared for the same reason. New styles bring new hazards or the return of old ones.

Systematic engineering design of the vehicle could minimize or prevent many pedestrian injuries. The majority of pedestrian-vehicle collisions produce injuries, not fatalities. Most of these collisions occur at impact speed of under twenty-five miles per hour, and New York City data show that in fatality cases about twenty-five per cent of the collisions occurred when the vehicles involved were moving at speeds below fourteen miles per hour. It seems quite obvious that the external design and not just the speed of the automobile contributes greatly to the severity of the injuries inflicted on the pedestrian. Yet the external design is so totally under the unfettered control of the stylist that no engineer employed by the automobile industry has ever delivered a technical paper concerning pedestrian collision. Nor have the automobile companies made any public mention of any crash testing or engineering safety research on the problem.

But two papers do exist in the technical literature, one by Henry Wakeland and the other by a group of engineers at the University of California in Los Angeles. Wakeland destroyed the lingering myth that when a pedestrian is struck by an automobile it does not make any difference which particular design feature hits him. He showed that heavy vehicles often strike people without causing fatality, and that even in fatal cases, the difference between life and death is often the difference between safe and unsafe design features. Wakeland's study was based on accident and autopsy reports of about 230 consecutive pedestrian fatalities occurring in Manhattan during 1958 and early 1959. In this sample,

case after case showed the victim's body penetrated by ornaments, sharp bumper and fender edges, headlight hoods, medal-
lions, and fins. He found that certain bumper configurations
tended to force the adult pedestrian's body down, which of course
greatly increased the risk of the car's running over him. Recent
models, with bumpers shaped like sled runners and sloping
grill work above the bumpers, which give the appearance of
"leaning into the wind," increase even further the car's potential
for exerting down-and-under pressures on the pedestrian.

The UCLA study, headed by Derwyn Severy, consisted of ex-
perimenting with dummies to produce force and deflection data
on vehicle-pedestrian impacts. The conclusion was that "the front
end geometry and resistance to deformation of a vehicle striking a
pedestrian will have a major influence on the forced movement of
the pedestrian following the impact." These design characteristics
are considered crucial to the level of injury received, since subsequent contact with the pavement may be even more harmful
than the initial impact. As additional designs for protections the
Severy group recommends the use of sheet metal that collapses,
greater bumper widths, and override guards to sweep away
struck pedestrians from the front wheels.

If the automobile companies are seeking more complaints about
the effects of styling in producing pedestrian hazards, they might
well refer to a widely used textbook on preventive medicine
written by Doctors Hilleboe and Larimore. Taking note of the many
tragic examples of unnecessarily dangerous design, the results of
which "are seen daily in surgical wards and autopsy tables," the
authors concluded that "if one were to attempt to produce a
pedestrian-injuring mechanism, one of the most theoretically efficient designs which might be developed would closely approach
that of the front end of some present-day automobiles."

The ultimate evidence that the work of the stylist is anything
but trivial is to be found in the effect styling has had on the
economic aspects of the automobile industry.

General Motors, which controls over fifty percent of the automobile market, whenever it introduces and promotes a particular styling feature can compel the other companies to follow suit.
The history of the wrap-around windshield, the tail fin, and the
hard-top convertible confirms this point. For although the wrap-

around windshield created visual distortion that shocked the optometry profession, and the tail fin and hard-top designs engendered the dangers discussed earlier, every one of the other automobile companies followed the lead of General Motors in order not to be out of date.

Economists call this phenomenon "protective imitation," but under any name, following suit involved tremendous tooling costs, the curtailment of engineering diversity and innovation, and, most important, the wholesale adoption of features that were intended to please the eye of the driver rather than to protect his life.

George Romney, then the president of American Motors, described the situation aptly when he told the Kefauver Senate antitrust subcommittee in 1958, "It is just like a woman's hat. The automobile business has some of the elements of the millinery industry in it, in that you can make style become the hallmark of modernity . . . A wrap-around windshield, through greater sums of money and greater domination of the market, can be identified as being more important than something that improves the whole automobile. . . . In an industry where style is a primary sales tool, public acceptance of a styling approach can be achieved by the sheer impact of product volume."

Still the industry has persisted in declaring that it merely "gives the customer what he wants." This hardly squares with Mr. Romney's statement or with the facts. The history of every successful style feature is that it was conceived in one of the automobile company style sections—often without reference to company engineers, let alone considerations of safety—and then turned over to marketing specialists for repetitive, emotional exploitation until it was an entrenched, accepted "fashion."

Entrenched, that is, until the need to make the customer dissatisfied with that fashion sent the styling staffs back to their drawing boards. The principle that governs them is in direct contradiction to the give-them-what-they-want defense. In the words of Gene Bordinat of Ford, the stylist at work must "take the lead in establishing standards of taste." That, in fact, is what they have done.

The follow-the-leader spiral of styling innovations has had other profound effects. One of the most important results is that by concentrating model "changes" in the area of styling, the manufacturers have focused consumer attention on those features of the automobile that are the most likely subject of "persuasive" rather than "informational" appeals. As in the fashion industry, dealing with emotions rather than dealing with the intellect has had the result that the car makers have rarely been threatened with consumer sovereignty over the automobile. On the contrary, car manufacturers have exerted self-determined control over the products they offer. This control is reflected in another statement from Mr. Mitchell, who said, "One thing today is that we have more cars than we have names. Maybe the public doesn't want all these kinds, but competition makes it necessary."

The narrowing of the difference between automobiles to minor styling distinctions is not the only unhealthy result of the stylists' dominance. Even more discouraging has been the concomitant drying-up of engineering ingenuity. As the stylists have steadily risen to pre-eminence, the technological imagination of automotive engineers has slowed to a point where automobile company executives themselves have deplored the lack of innovation. Ford vice-president Donald Frey recognized the problem clearly when he said in an address delivered in January 1964, "I believe that the amount of product innovation successfully introduced into the automobile is smaller today than in previous times and is still falling. The automatic transmission [adopted in 1939 on a mass-production basis] was the last major innovation of the industry."

The head of Mr. Frey's company, Henry Ford II, seemed troubled by the same question in his address to the same group. He said, "When you think of the enormous progress of science over the last two generations, it's astonishing to realize that there is very little about the basic principles of today's automobile that would seem strange and unfamiliar to the pioneers of our industry. . . . What we need even more than the refinement of old ideas is the ability to develop new ideas and put them to work."

Neither of these automobile executives, of course, makes the obvious connection that if an industry devotes its best efforts and its largest investment to styling concepts, it must follow that new ideas in engineering—and safety—will be tragically slow in coming.

7

The traffic safety establishment:
Damn the driver and spare the car

"Roads, laws, and cars are inanimate of themselves. They cannot give—or take—life. It is *people* who animate highway transportation; *people* who use the roads—obey or do not obey the laws —drive their cars carefully or carelessly." The speaker was H. E. Humphreys, Jr., chairman of the U. S. Rubber Company. In reiterating the basic creed of the private traffic safety movement, he bore down hard each time he said "people." Mr. Humphreys was addressing the tenth Highway Transportation Congress in Washington, D. C., in his capacity as chairman of the National Highway Users Conference, a lobby group. The date was May 6, 1964, but the words could have been uttered in 1924, the year this country's approach to highway safety was launched—to become later an ideology guarded and perpetuated by a network of trade associations, tax-exempt organizations, and other groups professing an interest in traffic safety.

In 1924, prompted by the United States Chamber of Commerce and the National Safety Council, Herbert Hoover—then Secretary of Commerce—called the first of two national conferences on street and highway safety. Out of these conferences, sponsored and financed by private funds, came a number of recommendations dealing with statistics, education, public relations, traffic control, and a model uniform vehicle code. Underlying all these efforts was the view that highways and vehicles were built about as well as could be expected under existing technology, and that traffic accidents were therefore traceable to willful, careless, irresponsible, or incompetent drivers.The problems of highway safety were considered essentially to be the result of the driver's behavior.

The 1924 and 1926 conferences were dominated by business leaders concerned about the tragic by-product of a new, fast-growing mode of transportation. "The three E's"—Enforcement, Education, and Engineering—became the slogan for a "balanced" traffic safety program. It was not long before the public was given to understand that "Enforcement" and "Education" meant the motorist, while "Engineering" meant the highway. The only reference to the vehicle itself pertained to its maintenance by the owner and the desirability of periodic inspection. In the subsequent decade, vehicle design was not an issue, apart from the insistent pleas and writings of a Detroit physician, Dr. Claire Straith, and a few critical insurance men.

During the 1930's the automobile death toll was the subject of some dramatic journalism, the most noteworthy being J. C. Furnas's article "And Sudden Death," which appeared in the October 1935 issue of the *Reader's Digest*. Millions of reprints of Furnas's piece were circulated which helped to generate public demands that "something be done." In the same year, the Detroit *News* called on the manufacturers to participate more actively in encouraging safer driving. The National Safety Council approached the automobile industry for financial support of several traffic accident prevention projects. In June 1936, Congress requested that the Bureau of Public Roads (then a part of the Department of Agriculture) make a survey of motor vehicle traffic conditions. The growing demand for action was not lost upon the alert leaders of the automobile industry. The move of events suggested that it was in order for them to take a forceful role in encouraging safer use of automobiles. A pattern of financing and guiding the major voluntary organizations concerned with the subject was established, and continues to the present day.

In January 1936 the Automobile Manufacturers Association announced with fanfare that it would contribute about $450,000 a year for traffic safety activities. That year, grants were awarded to the American Automobile Association, the American Legion, the General Federation of Women's Clubs, the International Association of Chiefs of Police, the National Congress of Parents and Teachers, the National Safety Council, and the National Grange—all for various projects in education, enforcement, and "public support" activities. Three months later, an Automobile Manufacturers Association committee assured the Secretay of Commerce: "The motor industry recognizes its obligation to produce the safest vehicle human ingenuity can devise, and dedicates every laboratory and engineering resource of the industry to that purpose. In addition, the industry is pledged to cooperate with public officials in their efforts to curb accidents. Further, it has, by direct grants of money, energized the expansion of highway safety activities of nine national organizations." It was not long before the automobile industry decided to associate its traffic safety activities with a less obviously commercially tainted organization, and it established the Automotive Safety Foundation in June 1937.

In 1938 the Bureau of Public Roads submitted a six-part report to Congress. This report was written with the help of a business and academic advisory committee and covered the need for better investigation at the accident scene, the deficiencies of state automobile accident reporting, the importance of vehicle inspection, the lack of uniformity in state laws, and the "accident-prone" driver. Nothing was said about vehicle design and construction. What makes the report noteworthy is that present-day programs display no advance in quality and are applied with an extraordinary emphasis on driver behavior—which is almost always considered apart from vehicle and highway.

Today almost every program is aimed at the driver—at educating him, exhorting him, watching him, judging him, punishing him, compiling records about his driving violations, and organizing him in citizen support activities. Resources and energy are directed into programs of enforcement, traffic laws, driver education, driver licensing, traffic courts, and vehicle inspection. The reasoning behind this philosophy of safety can be summarized in this way: Most accidents are in the class of driver fault; driver fault is in the class of violated traffic laws; therefore, observance of traffic laws by drivers would eliminate most accidents.

The prevailing view of traffic safety is much more a political strategy to defend special interests than it is an empirical program to save lives and prevent injuries. For "traffic safety" is not just an abstract value to which lip service is paid. In the automobile industry, safety could represent an investment in research, a priority in production design and manufacturing, and a theme of marketing policy. But under existing business values potential safety advances are subordinated to other investments, priorities, preferences, and themes designed to maximize profit. Industry insists on maintaining the freedom to rank safety anywhere it pleases on its list of commercial considerations. In the protection of these considerations the industry supports and fosters the traffic safety policy focused on driver behavior; through lobbying and other close relations with state and municipal administrators the efforts of the automobile manufacturers have resulted not only in the perpetuation of that policy but also in some side effects which help the industry preserve its exclusive control over vehicle design.

For one thing, a driver-oriented traffic safety program does not disrupt the traditional state jurisdiction over traffic safety matters. The industry has worked for many years to maintain state control against any "encroachments" or "interventions" by the federal government. Should the federal government become involved, it might upset the time-tested accommodation which the industry has developed with state administrators and legislators. The saying among automobile men is: "We know the state tiger and what it likes to eat." The federal government might want to see for itself whether the vehicle was really as innocent as automobile publicists have vigorously proclaimed.

Another advantage to the industry in seeing traffic safety in terms of driver responsibility is that the law has developed in conformity with this emphasis. Thus damage or injury in automobiles is attributed, by definition, to some legal violation by the driver. Traffic laws prescribe how people shall behave so as to avoid accidents on streets and highways. These rules are quite specific, such as those about overtaking or passing a school bus. But there are also general provisions prohibiting "reckless driving" or "driving so as to endanger," which cover almost any situation that is not explicitly cited. Therefore the contributing factors stemming from the vehicle's design can be imputed to the driver. The law embodies an invincible rationale: "He had an accident; therefore, he violated the law." No distinction is made between responsibility for the accident and responsibility for the injury due to unsafe vehicle design or construction. Manslaughter charges are filed routinely against drivers; there are yet to be recorded any similar charges against the manufacturers for vehicle defects. The statutes make no provision for including the manufacturers in traffic accident criminal penalties, and it is a rare prosecutor who would proceed against an automobile maker on common-law principles.

Laws that do not adequately reflect reality have predictably distorting consequences. It is to be expected that laws exclusively centered on the motorist will profoundly affect the kind of accident investigation, accident reporting, and insurance rating policy that develops. Accidents are investigated principally by police and investigators representing claimants and insurance companies. The primary purpose of police fact-gathering at the accident scene is to enforce the law, so the policeman's common assumption is driver responsibility. A typical police traffic accident report has a list of "contributing circumstances" which the officer is to check off: "Speed too fast; failed to yield right of way; drove left of center; improper overtaking; passed stop sign; ran traffic signal; improper lights; had been drinking and other improper driving." All of these are violations of the law by motorists. No distinction is drawn between the behavior of the driver and the behavior of the vehicle. Insofar as the law is violated, they are one. Thus the driver is heir to all the dangers created by the automobile designers, not only in terms of his bodily exposure but also in terms of legal exposure. The result of this drastic imbalance in the law is the very poor quality of accident investigation in this country. There is great pressure on the police officer to cut his investigation short in order to clear away the damaged car or cars and get traffic moving. He finds little incentive to probe beyond the facile explanation of the accident offered by the catch-all categories of driver error on the accident report form. The law does not encourage or provide for conscientious investigation. Consequently enforcement of the law brings no pressure on the car makers to increase the safety of vehicles.

The way traffic law is written and enforced also affects automobile insurance and claims investigation. Civil actions are brought in court on the basis of driver-to-driver or driver-to-passenger confrontations, with police reports and sometimes criminal proceedings (which usually are completed before civil actions come to trial) serving as principal tools of conflict. Since insurance company payments for damage claims are predicated on driver responsibility, insurance rates are almost exclusively based on differences in drivers—accident experience, use of the car, sex, age, marital status, place of residence, and the number of drivers in the family. Were manufacturers made more responsible by law for vehicle behavior in accident and injury causation, the entire actuarial and investigatory apparatus would be forced to consider vehicle engineering factors as an integral part of investigation.

Investigation stops with the driver in the vast majority of cases because our statutes ascribe all responsibilities to the driver. It is legal responsibility that forms the basis for compensation payments. Often, when the responsible agent is missing—in cases where there is no other driver, or the other driver is not financially responsible—the most thorough engineering investigations of the vehicle are conducted. Claims against the manufacturer for unsafe design or construction are obliged to proceed on the basis of the common law derived from the heritage of court decisions, not on statutes. The only statute law covering the vehicle simply requires certain basic automotive equipment such as brakes, windshield wipers, directional signals, and lighting systems.

Accident reporting and statistics also reflect the law's emphasis. A major purpose of accident reports is to lay the basis for preventive action, as well as to measure the effect of past accident-prevention efforts. Since the law ignores the cause of injury and concentrates on the cause of accident in terms of driver error, accident reports adhere to this outline. The statistics compiled inevitably emphasize the same point, as exemplified by the National Safety Council's annual proclamation that ninety per cent of all accidents are due to improper driving. To the extent that statistics outline problems, guide remedial action, and inspire or deter public authorities, vehicle design in such a statistical climate is not likely to come in for much attention. It is significant that the special

Cornell accident-injury reporting forms request information not required by law—information which is having important consequences in emphasizing the role of vehicle engineering.

The automobile makers have played an important role in the development of traffic law beyond their conventional advocacy at state legislatures. The industry's presence on the membership roll of the National Committee on Uniform Traffic Laws and Ordinances (NCUTLO) is an impressive display of how automobile companies and their trade associations and front organizations can saturate an organization. The financial and advisory support given the NCUTLO—which produces a periodically revised Uniform Motor Vehicle Code as a "Guide for State Motor Vehicle Laws" —is not without results. The code is a place for implementing the automotive lobby's determination to achieve uniformity in vehicle equipment laws throughout the fifty states, without the supervision of the federal government. While the code embraces sound and well-expressed provisions, the attention given the vehicle is an abuse of the integrity which the drafting of model laws has generally attained in the United States. The code is composed of nineteen chapters totaling 194 pages. It is designed as a comprehensive set of motor vehicle laws covering administration, licensing, financial responsibility, and other subjects. Thirty-nine pages are devoted to equipment, inspection, and the size, weight, and load of vehicles.

The provisions of these pages could not have been more solicitous of the manufacturers. Although the code is described by its authors as offering "a sound legal framework within which effective safety programs can be carried out" to "the ultimate service of highway users," not a single provision deals with any vehicle design features prominently associated with injuries suffered in an accident. Although two pages are devoted to rules governing pedestrian behavior, the code has no reference to protruding ornaments and other pedestrian hazards, as do similar statutes in Switzerland and other European nations. The vehicle equipment provisions cover only lighting equipment, brakes, horns, mufflers, mirrors, windshield wipers, flares, air conditioning equipment, but the code does not establish standards for the operating and crash safety of the basic vehicle structure. Where applicable, the language provides for adherence to standards established by the Society of Automotive Engineers. Performance levels for items such as brakes are written into the code and are well within the limits of existing designs.

The Chapter called "Inspection of Vehicles" recommends the use of the American Standards Association Code D7 on inspection requirements for motor vehicles. Code D7 was written by the automobile industry. The object of D7 is to provide the states with a checklist that will bring the operational adequacy of inspected vehicles somewhere near the level of the vehicles when they left the dealers' showrooms.

The legal structure for traffic safety that exempts motor vehicle design and quality from its purview—the only transport vehicle so exempted—has not come about haphazardly. Its evolution has been shaped by a political and propaganda machine directed by the traffic safety establishment. This establishment is not a conspiracy; it does not have to be. As the only organized constituency in traffic safety, one which represents the interests of the automotive and allied industries, it has been more like a great power with no challengers. By championing driver safety and resistance to federal "encroachment," and by providing funds to "sound" recipients, the establishment has enlisted the support or understanding of state and local officials and of volunteer groups and workers.

The dreary quality of traffic safety activities throughout the country year after year can be attributed to the impressive efficiency in the administration of the establishment's ideology. There are no autocratic impositions involved. The practice of going along with industry's way is simply a pleasant way of getting by. There are neither tangible incentives nor countering stimuli to do things in any other way.

An estimated nine million dollars a year is spent by non-government organizations and citizen traffic safety councils on national, state, and local levels. Out of this sum, about $4.2 million is expended by state and local safety councils accredited to the National Safety Council and supported chiefly by local business contributors. After subtracting the $2.6 million devoted by the National Safety Council to traffic safety services, the remaining $2.2 million goes for the most part to support the traffic safety activities of the so-called national service organizations. The automotive and insurance industries finance almost all the traffic safety work of these service groups—chiefly, the Auto Industries Highway Committee, the American Association of Motor Vehicles

Administrators, the American Bar Association, the International Association of Chiefs of Police, the National Commission on Safety Education (of the National Educational Association), and the National Committee on Uniform Laws and Ordinances. Together with the American Automobile Association, which is self-financing, these are the organizations which the National Safety Council describes as "the groups that stimulate public support for traffic safety programs."

The two key sources of funds for these groups are the Automotive Safety Foundation and the Insurance Institute for Highway Safety, both tax-exempt organizations.

The Automotive Safety Foundation (ASF) was founded in June 1937 by four automobile executives. For five years, the Automobile Manufacturers Association contributed all the funds for ASF, but increasingly the AMA has broadened the financial support to include contributions from companies dealing in petroleum, rubber tires, automobile finance, advertising, magazines, glass, steel, as well as from banks, automobile and tire dealers, and asphalt and cement companies and associations. This has been done through a highly successful fund-matching system that not only helps to commit these groups to ASF's mission but also saves the Automobile Manufacturers Association money while it enlarges the total funds over which the AMA possesses complete policy control. In 1963 the AMA contributed half ($764,086) of ASF's income of $1,528,173, which has been roughly the level of the foundation's income for the past few years.

The Automotive Safety Foundation's accomplishment in promoting the automobile industry's traffic safety objective far exceeds what might be expected of such modest finances. Contrary to what its name might imply, the Automotive Safety Foundation has no concern for the automobile *per se;* except that it be driven better, maintained properly, and provided with more highways and off-street parking. A recent ASF publication echoes Mr. Humphreys of the U. S. Rubber Company: "Being inanimate, no car, truck or bus can by itself cause an accident any more than a street or highway can do so. A driver is needed to put it into motion—after which it becomes an extension of his will."

From its very beginning the ASF has been a policy-oriented organization. One of its first projects was the Standard Highway Safety Program for States, which erected two cornerstones for the private traffic movement—a "balanced program" for accident prevention, and the necessity for official responsibility by state and local officials backed with organized citizen support groups. With refinement and expansion by ASF and other automobile representatives, this program in 1946 was changed to the Action Program for Traffic Safety, which continues to be the blueprint for concerted activity.

The president of the Automotive Safety Foundation, Joseph Mattson, and his assistants maintain close contact with federal officials. ASF headquarters appear to be in Washington primarily to see that Washington does as little as possible in traffic safety beyond that of supporting the "time-tested" state activities. The ASF has various opportunities for observing, influencing, or deterring action in the executive branch. One is its joint financial sponsorship of research projects and conferences with such agencies as the Public Health Service and the Bureau of Public Roads. Through such cooperation the ASF helps guide federal attention away from vehicle design and its relation to deaths and injuries. This kind of cooperation also ingratiates the ASF with some federal administrators who can stretch department budgets to hold more conferences. The mixing of private and public funds and personnel is a recurrent practice of the traffic safety establishment and assures the participation of industry people directly in official programs. The ASF also has often graduated its employees into positions in the Bureau of Public Roads.

Mattson has found his way onto the advisory committee to the U.S. Public Health Service's Division of Accident Prevention in spite of his lack of scientific qualifications to advise the division on its scientific work. The advisory committee to the division is supposed to represent experts, not interest groups. In the Bureau of Public Roads, Mattson is viewed as the veteran spokesman for the automobile industry on traffic safety and as the figure who dominates the President's Committee for Traffic Safety. For ten years Mattson was head of the executive committee on the advisory council to the President's committee. In this capacity, he selected the executive director of the committee, William Foulis, who had been Mattson's employee at the Automotive Safety Foundation. In 1965 Mattson relinquished his committee post to Howard Pyle of the National Safety Council, but no one interpreted this as any diminution of his influence. Behind his retiring, easygoing manner, he remains a person to be reckoned with by the Bureau of Public Roads and its Office of Highway Safety, even in preliminary consideration of traffic safety policy.

Mattson has long been the chief figure among staffs of the private traffic safety groups that are congregated in one section of Washington. Whatever discomfort his influence has caused others in the movement has not been made public. His conciliatory skills and his why-stir-things-up type of appeal has succeeded in maintaining a solid consensus within the establishment on all major issues.

Financial data concerning the Automotive Safety Foundation give some indication of the variety of unofficial missions expected of it by the automobile industry in addition to the processing and awarding of grants. A typical year was 1963, when ASF reported contributions totaling $1,528,173, of which $692,890 was disbursed as grants. The expense of distributing this amount was reported to total $826,148, which included $517,603 for salaries and wages; a lump sum of $259,474 was listed under "miscellaneous expenses." That year, the foundation neglected to report officers' salaries individually to the Internal Revenue Service. But in 1962, when they did provide these figures, Mattson received $45,517, and two vice-presidents were paid $27,700 and $26,183, plus full reimbursement for expenses. Thus, the compensation of the three top officers alone amounted to one-eighth of the funds disbursed and one-fifteenth of ASF's annual income. This unique foundation spent almost $1.20 on "administration" for every dollar it disbursed in grants.

A 1947 document put out by the foundation gave an indication of how diverse its interests were even at that early date:

> In addition to the studies of existing laws, the technicians on the Foundation staff also reviewed hundreds of bills proposed during the current legislative year, and passed along to interested national organizations the facts about those bills which failed to conform in substance with the [uniform vehicle] code and other accepted standards. . . .
> The Inter-Industry Highway Safety Committee is another new development. Throughout the country the vehicle, tire and petroleum retailers are in a position to offer valuable support to public officials and to civic groups in carrying on the highway safety program in their own states and communities. State and local groups are being organ-

ized throughout the country and already tangible and encouraging results have been reported. . . .

It is not possible in a report of this kind to illustrate pictorially the cooperative activities which the Foundation is conducting with a large number of national organizations. These groups—women, farmers, veterans, teachers, service clubs and others—offer enormous potentials in support of safer highway transportation. In each case, however, to make the activity sound and useful, the organization requires the expert direction and guidance which the staff here is able to provide. Financial assistance also is given.

At the present time the Automotive Safety Foundation awards grants, most of them on an annual basis, to about thirty groups, including the American Association of Industrial Editors, the American Association of Motor Vehicle Administrators, the American Bar Association, the American Municipal Association, the Association of State Universities and Land Grant Colleges, the General Federation of Women's Clubs, the Highway Research Board, the International Association of Chiefs of Police, the National Association of County Engineers, the National Commission on Safety Education, the National Committee on Uniform Traffic Laws and Ordinances, the National Grange, the National Safety Council, the National Congress of Parents and Teachers, the Northwestern University Traffic Institute, the Yale University Bureau of Highway Traffic, and some dozen other universities for small research projects or fellowships. Even those grants under $10,000 are of considerable consequence to the recipients because of the absence of other backing, either from public or private sources. The fellowships cover a number of subjects concerning highway safety, but never the vehicle itself. The foundation also administers the Alfred P. Sloan Radio and Television Awards for Highway Safety, which go to various radio and television stations throughout the country for constructive programing.

One of the ASF's largest annual grants—about $140,000—goes to form almost the entire support of the Auto Industries Highway Safety Committee (AIHSC), another tax-exempt organization. A project of which AIHSC is especially proud was the distribution of over six million "Man-to-Man and Dad-to-Daughter Good Driver Agreements." These were voluntary pledges signed by father and son or father and daughter wherein the children agreed to drive the family car safely.

AIHSC's principal activity is promoting vehicle inspection, high school driver education, safe holiday travel, adequate off-street parking facilities and better highways, and teen-age traffic safety conferences. These objectives are pursued, AIHSC says, "through contacts with officials charged with the responsibility of public safety on the nation's streets and highways, as well as organizations actively engaged in traffic safety work," and by "serving on national policy-setting committees such as the Advisory Council to the President's Committee for Traffic Safety."

In the automobile insurance industry, the counterpart organization to the Automotive Safety Foundation is the tax-exempt Insurance Institute for Highway Safety (IIHS). It was established in 1959 to bring together under one roof the scattered traffic safety efforts of the Association of Casualty and Surety Companies, the National Association of Automotive Mutual Insurance Companies, and the National Association of Independent Insurers. These three groups represent about five hundred insurance companies.

The traffic safety attitude of IIHS closely parallels that of ASF. For example, in January 1963 IIHS released this explanation of the record traffic accident toll in 1962: "The American public is not supporting the application of the Highway Safety Action Program, the blueprint recognized by traffic experts throughout the country. Officials are not administering the laws and regulations to the extent necessary to reduce traffic accidents. Dangerous confusion exists because of the lack of uniformity of traffic laws and traffic control devices."

IIHS president Russell Brown says that an additional five hundred million dollars of state and local funds are needed annually to support existing programs on a much greater scale and to augment the private budgets of the national service organizations. But neither he nor his organization's literature mentions vehicle design. The issue which appears to motivate the programs financed by IIHS and which makes it so cooperative with automobile industry interests is the threat of federal incursions into state jurisdiction over traffic safety. In almost every address Brown delivers the point is made, sometimes with constitutional embellishments: "In the management of our vast highway transportation system, public policy must be based on the premise that sovereignty rests with state governments, and that federal and local governments only have those rights that are given to them by sovereign states. Therefore, the focal point for all highway traffic control and safety activities is the state."

The institute's grants are fully consistent with this belief. With a budget totaling $1.7 million in 1964, IIHS provides grants to most of the service organizations funded by ASF, including the National Safety Council, the American Bar Association, and the American Association of Motor Vehicle Administrators.

It also provides assistance to state traffic safety programs, after soliciting a formal request by the governor. This aid takes the form of working with officials in developing safety programs and familiarizing them with other services available through the private traffic safety organizations. Direct financial support to state citizen traffic safety groups is the third activity of IIHS. In 1964, funds were allotted to ten such bodies, including the California Traffic Safety Foundation, the Missouri Safety Council, the New York State Citizens Council on Traffic Safety, and the Texas Safety Association. It is IIHS policy to encourage formation of these citizen units in all states to "influence personal behavior in traffic and create and express public support for official programs."

Plainly, insurance companies would seem to have every incentive to advocate measures for the prevention of loss in order to increase their underwriting profits. Insurance company engineers and inspectors routinely file reports to their superiors recommending as a condition of policy coverage the elimination of hazards on ships, in factories, and at construction sites. The work of the underwriter's laboratories in testing, inspecting, evaluating, and listing manufacturers' products with respect to their safety (especially electrical and fire-prevention equipment), indicates that companies take loss prevention seriously. In addition, premium rates usually have covered the entire risk situation in man-machine situations. Thus, for example, higher rates for fire coverage on factories with less than desirable conditions add an economic incentive for policyholders to achieve safer conditions.

In automobile insurance, the rules are different. Loss prevention and rate policy deal with the driver and avoid the automobile. Except for the discount for compact cars—a puzzling actuarial decision in light of their injury record—neither rating bureaus nor the large independent casualty underwriters have ever filed for approval by state insurance regulatory agencies any rating system covering various design features of automobiles.

For many years the insurance industry has known about and been disturbed by the role of unsafe vehicle design in producing accidents and injuries. Their files contain a secret horde of detailed accident investigations pinpointing design and construction hazards on particular models that caused deaths and injuries. There are instances where a company, after paying off a claim, has demanded in turn compensation from the offending automobile manufacturer and has obtained a confidential settlement. None of this vehicle design data has ever been publicly reported either by an individual underwriter or on an industry-wide basis. Contrary to every decent tradition of the casualty insurers (going back as far as their design and construction of lighthouses and lifeboats in the early days of the Lloyd's group in England), information of life-saving import, which connects vehicle features with statistically or clinically significant accident and injury experience, is being denied to the public, to the companies' own policy-holders, and to the industry's actuaries who could devise a vehicle-rating policy aimed at loss reduction. The same modern data-processing equipment used increasingly to refine the rating of drivers could be applied to the rating of vehicles.

During the past two years, several insurance company executives have commented in public about rising damage claims and the role of excessively powered vehicles. Articles in the industry trade publication, *The National Underwriter*, have called for an insurance rating structure for automobiles which reflects the relative safety of their design, as is done for factory and other transportation risks. All these statements are more indicative of the casualty industry's knowledge and concern about unsafe vehicle design than they are of its intention to do anything about that design.

This mixed attitude of worry and inaction is of many years' standing. In 1937 an editor of a monthly journal for casualty underwriters, *Safety Engineering*, studied some insurance company accident investigations made available to him and over a two-year period wrote a remarkable series of fifteen articles entitled "Make the Automobile Safer." Each article was devoted to a common vehicle design hazard. The editor emphasized the "second collision" and unnecessary dangers to pedestrians. For three years, *Safety Engineering* even graded the new automobiles by name, rating them on the basis of injury-producing hazards. The editor,

Harry Armand, wrote: "A building contractor realizes that tools and brick can fall from great heights, and he guards against possible injury by providing employees with protective headgear to minimize the effects of a possible accident, in addition to protective canopies and scaffolding to safeguard the public. This principle of 'preparing for the inevitable' should be the guiding factor in automobile design. The motor industry must face the fact that accidents occur. It is their duty, therefore, to so design the interior of automobiles that when the passenger is tossed around, he will get an even break and not suffer a preventable injury. It is not beyond the realm of reason to expect that in an interior designed for perfect safety a passenger may experience no more than a shaking up in many kinds of accidents that today are taking a heavy toll in life and limb."

Since those words were written, over a million Americans have been killed and an estimated eighty-five million injured. Harry Armand, still at his job, noted in 1964 that many of the hazards he described in the thirties still persist in one form or another in today's automobiles. Yet the insurance industry continues to treat the automobile as off-limits and restricts its public service to pamphlets published under such catchy titles as "Maim Street" and "Rushin Roulette," containing cartoons of driver carelessness.

The insurance trade associations are equally reticent. In March 1963 the motor vehicle bulletin of the Association of Casualty and Surety Companies noted that the "parking brake" of many new automobiles might appear firmly set but still allow rolling backward freely. The association added that this could be especially dangerous if a driver parks his car in the family driveway, many of which slope. It explained that this hazard arises because of recent changes in the design of parking and emergency brake systems in nearly all passenger cars and in many light trucks. If the parking brake is set without the simultaneous application of the hydraulic service (foot) brakes, it noted, the bottom of the brake shoes are brought into contact with the drums on the rear wheels, but the shoes are not fully engaged. With the parking brake in this position, the association said, the car cannot roll forward, but it can move freely to the rear. If, on the other hand, the motorist is pressing his foot on the hydraulic brake while he is setting the parking brake, the shoe and drum engage completely and the car will not move.

What did the association recommend? It urged the reader of this limited-circulation bulletin to get into the habit of applying the foot brake while he set the parking brake. "No problem can occur if a driver trains himself to do this," was the advice. Having told the reader how to adjust to a dangerous design, the association saw its task completed. It did not name the models which possessed such a hazard; it did not demand that the manufacturers change the design on future models and correct existing models; it did not notify appropriate state and federal officials, in spite of its knowledge of casualties proceeding from this hazard.

The deep-rooted reluctance of automobile insurers to take action is clearly demonstrated by the experience of Liberty Mutual Insurance Company—the only insurer to show concrete interest in vehicle design research. Between 1952 and 1961 Liberty Mutual developed and constructed two prototype safety cars called Survival Car I and Survival Car II. Working initially with the late Edward Dye at the Cornell Aeronautical Laboratory, Liberty Mutual's chief engineer, Frank Crandell, produced Survival Car I in 1957. This car was a non-operational vehicle featuring sixty safety design innovations, the combined purpose of which was to permit passengers to walk away from head-on collisions that had occurred at speeds up to forty miles per hour. In 1961, four models of Survival Car II were displayed. To show the feasibility of safety improvements within conventional production-line automobiles, Crandell used regular 1960 four-door Chevrolets. Based on his company's accident-injury investigations and forty crash tests, he built twenty-four major design features into these modified Chevrolets. The features included specially constructed "capsule seats" designed to stay moored on impact and protect the passenger from rear-end and side collisions. In addition to a safer steering assembly providing collision protection, improved maneuverability, and greater visibility, there was a fail-safe braking system, an automatic fire control system, a roll-over bar, safer windshields, and a smooth hood to reduce the severity of pedestrian injury.

Liberty Mutual no longer does any work in vehicle design. It considers its ten-year project, which cost $350,000, completed.

Company management has no intention of openly criticizing the automobile makers. President Bryan Smith closed the program with the statement: "In sponsoring the reconstruction and design of this completely functional passenger car solely for safety, our hope is that it will stimulate the forces already at work producing safer automobiles." That an insurance company had to produce the first prototype safety car itself constituted a stinging rebuke to the automobile makers. But Smith refused to draw the obvious conclusions and refused to follow through on Crandell's findings and make the project meaningful beyond that of building the company's reputation.

Predictably, the automobile industry's reaction to Liberty Mutual's prototypes was hostile. According to Frank Crandell, he was viewed by the industry as an enemy until 1962 when some communication was established with Ford. He saw some of his designs reflected in eight safety features that graced the experimental Mustang in 1963 and was severely disappointed to see all of them dropped when the car went into actual production.

If the automobile industry's reaction was hostile, the casualty insurance industry's was one of indifference. It did not see any policy-making significance, either private or public, in Liberty's promising engineering work on safer automobile design. Nor did it view the prototypes as stimulants for further research into injury prevention during collisions. There are three major reasons for this fundamental default by the insurance industry. First, the pressure of material self-interest is sharply diminished by the companies' ability to obtain approval from state regulators for higher insurance rates to cover higher loss experiences. Since the ceiling for rates can be raised as the level of claims payments rises, the monetary incentive to reduce the causes of deaths and injuries in automobile accidents by advocating safer vehicles is reduced. Moreover, the profits of the casualty industry now come much more from investment income than from earned premiums. Between 1959 and 1963, for example, the casualty industry had an underwriting profit of $1.38 billion and a net investment income of $4.01 billion. The higher the volume of prepaid insurance premiums, the more funds are available to produce investment income. The second reason for default by the insurance industry is that the automobile manufacturers and their ancillary industries represent important customers for casualty insurers. The third and most important reason is the unwritten law that large business groups never attack one another over a fundamental issue publicly unless they see their survival at stake. A determined and unilateral program by underwriters for safer automobiles would strike the automobile industry at its most sensitive level—that of marketing strategy and possible exposure to government regulation. The consequences of such an upheaval would be likely to unleash forces for change in more than one direction—forces beyond the control of both industries. Marketing freedom and minimum government control are very important to the insurance industry as well as to the automobile industry. But government control is not the only inhibition the insurance companies might feel. General Motors keeps a small automobile insurance subsidiary as a reminder that the underwriters are not immune from a possibly devastating competitive program with impressive distribution outlets through automobile dealers.

In addition, the view in insurance circles is that any radical change in the country's perspective on traffic safety will inevitably mean a larger role for the federal government. Insurance companies have learned how to handle state insurance commissioners, and the prospect of any federal attention to their business alarms them greatly. Even a bill by Congressman Kenneth Roberts to establish a national accident prevention research center was attacked in 1964 by insurance people as a move toward monopoly control over the discovery and dissemination of research information and as a costly effort that would duplicate the one now being satisfactorily performed by employers, insurance companies, trade associations, and safety organizations like the Insurance Institute for Highway Safety and the National Safety Council.

The most candid commentary on the insurance companies' attitude toward the automobile makers came from Leonard McEnnis, Jr., director of public relations for the IIHS, who said, "They don't want us telling them how to build autos and we don't want them telling us how to sell insurance."

Another instance of surprising default is the inaction of the American Automobile Association (AAA). With clubs in every state and a total membership of nine million motorists, AAA is by far the largest representative of automobile drivers. But however vigorous it may be in fighting highway tolls, unfair motor vehicle taxes, and other pocketbook threats to its membership, its position on automobile design has until recently been altogether one of curtsying whenever the automobile industry nodded. AAA has produced the usual brochures and reflected the accepted traffic safety views. Since the thirties it has singled out pedestrian protection as a special AAA program, but it has carefully excluded from its concern external vehicle design hazards such as protruding ornaments and sharp edges and points.

Closely tied to AAA's Washington headquarters is the AAA Foundation for Traffic Safety whose major activity is supporting safety film productions. It also grants $35,000 a year to serious research on driver behavior by Dr. James Malfetti at Columbia University.

AAA is a state-oriented organization. Member clubs finance national headquarters and establish the policies of the national organization. Traditionally, AAA and member clubs have strongly backed exclusive state jurisdiction over traffic safety, placing AAA in full accord with other private safety groups. Until 1961, AAA has not taken a determined position on vehicle design and safety beyond occasional denunciations of braking performance and tire failure. In that year, AAA passed a weak resolution urging the manufacturers to build more safety into their vehicles so as to reduce "the severity of injury to operators and passengers involved in auto accidents." The following year for the first time in AAA history a state club got serious. Led by Robert Kretschmar and Richard Hoover, the Massachusetts AAA was instrumental in having introduced in the legislature a state bill that would establish a special commission to draft a code of minimum safety standards for the construction of motor vehicles. The bill listed forty-five design features for the proposed commission's consideration. Mark Bauer, the mobile eastern field representative for the Automobile Manufacturers Association, paraded his lobbying skills before his old legislative committee friends who had the bill before them. In 1963, shortly before the hearing on the bill, a special trip to Detroit for the committee was arranged, with all expenses paid. The bill has never gotten out of committee.

Kretschmar and Hoover pressed further. With the support of the New York AAA, they persuaded the Eastern Conference of AAA Motor Clubs to adopt their position for safer vehicles at the annual meeting in the fall of 1963. It was also decided that the

American Automobile Association Foundation for Traffic Safety would finance a project to investigate vehicle hazards and develop standards that could be embodied into law.

On January 22, 1964, Kretschmar delivered an address in New York City accusing the automobile industry of "putting up organized resistance against making cars safer." He pointed out that in the past the manufacturers opposed putting on all cars such equipment as stop lights, directional signals, and windshield wipers until, after years of delay, legislation compelled them to do so. "Safety glass was legislated into cars literally window by window, starting in Massachusetts," he declared. In urging complete safety standards, he cited the results of a Massachusetts state investigation that showed that "the 1963 models of two brands of cars develop steering weakness after about 20,000 miles of use."

In June 1964, the New York AAA's safety director, Charles Murphy, told the Pennsylvania AAA club: "We must try to change the image carefully cultivated over the years of the motorist as the fellow responsible for eighty-five to ninety per cent of the accidents. I look forward to the results of the massive research job being undertaken by the AAA Foundation for Traffic Safety on this entire question. And I am sure it will be revealing and will lead to constructive public consideration to which manufacturers must eventually respond."

This was the small progressive wing of the AAA speaking. The old guard, especially those in Washington, opposed such a research job but not because of insufficient funds. The AAA Foundation, which receives about $165,000 yearly from AAA clubs, has a substantial financial surplus each year. As of mid-1965, no action had been initiated concerning this projected study.

The national AAA, along with most AAA state clubs, has long maintained close relationships with automobile industry personnel. In the thirties and forties AAA received safety grants from the industry. Commanding positions in AAA club membership are held by employees of automobile companies, suppliers, and automobile dealers. When in early 1964 the Michigan Automobile Club released a fifteen-point plan that included a statement urging the manufacturers to "give increasing attention to design and production of features which make cars safer to drive," automobile industry publicists were angered at not being sent a draft for advance clearance. Out-of-state AAA observers conceded that the Michigan club's unilateral move was a bit bold, considering the state in which it is lodged. These observers add that it is quite understandable why the club has maintained a complete silence since its "indiscretion."

Automobile men cultivate the AAA since the clubs make good impressions before state legislative committees. The industry and AAA find that they share common interests. Among these are their opposition to federal "intervention," their desire for more highways, their coolness toward rapid transit, and their encouragement of improved motoring conditions and services. The whole administrative apparatus of AAA is geared to dealing with state officials, and a reorientation to federal activity would be a difficult adjustment, one that would weaken the state clubs at the expense of the national association.

Considerations such as these have kept the AAA, the largest car user group in the nation, from advancing forcefully the safety interests of its members on the issue of vehicle design. The attempt by the Massachusetts and New York clubs to breathe new life into AAA on this issue has not made much headway. The few courageous men who are trying find that regeneration from within is a difficult task. By not backing a determined policy that demands safer automotive engineering, the dominant leaders continue to allow the nine million members of the AAA to suffer the consequences of unsafe vehicles.

While the AAA may occasionally raise a voice that is displeasing to the automobile industry, that "hub of the safety movement," the National Safety Council, remains the unswerving keeper of the traditional faith. Almost everyone in America has heard the council's repeated injunction that to be safe one simply has to be careful. Before every holiday weekend, the council makes its highly publicized prediction of the number of highway deaths. Should the prediction be exceeded, it shows how important are the council's warnings against carelessness; if the prediction exceeded the actual toll, then the council concludes that its warnings made people drive more carefully. Either outcome serves to nourish the council's image of always being on the side of the angels. The council gets enormous publicity as the nation's caretaker of traffic safety. Since its founding in 1915, the council has saturated the country with slogans, printed material, and broadcasted exhortations for safer driving. It has helped to form state and local safety councils, accrediting seventy-two of them as council affiliates, all devoted to persuading the public to drive carefully. This may be a generally useless endeavor but it is not a harmless one. What seems to fill a need in form succeeds very well in excluding alternative methods that could fill it in fact. Every National Safety Council message disseminates a view of highway safety that lulls even the alert segment of the public into thinking that the council knows how to reduce casualties. Stripped to its fundamentals, the council view is that man must be the element adapted to the accident and injury risks of automobile driving, not that the automobile must be designed for maximum possible adaptation to man's requirements. This prejudiced view of the highway safety problem quite expectedly has led to prejudiced solutions. To administer these biased solutions, biased organizations arise. Of these, the National Safety Council is the most prominent example.

The powerful support enjoyed by the council goes far to explain why it refuses to pursue any policies that might imply criticism of the automobile industry's safety performance. Industry and commerce animate the council, provide the major source of its dues (600 of its 10,000 members are business firms which pay dues according to size, dues that far exceed the individual dues of $7.50), and dominate its board of directors. The automobile manufacturers and their safety organizations are heavily represented on the board. Further, the Automotive Safety Foundation annually grants nearly $150,000 for the council's yearly inventory of how closely communities are adhering to the "Action Program." About the same amount is granted by the Insurance Institute for Highway Safety. The Automobile Manufacturers Association provides the council with funds for special projects.

Overt pressure by the automobile industry, however, rarely has to be exerted; the council has always attracted the kind of men who reflect the industry's viewpoint. As late as 1965 council president Howard Pyle had this reaction to industry critics who are pressing for a crashworthy car: "The question is, does this nation want a packaged car or a free car?" Once, in the late fifties, a high council executive found the council's taboo on discussion of car design so demeaning that he attempted to effect a modest change in policy. A weekend meeting between the council's board of directors and automobile executives aboard a yacht on Lake Michigan squashed that attempt.

The difference between the National Safety Council's avowed missions and its actual performance shows the extent to which it has subordinated the promotion of safety to the interests of industry. During its quest to win a federal charter (a prestige imprimatur with little legal significance) from Congress in 1953, the council supplied the following description of its work in a report to the House judiciary committee: "The National Safety Council is presently engaged in a continuous and unified program of accident prevention which includes research into the causes of accident occurrence, devising measures for accident prevention, determination of engineering requirements for safe design, construction and use of machines and equipment, formulation of modern safety legislation by providing needed technical information and advice, participation in educational safety projects, dissemination of material on accident cause and prevention, and cooperation with national, state and local agencies in accident prevention. One of its major functions is to act as a national coordinating agency for all private and public bodies interested in matters of safety."

Weighed against such intentions, what is the council's actual achievement in traffic safety, apart from its publicity campaigns aimed at the driver? First, measured against even a minimal standard, the council conducts no research. No one is more painfully aware of this fact than its research director, Dr. Murray Blumenthal, whose duties are primarily administrative and whose hope of any improvement in this condition is dwindling. Second, the council has not devised any accident prevention measures or determined any engineering requirements for safe design of automobiles. It has sedulously avoided providing to the public, directly or indirectly, any technical information or advice concerning the formulation of safety legislation which concerns vehicle design. Nor has it cooperated in the slightest with any national, state, or local agencies interested in safer vehicle construction.

Avoidance is not the only path followed by the council in order to continue its unblemished record of never differing with the automobile industry. In a detailed chart included in the distribution literature and presented before legislative committees, entitled "Quantitative Analysis of Traffic Safety Services of National Organizations," the council categorically asserts that present research, standards, and recommendations of the automobile manufacturers pertaining to the operational and crashworthy qualities of vehicles are adequate. The council's basis for such an unequivocal evaluation is a letter from the Automobile Manufacturers Association saying so!

A more important protective service the council performs for the automobile industry lies in the nature of the traffic accident statistics that it compiles and reports every year. It has been the practice in this country to rely on the council to provide nationwide data on motor vehicle accidents and injuries. This represents a rather unusual delegation of a public function to a private organization. The council has not failed to abuse the privilege. It has not encouraged the compilation, analysis, or reporting of data by state and local agencies relating to the accident injury experience of different makes and models of automobiles. Nor has it done any sample studies of its own regarding these differences, although its alleged research mission would certainly include studies of this kind. The council's default is all the more insupportable in view of the fact that standard motor vehicle accident report forms include data on the make and year of vehicles involved, providing at least the rudiments for such studies. The first statistical reports in this area, dealing with small car–large car comparisons, have come in the last three years from five state agencies and the Cornell program. Neither central National Safety Council headquarters in Chicago nor its highly publicized field service personnel were involved in these efforts.

In addition, the council is a staunch adherent of measuring traffic safety progress by the death rate per vehicle miles traveled. In a council pamphlet called "The Fight for Life," the decline in the traffic death rate over the years is cited as the answer to the question, "Does all this work and activity by the Council really make things safer for the people of the United States?" This declining death rate, measured in relation to the number of miles traveled by automobiles, is the standard by which the private traffic safety movement measures the success of its programs, assuming without any evidence that such a cause-and-effect relationship exists.

There are many questions that can be raised about the consistency of methods in calculating vehicle miles traveled, but the pertinent factor here is that any claim of a reduced death rate per vehicle miles traveled gives an illusion of progress which is definitely misleading. The fatality rate per hundred million vehicle miles traveled had gone down steadily from 11.4 in 1940 to 5.2 in 1962, then began rising again in 1963 and registered 5.7 in 1964. But fatality rates have remained basically unchanged when the total population of the United States is used as a base. For example, traffic deaths per 100,000 population totaled 26.1 in 1940, 23.0 in 1950 and 24.9 in 1964. What this means is that a motorist can expect to drive farther in any given year without being killed, but he is just as likely as in previous years to be killed within that year. Most important, the council's emphasis on the vehicle-mile death rate has greatly obscured the tremendous injury totals and rates that are produced by automobile collisions. For every death by automobile, there are about ninety injuries, including three totally crippling disabilities. National injury statistics are arrived at only by sample, but evidence in various states indicates a sharp increase in injury rates during the postwar years, reflecting in part a greater density of vehicles in urban areas and more rapid modern medical care that is saving lives. In Connecticut, during Governor Ribicoff's well-known crackdown on speeders, the number of accidents and injuries increased and so did the injury rate per vehicle miles traveled. Connecticut, which compiles better statistics on motor vehicle accidents than most states, reflects the National Safety Council's traditional inattention to injury rates. Between 1961 and 1962 Connecticut reported a staggering 21.8 per cent increase in persons injured. When asked what could explain such an increase, the statistical office of the Department of Motor Vehicles replied that it had no explanation and did not contemplate any study to find one. Robert Catlin, a retired insurance executive and member of the President's Committee for Traffic Safety, proposed at a committee meeting in 1964 that a serious study be undertaken to determine with some exactness the number and pattern of injuries arising out of motor vehicle accidents. He suggested there was reason to believe that the increase has been alarmingly high in recent years. His suggestion received a frosty reception by council and automobile representatives at the meeting.

The focus of the National Safety Council's traffic safety activities is the support and promotion of the "Action Program" of the President's Committee for Traffic Safety. A council publication outlining in great detail how to form a local volunteer safety group states: "The Action Program is a compilation of the best knowledge in the traffic safety field and incorporates accepted standards of national organizations concerned with traffic accident prevention. It is the master plan for all traffic safety activities. The basic objective of your local traffic program should be the adoption of the Action Program in your area."

The Action Program was launched by the traffic safety establishment in 1946 after a White House conference on traffic safety. It consists of ten separate subjects, each represented by a booklet distributed by the President's Committee for Traffic Safety.*

The council president, Howard Pyle, recently made some ambitious claims for this master plan. He said it was developed "through a sound and democratic process," that "every feature in it had been proven workable," that it brings "to each governmental jurisdiction the best of fifty years of ideas, experience and research findings in traffic safety," and that if state and local governments would only invest annually an additional three dollars per capita to apply the program more fully, the traffic death and injury toll would be cut in half.

The facts contradict Mr. Pyle's assertions. The program was drawn up by a clique representing private economic and bureaucratic interests. It was prepared without any participation of the formal institutions, legislative or administrative, that would ordinarily be associated with democratic policy-making. Even technical expertise was not involved. Those who passed on the drafts of the program and determined what was to be included in it, and what emphasized, had no scientific, engineering, or medical qualifications that might have substantial bearing on the drafting of a traffic safety program. Since the program has been unchanged since 1949, it is hard to understand how it could bring "the best of fifty years of ideas, experience and research findings in traffic safety," particularly since the greatest advance in

---

* The subjects are: (1) laws and ordinances; (2) traffic accident records; (3) education; (4) engineering; (5) motor vehicle administration; (6) police traffic supervision; (7) traffic courts; (8) public information; (9) organized citizen support; and (10) research.

knowledge and experimentation in the traffic safety field has come during the last fifteen years.

The effectiveness of the program has never been determined. The council's annual traffic inventory, purporting to show how many states and cities apply the Action Program, is based on inventory forms filled out by various state officials. From the answers on these forms the council concludes that fifty-six per cent of the Action Program standards have been applied at the city level and seventy per cent at the state level. If one asks how this conclusion was reached, the answer is, "The state officials told us so." Aside from the likely distortions of self-serving statements, what is more interesting is that the council has never compiled comparative evidence showing the accident experience in areas applying the Action Program and those areas not applying it. This failure suggests that the outcome of any comparisons might prove embarrassing to the council and the authoritative mystique which surrounds the program. It is known that some unpublished correlations made by the National Safety Council staff in the postwar years have shown negative or inconclusive results. At any rate, the failure of the program to prove its workability is no surprise to the handful of competent accident researchers in this country. They look upon the program as a statement of general aspirations designed to offend none of the interests it was prepared to protect in the first place. Emerging from such a context, it is not surprising that the program gives only the briefest formal attention to the vehicle, that it contains no ranking of priorities for the many subjects it treats, and is almost entirely useless for operating and test purposes.

The council's bankrupt performance is clearly visible when its leaders are interviewed on the subject of the traffic safety problem. The impression received is well summarized by one sympathetic interpreter, Nick Thimmesch, who wrote in *Car and Driver* of the understanding he carried away from long discussions with council people: "But all of man's programs deliver only promise and perhaps progress, and people will forever fuss over traffic safety. The NSC men know people will always be killed on highways; that Detroit's products and the imports are about as safe as can be; that 'vehicle failure' comes from poor maintenance by owners; that driving environment in the U.S. is spectacularly improved; and that the principal cause of accidents is species homo sapiens, few of whom ever really learn to drive well."

"The National Safety Council, the Great Green Giant, has learned that sin will always be with us. After two generations of trying to reform human nature, the Council now wisely realizes it can only be treated. Besides, life isn't that bad anyway.

"'We can only do so much,' says Ed Kirby [Edwin Kirby, a National Safety Council traffic safety specialist], the look of knowledge on his face."

On the ground floor of the building at 1711 H Street N.W. in Washington, the safety establishment displays a creativity in political science not approached by the most powerful of private lobbies. The door at that address identifies it as the office of the President's Committee for Traffic Safety. The drawn Venetian blinds covering the long front window do not allow those passing by to see inside. But any interested visitor is greeted by a friendly secretary and on request may meet the committee's executive director, William Foulis, or its assistant director, Richard Tossell. Foulis is a former radio broadcaster and a genuinely talented practitioner of the art of double-talk. Tossell is an unpretentious holder of a doctorate in safety education.

The inquirer would never suspect that behind this smooth façade a federal institution quite without parallel in the history of American government is administered. There has never been another agency created by and then leased back outright to private enterprise. The price for this continuing experiment of business in government is about $50,000 a year—a rather modest fee for maintaining an agency that (as the committee's chairman, William Randolph Hearst, Jr., put it) "by virtue of its identification with the office of the President, provides the traffic safety movement with the prestige of the President, which no other organization could accomplish."

Foulis and Tossell labor in government office space and give instructions to civil servants under their authority, but on pay day their checks carry the name of a private, tax-exempt organization called the President's Action Committee for Traffic Safety. Most of the $50,000 which this "paper" organization receives is contributed by the Automotive Safety Foundation and the Insurance Institute for Highway Safety. The remainder comes from a few other private business groups having similar traffic safety interests. With such generosity, the ASF and IIHS have become the dominant members of the President's Committee's advisory council, composed of thirty-seven people, most representing automotive, insurance, transportation, and "professional" safety associations. On paper, the advisory council makes the policy for the committee to follow, but in reality it is the advisory council's executive committee (renamed the administrative committee in September 1964) which is the decision-making group within the council. The actions of the President's Committee are the actions of this executive committee run by Mattson, Brown, Pyle, and Arthur Butler (through his aides) of the National Highway Users Conference. The President's Committee is composed of eighteen patronage positions filled by fairly prominent individuals, most of whom know nothing whatever about traffic safety.

It took considerable ingenuity for the automobile industry leaders to develop the idea of the President's Committee. It was created in 1954 simply by a letter from President Eisenhower to Mr. Harlow Curtice, head of General Motors and chairman of the then Business Advisory Committee on Highway Safety. In the tone of the solicited message, the President's letter, dated April 13, 1954, noted that the recent White House Conference on Traffic Safety (sponsored by private industry) had generated an enthusiasm which should not be lost, and expressed the President's wish to "have a national committee for traffic safety formed to follow through on the fine work begun by the business group."

The Committee's organizational meeting was held two weeks later in Room 4426 of the Treasury Building, where Mr. Curtice stated the new group's purposes. These were to organize local communities for a continuing traffic safety effort and to serve in an advisory capacity to the President on matters pertaining to traffic accident prevention. It was also decided by those present that, contingent upon approval of the American Petroleum Institute, Rear Admiral H. B. Miller (USN, Ret.) would become the committee's volunteer director. These private citizens then voted to obtain $16,000 to $20,000 by private subscription to finance salary and travel expenses of a staff director who would be responsible to Admiral Miller. Mr. Curtice offered to raise the necessary funds. Mr. Light Yost of General Motors was appointed as secretary of the committee. In considering a formal name for the committee, all in attendance agreed that it was essential for "President" to be in the title. A government staff responsible to the staff director was to be made available to the committee, Mr. Curtice announced. Thus General Motors required only two weeks to establish an executive organization whose essential structure remains unchanged to the present day.

In 1960, the committee was given a more permanent legal status within the administration by Executive Order 10858, issued by President Eisenhower. It is vaguely worded, permitting the committee's ruling advisory council wide latitude in interpreting its own role and the role of the committee. Executive Order 10858 associated the committee with the White House explicitly in Section Two, which states: "The Committee, on behalf of the President, shall promote State and community application of the Action Program of traffic safety measures established by the President's Highway Safety Conference in 1946 and revised in 1949."

At the beginning of the Kennedy administration there was some question whether the committee would be continued, but this uncertainty was resolved when Mr. Hearst reached an understanding with the President that he would remain as committee chairman. However, in October 1961 the President signed an amendment to the executive order, permitting the Secretaries of Defense, Commerce, Labor, and Health, Education, and Welfare to sit as ex-officio members. Whatever hope existed that this amendment would bring a greater government voice to the committee's actions has not materialized. The representatives of the Departments of Commerce and Health, Education, and Welfare on the advisory council's administrative committee (formerly the executive committee) have played an entirely secondary and almost obsequious role, leaving the entire show to Mattson and his associates.

The committee's formal purpose is to promote state and community application of the Action Program. It tries to do this in part by conducting conferences and seminars of women's groups, state legislators, and county and municipal officials with federal funds. These activities keep Foulis on the road many days, with all the expenses paid by his private employers, who also supply volunteer assistance and absorb some entertainment expenses at these meetings.

William Bethea, Foulis' predecessor, was the committee's privately salaried staff director from 1954 until 1961 when he resigned, partly due to the selfishness of the interest groups on the advisory council, which finally persuaded him that nothing effective could be done. "They close in on you," he said. According to Bethea, the advisory council "is completely hostile to the federal government. . . . They never want to talk about the vehicle, which is the primary bugaboo," he said. Bethea ridiculed the idea that the committee staff and committee advisers were "safety professionals," saying, "we were just organization and public relations men." In describing how he protected the committee's favored position with the government, he honestly admitted: "I kept the White House wrapped around me all the time." He specifically referred to Howard Pyle, then an aide to President Eisenhower, and Frederick Dutton, an assistant to President Kennedy, as the two key contacts there who "would back you up all the way."

The committee's work includes preparation and distribution of audio and visual aids and the printing and distributing of slick progress reports. The latest such report, released in September 1964, devoted thirty-four pages to the Action Program. Vehicle engineering was discussed in twelve lines, alleging safety gains in recent models. All committee projects are developed and approved by the heads of the advisory council before being sent to the Bureau of Public Roads in the Department of Commerce for financing. A law authorizes the Department of Commerce to spend up to $150,000 a year for the committee's projects. The Bureau of Public Roads' approval of these projects, rendered with little written justification, is a more or less rubber-stamp affair.

The importance of the committee does not come from receipt and expenditures of these small sums, but from the exploitation of its greatest capital asset—the prestige of the President's office. This is the attraction for all those who work in and around the committee. As James Lake of the Automotive Safety Foundation said at a meeting of the advisory council's executive committee, "The President's name is magic; his appearance is magic." And the committee has made sure that it alone in the traffic safety field has access to that magic. Ever since Eisenhower took office, every

President has spoken on the traffic safety problem only in connection with a function of the committee, such as the presentation of a report or an annual meeting. The proper expressions are drafted by the committee's privately paid staff and sent over to the White House for almost verbatim incorporation into the President's formal statement.

On September 10, 1964, President Johnson issued a statement in response to the committee's report on the Action Program's community application. In the statement he called for an intensified effort toward accident prevention as the program directs, and he praised the committee's work, taking note of the advisory council's supportive role. He thus became the latest President in a line going back to Calvin Coolidge to say, "Primary responsibility [for traffic safety] rests in our States, counties and municipalities."

The committee rarely loses an opportunity to display the President's committee seal on its publications, which leads the reader to believe that their contents have the full approval of the President. Foulis, the committee's executive director, wanted to go even further last year when he unsuccessfully attempted to get Department of Commerce support for the seal's being employed by any safety council or committee-approved group on literature supporting the Action Program.

The President's committee seal has come in handy for more overt political policies which the advisory council of the President's Committee for Traffic Safety supports. One such instance is the promotion of interstate traffic safety compacts as a means of heading off federal action and at the same time of achieving a *de facto* delegation of state legislative initiatives to industry-dominated compact commissions. The most important compact to Mattson and the Automotive Safety Foundation is the Vehicle Equipment Safety Compact, which the tax-exempt ASF has helped promote with men and money. This compact was drafted by the Automobile Manufacturers Association and the Council of State Governments. It was launched in 1962 after an exceptionally vague enabling resolution was whisked through Congress, and it is now adhered to by a majority of states. A commission to administer the compact's business has been created and is nestling in the Washington headquarters of the American Association of Motor Vehicle Administrators. AAMVA—a private association of state administrators—has long been the recipient of grants from the ASF and lavish automobile industry hospitality at its annual meetings. The object of the commission is to control the content and pace of motor vehicle safety standards, which are sent to the state legislatures or (where the state law permits) to state motor vehicle departments for approval. The initiatives come from commission "experts" who thus far have all been from the tire and automobile industries.

Three years ago the President's Committee on Traffic Safety began circulating a pamphlet entitled the "Vehicle Equipment Safety Compact" with the President's committee seal prominently displayed on its cover. The pamphlet contained a glowing description of the compact's promise and emphasized the message that highway safety is entirely the states' and not the federal government's responsibility. This pamphlet was printed and paid for by the Automobile Manufacturers Association. There is no record of either the committee or any other federal agency approving this bold move. It was strictly a staff operation carried out by Foulis and industry advisers.

To foster the impression that they are right on top of the traffic safety problem, the advisory council's "professionals" have pursued strange paths to publicize their "make-work" activity. The transcripts of the advisory council's executive committee meetings over the years are laborious records of the deliberations of self-seeking publicists. One of the more coherent subjects that absorbed their energies was discussed at several meetings in early 1963 and centered around information supplied by Howard Pyle that the National Safety Council would soon announce the 1962 traffic fatality toll (40,804) as being the highest ever. All readily agreed that the committee might, in Mattson's words, "offset the negative aspects of last year's all-time high in traffic deaths" by "capitalizing on the public interest generated" by so hideous a record. Mattson said that he and Pyle thought "the President ought to be pulled into this in some manner." There would be some kind of meeting where the President would appear, Mattson foresaw, in front of the members of the President's Committee for Traffic Safety and several representatives of each organization on the advisory council. "This could serve as a springboard for the President to make a speech and this would be the platform from which all the publicity would generate as to the concern that the President has over this," he said. Then with an expectation born of past experience, Mattson added: "In all probability the President would say to the President's Committee and to the members of the Advisory Council that this is an urgent situation, an emergency situation, that this is a grass roots problem and therefore, what we ought to do is to get the Action Program of the President's Committee out to the various states."

Foulis and the members of the executive committee then began to discuss strategy about how best to "deliver" the President. Pyle advised his confreres that he had a "fair knowledge of how that white pagoda operates there," and that the object should be to publicize the Action Program by showing that the President believed in it. The President would call the committee and advisory council into emergency session, "as his core of advisers," and charge these advisers to see that this community plan of action was implemented. Pyle told his colleagues that getting wider acceptance of the Action Program required repetition. "I have seen my father stand in the pulpit for fifty years," he said, "and talk about the Ten Commandments, and they are going to do that from now until hell freezes over. There is no new way to say this. You have just got to keep saying it over and over and over again. You tell them what you have got to tell them, and you tell them what you told them."

Russell Singer of the American Automobile Association cautioned not to make too much of the 1962 death toll. "This thing could get away from us," he said, referring to the risk of inciting alarmist and radical ideas. He counseled that to give the proper perspective, the fact that people traveled more in 1962 than in 1961 should be attached to the death toll announcement. Discussion followed, off the record, about the danger "of misdirected or undirected public reaction to the 1962 figures."

Back on the record, Pyle stressed the short time available before the council's death toll announcement and how quickly they on the executive committee had to act. Russell Brown wondered about the matter of getting "the skids greased at the White House." Pyle replied that this was a detail to be worked out. Mattson informed Brown that the White House was not aware of any of these plans. Foulis added that neither was Hearst, the committee chairman, indicating that there was "a very strong possibility we can see the chairman in the morning. Whether we want to or not is another thing." Pyle suggested that Hearst "could contact the White House immediately and ask for an audience with the President."

The executive committee moved rapidly. Hearst and Foulis met briefly with President Kennedy on February 8, 1963, to make arrangements. Five days later, the executive committee met in a government office to discuss in more detail what points should come out of the meeting at which the President would appear. William Simon of the National Highway Users Conference advocated getting the White House committed to the kinds of state action that could only end up with state legislation (like backing the Uniform Vehicle Code program). This, Simon reasoned, would by simple logic stop the White House from supporting competitive federal laws for highway safety. He thought that "that would be a good policy position to get the Administration into." Simon expressed added concern that with the "White House dipping their fingers into all kinds of state legislative programs" such as civil rights and getting rid of poll tax laws, it wouldn't seem "that the White House would be out of character if they would dip into this highway safety thing."

Others around the table preferred to suggest that the President say something that would not arouse his suspicions. Foulis offered an alternative: "If we could provide the President with something that would give a public image, give the proper public image of what is being done and how it is being done, we would be much better off . . ." This seemed to the group like a good idea, so it was decided that the announced purpose of the meeting would be "the acceleration of the application of the Action Program."

The next matter to which they turned their attention was how to publicize the meeting, and whether federal funds could be used to hire a public relations firm, as was done on prior occasions for the conferences the President's Committee on Traffic Safety sponsored around the country. The Automotive Safety Foundation's James Lake estimated the cost at $5000 and thought that maybe *Life* magazine could be persuaded to do a story on the general subject of traffic safety, "tying the President into this thing." When Foulis asked, "You think we ought to hire somebody to get *Life* magazine to cover it?" Lake suddenly dropped the subject. The deliberations continued over who should be invited from the government, whether too many government people would unbalance the private participants' presence, how to handle Capitol Hill, especially Congressman Kenneth Roberts, who was not thought to be properly enthusiastic over either the Action Program or the President's Committee operations.

Russell Brown broke in with exasperation at one point, urging his associates to concentrate on getting President Kennedy to speak before a small group at the White House rather than before a large group in an auditorium, which would dilute the whole idea of the meeting. "I'd like to get this guy on the record to make a statement. He hasn't said boo about traffic safety as far as I am concerned, and I think that is why I am even willing to have him make a statement to the press," he said. Brown clearly thought the time had come to be more aggressive. He declared that Hearst, Mattson, Mrs. Katharine White (a member of the President's Committee) and Foulis "ought to go up there and gang up on the guy. I think it is important that he finally gets on his feet." Dr. Paul Joliet, chief of the Public Health Service's division of accident prevention, concurred. "He will find it more difficult to be negative before four than before one," Joliet said, and Brown replied, "Particularly before a woman."

Mattson was a little worried that "we might look kind of bad if both Mr. Hearst and Mrs. White went in there and neither one knew a damn thing," especially, as Mattson allowed, the President was "no fool." But he went along with the idea of sending four people up there, relying on his own capacity to meet any contingencies.

Nobody, including Dr. Joliet or Mr. James Williams (director of the Bureau of Public Roads' office of highway safety), who ostensibly were representing President Kennedy's administration, raised the question of why the President should stand up for a set of policies created and promoted by what Mr. Williams himself has called, on other occasions, special interest groups abusing the President's prestige. Admittedly, raising such a question would have taken a little courage. The leaders of the President's Committee on Traffic Safety can change moods on short notice. Williams later discovered this at a June 1963 meeting of the executive committee. At that time, he notified the "pillars" of the traffic safety establishment that the Bureau of Public Roads' budget for highway safety had been cut for fiscal 1964 by twenty-five per cent and that this cut would have to be absorbed down the line, including the amount the bureau supplied to the President's Committee. Whereupon the "pillars" subjected Williams to a humiliating session of outraged reactions.

"Who stands up for us when you come to a budget hearing?" demanded Pyle.

"You are operating out of the trust fund, which is rather lush with dough right now," Simon asserted.

"Why haven't we the right to seek to correct it?" asked Burton Marsh of the AAA.

Mattson wanted to know if the decision couldn't be changed. He was undisturbed by the fact that the fiscal year was to begin just two weeks later.

Pyle, whose fury was building up, finally exploded: "I think this is murder, absolutely murder, and if I were in a position where I was called on for a public statement about this, I would have to cut this thing to ribbons in public. I don't think the Bureau of Public Roads wants this done."

Williams said, "I think that this decision was made in the best of faith."

"It doesn't make any difference," Pyle told him. "We in the private community are expected to boast of our strength and we are criticized if we don't get something done." What Pyle was indignant over was that fewer taxpayer funds would be available during the forthcoming year to make his "private community" look good.

Simon, of the National Highway Users Conference, interjected that he thought the money representing the twenty-five per cent cut was really going into research instead of traffic safety. "They are researching a way to invent a new transportation device to do away with the automobile. That is one project they have got projected. They are going to find a better form of transportation than the automobile. My people don't like that. Neither will yours." "Neither will ours," chimed in Richard Bennett of the Insurance Institute for Highway Safety. Simon wanted James Roche, the executive vice president of General Motors, and Mr. Hearst to go directly to Mr. Whitton, the federal highway administrator, and bring about "a better understanding or adjustment." The discussion was then off the record.

Back on the record, Russell Brown recommended calling Hearst, who was in Europe.

"Have you ever tried to catch him?" answered Mattson. "There is not enough money in this committee's function to run down that guy." It was finally decided not to pass a formal motion but simply to communicate the committee's displeasure over the cut in other ways and plan so that it would not be repeated in future years.

The executive committee members always have been troubled by Hearst's casualness and inattention to formal operations of the President's Committee for Traffic Safety. Mattson recounted how "terribly embarrassed" he was one time "when Hearst had to get up and leave the President's Committee and said, 'Joe, you take over,' and I said, 'No, I am not a member of the committee.' And he said, 'It doesn't matter; get up there.' And he walked out of the room."

Notwithstanding such behavior, Hearst is an important figure whenever the traffic safety establishment has to beat down efforts by Presidential advisers to abolish or downgrade the committee. As chief executive of a large newspaper chain, William Randolph Hearst, Jr. is a good man for approaching Presidents. In December 1963 he met with President Johnson and obtained the President's acquiescence to the continuance of the committee. The newspaper mogul values highly his being Chairman of the Committee and actively worked for reappointment in 1961. Apparently he sees every compatability between his newspaper holdings and his reliance on the advice of the automobile and insurance safety professionals on the advisory council to whom he defers openly.

Between 1962 and 1964, high officials in the Department of Commerce and certain government agencies tried in vain to dissolve or at least to curb the committee, so anomalous and notorious had been its status and activities under the domination of its advisory council. A host of arguments was advanced to support their case: the untenable fiscal and administrative practices resulting from the mixing of private funds and staff with public funds and staff; the inherent inability of the committee to be adequately responsive to the public interest when its direction comes from private groups; the obstruction, duplication, and complications it poses for the Office of Highway Safety; the false impression it gives to the public that the federal government is playing an important role in highway safety when the committee is actually being used to make sure that precisely the opposite is the case; the use of the committee's Presidential prestige to preserve the status quo in safety policy at the state and community level; the superfluous nature of the committee in the light of the creation of the Office of Highway Safety, the Division of Accident Prevention, and the Interdepartmental Highway Safety Board in the years since the committee was organized; and the more efficient and more appropriate exercise by the Office of Highway Safety of whatever useful endeavors the committee is supposed to perform as outlined in its executive order.

The argument was clear: a privately owned and run government agency should not be tolerated. It was not even good form. But tolerated it was—and still is. The movement against the committee was reaching a decisive stage in the Department of Commerce, with James Williams, Lowell Bridwell, Acting Deputy Federal Highway Administrator, and Clarence Martin, Under Secretary for Transportation, comprising the chain of command behind it. White House aides were persuaded that something had to be done. But the assassination of President Kennedy on November 22, 1963, shattered all the plans. In January 1964 Secretary of Commerce Luther Hodges submitted to the White House a draft executive order upgrading the Interdepartmental Highway Safety Board (a coordinating group for federal agencies involved in highway safety) and reducing the President's Committee on Traffic Safety to a subordinate advisory role. Presidential assistant Walter Jenkins did not think such a change was timely, though he said he saw value in it. What this really meant was that during the previous month Hearst had spoken to the President, who, burdened with the problems of a painful transition, assented to keeping the committee as it was.

In September 1964 Mattson and his associates forged ahead, changing the rules governing the advisory council in order to increase its control over the committee and strengthen its own autonomy. This just brought the formalities closer to the realities. Hearst was delighted to relinquish more of his formal powers as chairman. He had the title and that was what counted.

The committee continues as the Presidential voice on traffic safety with no supervision from the White House. Its wide latitude in employing the President's prestige simply dilutes the respect which the highest office in the nation should be granted. It is scarcely fitting for private interest groups to run an executive agency that speaks for the President; this seems clearly to be a situation that violates the basic canons of democratic government and executive organization. What has enabled the advisory council to manipulate the President's Committee on Traffic Safety in this manner without fear of being disciplined has been its essentially negative mission to see that the federal government stays out of traffic safety and that the entrenched view of accidents and injuries as being due to driver behavior is not disturbed. A status quo policy makes very good camouflage.

The rule of the traffic safety establishment has been a reign of darkness. Few who have observed closely its infidelity to the cause of human life have been in a position or felt a duty to articulate these observations publicly. One exception is Dr. Daniel P. Moynihan, former Assistant Secretary of Labor and the only political scientist who has ever taken a sustained interest in traffic safety. Moynihan found that the establishment's great emphasis on retaining complete state responsibility for traffic safety was not based on any useful analysis of which government jurisdictions can best meet which aspects of the safety problem. It was based instead on an analysis of which jurisdiction can be best manipulated. Moynihan described the situation in state administrations thus: "The typical bureau of motor vehicles is filled with deservedly low-paid clerks and run by an assortment of genial 'pols' with utterly no training or interest in traffic safety except as it provides an opportunity to do small favors—passing out low-number license plates, lifting a suspension, restoring a license here and there, and so on." It is not surprising that the automobile industry is so proud of its long and close relationships with the state authorities responsible for motor vehicle regulation. In numerous statements, automobile industry spokesmen talk of the "constructive" cooperation between the Automobile Manufacturers Association and the American Association of Motor Vehicle Administrators. Although the AAMVA is a private organization, the industry representatives regard it as an official body of state administrators, and the AAMVA does nothing to dispel this idea. General Motors' Charles Chayne has given the customary description: "This industry-government link for many years has proved highly effective as a means of facilitating exchange of information and suggestions and as a medium for the cooperative solution of many of the technical and legal problems involved in automotive safety."

So close is the relationship between the industry and most state administrators and their key aides that the Automobile Manufacturers Association's legislative lobbyists, such as Karl Richards and Mark Bauer, need only call their friends at the motor vehicle department to learn whether a given bill introduced by a given legislator has any strength behind it, or whether it is just a "hopper filler."

While Moynihan was an aide to Governor Averell Harriman in the late fifties, he was also dismayed by the nature and use of traffic-accident data. In 1963, representing the Department of Labor, he testified before the Roberts subcommittee that traffic accident and injury statistics, with very few exceptions, have been collected uncritically for decades by state and local governments and analyzed uncritically by those who process them for national dissemination—meaning largely the National Safety Council. As a result, he said, these statistics have contributed almost nothing to accident injury prevention. The reception given Moynihan's testimony by those to whom it presented a direct challenge further confirmed Moynihan's characterization of the traffic safety movement as lacking in self-criticism. He told the Ribicoff subcommittee two years later about his experience before the Roberts subcommittee: "First, the hearing room in which I made that statement was filled with persons representing the major institutions concerned with traffic safety. Second, it was of course a public statement and was printed in the published record of the hearing. Finally, it was rather an emphatic statement, which had not, to my knowledge, been made before.

"For these reasons, it seems to me that the reaction to the statement was rather remarkable.

"There was no reaction.

"So far as I know the statement never appeared in any traffic safety publication. No one commented on it. No one attempted to refute it. I certainly do not wish to suggest that silence inferred agreement, but it could indicate a measure of indifference."

Indifference to evidence or the lack of it has been the trademark of the establishment even within its chosen field of concentration —driver behavior. It has laid great stress on driver education as a principal accident-prevention measure. This measure never was based on any evidence that would substantiate its pretensions. To this day it remains at best a hypothesis that costs millions of dollars and crowds an already congested high school curriculum. Despite numerous reports allegedly proving that youths with driver education (largely classroom lectures) have fewer accidents than those who have not taken such courses, every one of them contains deficiencies that render its conclusions useless, according to Dr. Richard Michaels of the Bureau of Public Roads. Among the control groups chosen for statistical comparison, the driver education group, for example, often has been mainly composed of girls, who drive much less than boys and drive less at night. Or it was found that prosecutors would not pursue first charges involving minor accidents against youths who had taken such courses. This does not mean that the concept of driver training is worthless; it does strongly indicate, however, that the statistics need a firmer foundation before meaningful comparisons can be made. Even after the elements of the driving task are understood, it may be revealed that the time and resources necessary to upgrade driver control and response to highway situations are not practical and are replaceable by cheaper and more effective engineering innovations which adapt to human limitations. The organized forces of safety are unmoved; they want millions of dollars more for the same "proven" kind of driver education of high school students, college students, and adults. The burgeoning driver-education industry, well into its third decade, agrees vigorously.

Enforcement is another "time-tested" preventive measure that has not been subjected to much scientific scrutiny. In an article by Dr. Michaels entitled "The Effects of Enforcement on Traffic Behavior," which appeared in *Public Roads* in December 1960, the author examined data comparing highly patrolled roads in Wisconsin with comparable roads having fewer patrolmen. The author concluded that different amounts of highway police patrol between the test roads and the non-test roads showed no reliable difference in the number of accidents on those roads. Since studies like this are very rare and since the competence of the researcher, Dr. Michaels, is well known, his conclusion was a challenge to one of the main foundations of the traditional safety policy. (Michaels was trying to open a line of inquiry, not close one.) There was some grumbling about the article along the line of its undermining enforcement efforts, but by and large the establishment held to the standard operating procedure: When challenged, ignore.

Closely allied to the enforcement approach is the long-held belief that a small percentage of incorrigible or accident-prone drivers account for the majority of accidents. If these people could either be adequately punished or taken off the roads, according to this belief, the highway accident problem would be greatly diminished. This exaggerated assertion would never have been taken seriously if its advocates had paused to apply the Poisson distribution—a mathematical technique for describing the probable occurrence of infrequent events. Using the Poisson method, and purely as a result of chance, nine per cent of the drivers would be expected to have forty per cent of all the accidents. Actual accident studies indicate that nine per cent of the drivers have forty-eight per cent of all the accidents. The difference between the Poisson result and the results of these studies is really the small number of drivers who have repeated accidents in excess of the number expected by chance. In a review of studies on the accident-proneness of drivers, Professor Ross McFarland concluded that "close and invariable relationships between particular characteristics of drivers and the frequency of accidents have rarely been found."

For decades, speed was the subject of the most widespread slogans drummed into the public. "Speed kills" and "slow down and live" are familiar ones peddled by the National Safety Council. But of late the council is underplaying these messages, owing in part to the embarrassing effects of the automobile companies' promotional emphasis on horsepower, speed, and racing and—encouragingly enough—due in part to the results of a study by the Bureau of Public Roads six years ago. This study, conducted by David Solomon, concerned the relationship between accidents and highway speed on rural highways. The findings showed a more complex picture of the role of speed than had been assumed before. Accident involvement rates are at a minimum at speeds between fifty and seventy-five miles per hour. As the speed goes below fifty miles per hour or above seventy-five miles per hour, the involvement rate increases rapidly. Solomon emphasized the importance of variations from average speed on a given section of highway in contributing to accidents. Although obviously the severity of accidents is greater at higher speeds, the study revealed that considering accident frequency rates and severity, the number of injuries per vehicle miles traveled is at its minimum in the speed range of forty-five to seventy miles per hour.

The failure of the establishment to provide some empirical basis for its driver-oriented nostrums is fully consistent with the purpose of concentrating on the driver in the first place. That purpose is to divert attention from the vehicle, not really to understand driver behavior, because a sincere attempt to understand driver behavior would inevitably bring under discussion the engineering of the vehicle. To take a fairly simple example, many drivers respond to an emergency situation by a sudden application of the brakes, which can easily make the brakes lock and lead to the loss of steering control. There is substantial evidence that the loss of steering control with locked brakes is highly dangerous and has led to many collisions with other vehicles or roadside objects. There are two approaches to solving this problem: either trying to teach drivers that during emergencies they must not resort to a sudden application of brakes which, because of their design, will lock; or trying to persuade the manufacturers to provide cars with anti-locking brakes. It is not difficult to choose the more feasible approach. But although anti-locking brakes have been in use in aircraft since the thirties, the automobile makers have done very little research and development in this area—at least, very little that is publicly known.

The first-rate accident research that is being done in this country, backed mainly by federal funds, is producing mounting evidence that the more that is known about human behavior, the more the fundamental solutions will lie in the engineering of the highway transport system. The vehicle is the basic unit of that system; the driver's adequacy is a function of his vehicle's adequacy. The traffic safety establishment sees the basic problem of accident prevention in the light of an existing system that requires the driver to judge and act perfectly without fail. But the limitations of human beings in coping with the increasingly complex driving task, even under the most rigid law-enforcement or the most ambitious education programs, make it unrealistic to expect all drivers to control their vehicles perfectly all the time.

Before an engineering audience recently, Dr. Michaels described in these words the orientation of modern research on highway safety: "This historical failure has been to arbitrarily assign the control function to the driver without fully knowing whether he could carry out that function with the required accuracy and reliability. And the more we have examined the requirements of the system in its control dimension, the more evidence we have uncovered that those requirements are neither sufficiently adapted to human capabilities nor do they adequately take into account his limitations as a controller." Dr. Michaels offered an example of how electronic communication instruments can greatly improve the driver's ease of perceptual judgments and prevent an accident. "Most of the basic dynamics of the free overtaking rear-end collision accident are known," he said, "and it is possible to design systems for aiding the driver in solving the discrimination and judgment problems inherent in these situations."

Appearing before the National Safety Congress in 1963, Rex Whitton, the Federal Highway Administrator, delivered a significant analysis of the highway safety problem which his Bureau of Public Roads researchers were prepared to explain and defend. "Perhaps the time has come," Mr. Whitton said, "to examine some of our present safety programs and some of our present safety concepts. The truth, as I see it, may be painful. . . . I am concerned about the great amount of energy being devoted to 'hard sell' efforts to reform the driver—to scare or shame him into being a better one. I believe we have exhausted the value of this continuing assault on human nature. And I have grave doubts that it works. . . . In many cases haven't we given the driver a task beyond the capacity of his senses, nerves, and muscles? . . . I believe that because of these attacks [on the drivers], our attention is being distracted and our energy is being diverted from the essential things we could and should be doing to reduce the traffic accident toll.

"We must face up squarely to this premise: the majority of drivers are performing as well as we can reasonably expect, under existing conditions. From that premise it is logical to reason that the conditions must be changed—we must improve the road, the vehicle, and the basic control measures of the system. We already have in our hands much proven technology, which if widely applied can bring about great improvement in highway safety. And such improvement is within our financial resources. Indeed, we cannot afford *not* to move ahead."

Whitton's remarks were as direct a condemnation of the conventional traffic safety theory as a high federal official could make and still observe the Department of Commerce's polite rule not to condemn the vehicle. And he offered an alternate way.

The establishment ignored the address. Whitton's remarks, which at the very least should have sparked debate and self-examination, never went further than his voice carried the day he delivered them. The forces of safety were not interested in the bright expectations of applicable technology, since they have always feared the unforeseen consequences of progress. It is this fear which has helped keep traffic safety efforts more in the hands of unqualified laymen than in the hands of unfettered scientists and engineers. This is why the establishment must keep its policies trivial and stagnant. To raise the saving of 50,000 lives and prevention of over four million injuries yearly to the level of a well defined mission of national importance, excitement, and innovation would attract disturbing talents and resources and the serious attention of the President and Congress. The measure of the establishment's success in keeping traffic safety a subordinate goal in the nation's scale of priorities can be gauged by a news item from the *Wall Street Journal* of Sept. 17, 1965. It reported: "The Senate passed a two-year $320 million highway-beautification bill designed to eliminate thousands of advertising billboards and junkyards from the nation's major roads. The measure would also provide $5 million for a study of ways to dispose of scrapped cars and $500,000 for a Commerce Department study of highway safety."

8
The coming struggle for safety

On a September day in 1899, Mr. H. H. Bliss stepped down from a trolley car in New York City and, while graciously assisting a lady passenger to alight, was fatally struck by a horseless carriage—the first recorded death by automobile. Not until 1,125,000 more fatalities and tens of millions of injuries had occurred did a Congressional Committee open hearings on the conditions that cause this massive casualty count. On July 16, 1956, Congressman Kenneth Roberts, an Alabaman and a firm believer in minimum federal government, opened the first session of the new House subcommittee on traffic safety by proceeding immediately to the subject of automobile design hazards. It was a promising start but one that remained little fulfilled in hearing after hearing through 1963. Congressman Roberts was surrounded by apathy and opposition in Congress and with hostility from the automobile industry and its traffic safety establishment. Even taking a look at the problem was suspect.

In spite of these obstacles and the lack of a full time subcommittee staff, Roberts performed some important services for the cause of traffic safety. One was to provide the first public forum for presentations on the vehicle safety issue by industry representatives and by physicians, engineers, and other specialists in crash injury research. These presentations have a continuing significance. The automobile makers' testimony, for example, reveals how little their present attitude, performance, and excuses have changed from a decade ago. They offered the jaded themes of their supposed concern with safety; their past progress in matters such as sealed beam headlamps and windshield wipers; the necessity of high-horsepower engines; the industry's thorough methods of quality control; the reasons why safety devices must begin on an optional, extra-cost basis; and the usual tributes to the American Association of Motor Vehicle Administrators and the safety standards of the Society of Automotive Engineers.

The subcommittee members were taken on a tour of company proving grounds, were shown some barrier crashes, and were given lectures about National Safety Council figures showing that the vast majority of accidents and fatalities are caused by bad driving. General Motors' director of public relations, Anthony De Lorenzo, gave an extended account of General Motors' support of traffic safety councils throughout the country with funds and printed materials, and the involvement of company executives and personnel in helping to orient local safety activities of clubs, schools, and government agencies. "In this way," declared De Lorenzo, "General Motors has put its shoulder to the safety wheel in virtually every village, town, and metropolis in America."

Roberts also invited independent specialists to testify. The subcommittee heard from numerous physicians, such as Dr. Fletcher Woodward, Dr. Arnold Griswold, and Dr. Horace Campbell, who for so many years have observed at first hand the bloody consequences of interior vehicle design and have tried in vain to galvanize their profession into action for safer cars beyond the easy passage of medical association resolutions. The subcommittee also heard from engineers such as Professor James Ryan, William Stieglitz, Frank Crandell, Henry Wakeland, and Andrew White, a man who left the automobile industry to establish motor vehicle safety research facilities in rural New Hampshire. The subcommittee heard, as well, from representatives of the American Public Health Association, the American College of Surgeons, and the American Medical Association. All of those representatives underlined the ability of the automobile makers to make the inevitable accident safer. These dedicated physicians and engineers were farsighted not because they perceived some hidden truths but because the society around them and the major decision-making bodies that could discipline the automobile manufacturers were so near-sighted.

What disturbed Roberts most was the response from the executive branch of the federal government. He found it very difficult to get information from federal agencies that dealt with highway safety matters; nor did his committee enjoy any of the other forms of cooperation that nourish good legislative policy-making. Very soon it became clear that the automobile was a taboo subject for most federal officials. What particularly incensed Roberts was the attitude of the Department of Commerce. In a rare flush of anger, he made known his displeasure during testimony on H.R. 2446— a bill providing that hydraulic brake fluid meet safety standards prescribed by the Secretary of Commerce. Roberts introduced the bill in 1961 after receiving evidence that many brands of brake fluid came to a boil at a dangerously low temperature. Such fluids are called "phantom killers" by automotive experts because under hard stopping conditions they vaporize, leading to total brake failure. By the time the damaged vehicle is investigated, the brakes have cooled, the vapor has returned to a fluid state, and the brakes are operable.

This had been a serious problem for many years before the first state law was passed by Minnesota in 1953. In 1961 only half the states had passed laws regulating brake fluid, and these mostly required conformity with the tolerant SAE minimum standards. All the laws were chiefly exhortatory in nature with nominal, if any, enforcement provisions.

Roberts thought federal legislation was needed. The official reaction from the Commerce Department was: "This Department is certainly sympathetic with the safety objectives contemplated by H.R. 2446. However, we would also emphasize that the several States have traditionally exercised regulatory authority over motor vehicle safety features; and it would seem that the entry of the Federal Government into the field of brake fluid standards regulation presents the basic question of the proper role of the Federal Government generally in the regulation of motor vehicle equipment." After thus lecturing the subcommittee about the bill's jurisdictional propriety in the light of "tradition," the department made this astonishing recommendation: "We would like to suggest that it might be helpful for the President's Commission on Intergovernmental Relations to give careful study to the basic question of the Federal Government's role in the regulation of motor vehicle equipment, before decision is made with respect to brake fluid standards." It might have been expected that the department would know its position on motor vehicle regulation, since it had finished in 1959 a $200,000 study entitled "The Federal Role in Highway Safety," which was ordered by Congress in 1956 specifically to "determine what action can be taken by the Federal Government to promote the public welfare by increasing highway safety." A draft version of this study was sent for review to the Automotive Safety Foundation and the National Safety Council, which may help to explain why by the time the study was published the government's role in vehicle safety was never defined.

Roberts told the department's spokesman, Charles Prisk, a cautious veteran of the Bureau of Public Roads and the principal author of the 1959 report: "Mr. Prisk, you know I have had a good deal of experience with departmental reports. This is not the first time that I have been confronted with the reluctance of the Commerce Department to go along with safety regulations."

Roberts also said: "I am getting tired of introducing bills and holding hearings on safety matters. This is certainly not a far-reaching bill. But it is a bill that can save a lot of lives. And when the Department continually comes up here and recommends against a very small step in the direction of the safety of our people on the highways, roads, and streets of this country, it seems to me that certainly we ought to investigate and find out what is wrong with the Department of Commerce. . . . They constantly opposed every effort the Congress made for safety in that field. I am not going to be satisfied until we find out what is happening at the Department level."

Roberts never carried through on what would have been a significant inquiry. But he did modify H.R. 1341, authorizing the federal government to establish safety standards for the motor vehicles it purchases, so that the General Services Administration got the job, instead of the Department of Commerce, which did not want the responsibility. In view of the odds against the success of Roberts' efforts, H.R. 1341 was a stroke of legislative genius. It was difficult for the automobile lobby to oppose a law restricted to government procurement of some 36,000 vehicles a year. Nevertheless, the lobby did oppose it. Although the bill passed the House in 1959 and 1962 by large majorities, the automobile industry managed to block it in Senator Smathers' subcommittee on surface transportation. The Automobile Manufacturers Association testimony against the bill argued that "nationally recognized performance standards already are available," and only duplication and expense would result from passage. The American Association of Motor Vehicle · Administrators echoed the AMA, declaring that the bill "would probably result in serious injury to the economy of this Nation . . . and would create stagnation among automotive engineers and designers." The Automobile Manufacturers Association made clear that when it referred to "nationally recognized performance standards" it meant those of the American Standards Association and the Society of Automotive Engineers.

In the summer of 1964, with Senator Smathers no longer chairman of the subcommittee on surface transportation, Roberts spoke with Senator Warren Magnuson, chairman of the parent Senate commerce committee, and secured his endorsement of the bill in return for Roberts' support of a Magnuson bill providing medical care for commercial fishermen. After that the bill sailed through the Senate and was signed by President Johnson at his Texas ranch on August 30, 1964.

The clear legislative intent behind the law, now Public Law 88-515, was for the General Services Administration to emphasize vehicle safety in its purchase standards so as to exert pressure on the industry and get it moving faster in the engineering of all its vehicles for accident and injury prevention. GSA's administration of Public Law 88-515 during the first year of its enactment failed to carry out this mission.

The task of developing the standards fell initially to Willis MacLeod of GSA's standardization division, and to his deputy, John Scott. Congress did not make their job any easier. No special appropriations were made available with Public Law 88-515 to facilitate the hiring of specialists and services of expert consultants by GSA.

However, the Roberts law was written in a very permissive manner. It did not limit GSA to prescribing only those standards whose features it could obtain and pay for in the next procurement year. The agency was perfectly free to establish standards that could point the way to future adoption and thus not only give the automobile makers advance notice but also provide a basis for stimulating greater competition in bidding for government business. GSA chose not to avail itself of this flexibility.

MacLeod and Scott did begin their work with sincerity and showed a determination to explore available knowledge from a variety of sources—industry, government, universities, independent specialists, and physicians. Two advisory committees were created, one consisting of representatives from other federal departments and the other composed of the automobile companies, standards groups, and trade associations. The first standards had to be published by the summer of 1965 for application to 1967 model vehicles.

The Automobile Manufacturers Association invited the General Services Administration officials and members of the government advisory committee to a three-day tour of company facilities and consultations with company engineers. Soon after this early November meeting, General Services Administration officials held a formal specification-development conference attended largely by government and industry people. The synchronized performance of the four automobile companies, the Automobile Manufacturers Association, and the Society of Automotive Engineers almost appeared as if it had been preceded by a dress rehearsal. Their strategy was to point out what they could *not* do to insure greater safety, never to offer suggestions about what they could do. No data were volunteered to back up their restrictive assertions, nor was any information released about their work on safety, such as what they had done on steering wheel assemblies. They advised the General Services Administration to adhere to the "proven" safety features available as optional equipment and cautioned that within a few months the 1967 models would be "in the pan" except for minor alterations. To emphasize that the industry was not being overly parochial, the redoubtable satellites—SAE, ASA, AAMVA, and NSC —either rose in active support or implied concurrence by staying silent.

GSA published seventeen preliminary safety standards in January 1965* and invited comments. Some GSA personnel believed

---

* These were: anchorages for seat belt assemblies; padded dashboard and visors; recessed dashboard instruments and control devices; impact-absorbing steering wheel and column displacement; safety door latches and hinges; anchorage of seats; four-way flasher; safety glass; dual operation of braking system; standard gear quadrant P R N D L automatic transmission; sweep design of windshield wipers-washers; glare-reduction surfaces; exhaust emission

that these standards would be substantially toughened by the June 30th deadline for the issuing of the final standards. Just the opposite occurred.

In February and March numerous detailed commentaries were received. The industry comments expressed approval of the standards that adhered to SAE or ASA standards or simply detailed optional equipment (without any performance requirements) that they were currently selling, or pressed recommendations for lowering or altogether dismissing other standards. Comments from independent specialists and government agencies recommend that many of the proposed standards be strengthened.

During this period a shift to the industry's viewpoints began. MacLeod's superiors, H. A. Abersfeller, Commissioner of the Federal Supply Service, and his assistants, George Ritter and Walter Roberts, began to take over more of the details and the communication with the industry. A final specification-development conference was held on May 19 and 20, 1965. A revised list of preliminary standards was presented by GSA for consideration. There was little indication then that the final standards which came out on June 30 would be even weaker than the draft standards. For example, the standards for padded instrument panels were reduced to the point of uselessness. A GSA proposed standard regarding the decelerative force of the head upon impact was reduced from a required 44 feet per second and 40 g's in 40 milliseconds in May to a required 22 feet per second and 80 g's in 60 milliseconds in June. This standard was such that out of a group of sixteen automobile makes built between 1953 and 1959 that were tested by John Swearingen of the Federal Aviation Agency, nine would have met or exceeded the present GSA requirement without padding. Swearingen considers all sixteen makes he tested as excessively dangerous. Another illustration of how the standards were watered down relates to the instrument panel control devices, which, according to the preliminary standard, were to be designed so as to be flush with the panel surface or be detached by a force not exceeding forty pounds; this was weakened to ninety pounds in June. The steering column standard had provided for a permissible rearward displacement not ex-

---

control system; tires and tire safety rims; back-up lights; an outside rear-view mirror. All these items were retained in the final standards, which were significantly weaker in many instances. Pedestrian protection was not considered by GSA, though its general counsel interpreted the law as permitting it to do so.

ceeding five inches during a barrier collision test at thirty miles per hour; despite much data and expert judgment to the contrary it was changed to five inches at twenty miles per hour on the basis of some uncritically evaluated cases presented by an anatomist, Dr. Donald Huelke, a protege of GM's Kenneth Stonex and consultant to General Motors and Ford. The glare-reduction standards were weaker than their January levels, to the extent that many 1964 and 1965 glare-ridden models meet the GSA requirements. What makes the GSA standards even more accommodating to the industry is that they assume the occupant is belted to the seat. This assumption means, for example, that the standards do not take knee contact areas into consideration.

Nothing particularly new happened between May 20 and the deadline for the final standards on June 30. Civil servants tend to shape their jobs along paths that avoid strong adverse reaction and great controversy. Reaction and controversy mean more work. The industry and its satellites are most capable of having a strong re-action and creating controversy. The consumer is not.

The General Services Administration says that it did not have the data on which to base standards stronger than the ones it es-tablished the first year. This "lack of data" argument seems largely specious. It does not take any more data, for instance, to have more stringent glare reduction standards, more complete tests for door latches and hinges, and a stipulation of the area adequately wiped by the windshield wiper. The General Services Administra-tion, in a landmark study by John Swearingen on instrument panel design hazards, had data that it ignored completely.

The fact that during the month preceding the June 30 deadline the General Services Administration did not inform other federal agency representatives on the government advisory committee of its decision to weaken the standards was entirely inexcusable. GSA was far more solicitous of the industry than of the government. It permitted company engineers to see and comment on the final draft of the standards, right up to the time when the draft had to be sent to the printers. The final standards in general represented quite a triumph for the automobile makers. They obtained a government endorsement of existing optional safety devices and approval, by and large, of existing levels of safety. GSA was directed toward the "gadget" approach to safety and away from the much more fundamental structural approach. After extensive interviewing of automobile company engineers, *Automotive News* reported that "most automotive people are quite receptive to the General Services Administration approach because they have representatives on the General Services Administration committee permitting them to influence the selection of reasonable features."

Comments by two top industry executives illustrate the extent to which the General Services Administration officials fulfilled the law's intent to exert influence on the manufacturers to engineer higher safety levels for their 1967 models than contemporary vehicles offered. Arjay Miller, president of the Ford Motor Company, said in May 1965, "Although some reports may lead the public to believe that the GSA standards will be new, in most instances they are similar to or stem from our current engineering practice." In July 1965, Mr. Miller said, "Our newest [door] latches exceed . . . General Services Administration requirements. The safety features we have added to our cars over the years include almost all the requirements recently announced by the General Services Administration for vehicles purchased by the government starting with 1967 models." In the same month, July 1965, James Roche, the president of General Motors, made note of six GSA standards that covered optional equipment long offered by GM. Then he added, "With respect to other GSA specifications, I would like to point out that General Motors' cars already have a standard gear quadrant, safety glass, standard height bumpers, as well as door latches, hinges and anchorages for seats and seat belts—all of which meet or exceed the standards established. Our current steering wheels more than satisfy these GSA requirements." In a statement submitted to the Ribicoff subcommittee, General Motors even claimed that its door hinges, which the Cornell study showed to have failed in collisions at a rate many times higher than competing vehicle hinges, "for all of these years from 1959 through 1965 more than satisfy the 1967 GSA requirements."

It is understandable why, in view of such a dismal performance, GSA officials did not present any technical justification for their standards, either on a formal basis or when requested by nonindustry sources to do so. Instead, inquirers were given useless generalities which only confirmed the shallowness of the specifications. GSA's administration of Public Law 88-515 during 1964 and 1965 does not provide much ground for optimism over standards the agency is committed to develop in succeeding years.

Less than two weeks after the GSA standards were published, the United States Senate broke a sixty-year silence on the vehicle safety issue and, through Senator Abraham Ribicoff's subcommittee on executive reorganization, opened its first hearings. Each of the four domestic manufacturers was invited to testify. General Motors led off with its chief executives, Chairman Frederic Donner and President James Roche. From their testimony and attitude, it appears that Donner and Roche walked into that crowded hearing room on July 13 thinking that it would be just like 1956 and the Roberts subcommittee all over again, with perhaps a bone or two thrown in to pacify some headline-hunting Senators. Both presented statements which once again repeated the routine that has characterized all of General Motors' statements on safety through the years. Roche spoke about the progress of the past, beginning with 1910 models. It was just after that date, he reminded his audience, that "all driver compartments were equipped with doors to keep the occupants from falling out." After devoting a quarter of his testimony to cataloguing past advances, he went on to discuss the company proving grounds, the rigorous company testing, the need for better vehicle maintenance by car owners, the support General Motors gives to driver education, and other financial support the company gives to the private safety movement. Then Roche told the Senators that the proper role for the federal government was to encourage and assist the states and local communities, whose traffic safety responsibilities include the vehicle itself, since these communities "are obviously most familiar with their own conditions with respect to the safe operation of automobiles."

Donner's testimony reaffirmed the optional approach to safety which goes back to the days when headlamps and bumpers were options. "Some things must be built into the motor car because they are essential to its operation. Examples are brakes, steering and lights. Other items must be sold to the customer on their merits." He cited directional signals—first introduced by General Motors on an optional basis in 1939—as a self-evident safety device and deplored the lack of prompt customer acceptance, which impeded General Motors from standardizing this device on all its cars. Donner said that the "decision to offer an item as optional equipment recognizes what I believe is the basic freedom of the customer to pay the cost of tailoring a car to his own specifications or rejecting whatever he may not want." He neglected to explain why costly styling features were non-optionally imposed on the consumer, or whether General Motors ever clearly informs the car buyer about the safety purposes of particular options. He ignored the obligation of a manufacturer to make such features standard and not leave the decision to endanger innocent third parties, in other cars or on foot, up to the customer's acceptance of an inflated-price option. Rather, Donner was insistent that this optional policy "must be the approach" until there is high general acceptance or "there are other compelling reasons for standard installation." Since he was speaking of attachable safety features, "safety" (without legislation) was not such a compelling reason. He re-emphasized his point: "I come back again to the climate of public acceptance. If we were to force on people things they are not prepared to buy, we would face a customer revolt," and departing from his prepared text, Donner added, "and we want to stay in business."*

At the time Donner was speaking, an advertisement about the Skylark Gran Sport run by his company's Buick division was circulating the country under the title "Son of Gun." The advertisement asked: "Ever prodded a throttle with 445-pound-feet of torque coiled tightly at the end of it? Do that with one of these and you can start billing yourself as The Human Cannonball." It is obvious that automobile company management is taking little responsibility for the climate of public acceptance which its torrent of advertisements are helping to nurture throughout the country. As American Motors' Roy Abernathy once stated: "The influence of advertising on consumer attitudes is widely accepted as a substantial one."

What prompts automobile makers to refer in testimony or speeches to safety devices or other distinct, observable features instead of the far more important structural advances in safety engineering is the ease with which devices can help shift attention to the area of consumer acceptance and extra-cost options instead of the manufacturers' responsibility.

Donner did have an olive branch for Ribicoff's subcommittee. Just the week before the hearings it had happened that General Motors had arranged to give the Massachusetts Institute of Tech-

---

* *Medical Tribune,* long a reasoned critic of unsafe vehicle design, commented on Donner's statement with unconcealed acidity; "It is somewhat difficult to picture a horde of sans-culotte consumers, waving red flags, attacking the castles of General Motors' dealers, determined to rip seat belts, dual-braking systems, left-hand mirrors, safety tires, padded dashboards, etc., out of every car or die in the attempt."

nology a $1,000,000 grant to be spread over the next four years for a "long-range, in-depth, quantitative analysis of all facets of the safety problem—the car, the road, the driver, and their various interactions." This grant breaks down to $250,000 a year, less than a third of Donner's annual earnings from General Motors. Though no Senator inquired how much "in-depth" analysis of anything such a modest sum would buy, given the majestic sweep of the grant's subject matter, General Motors' testimony did not satisfy either Senator Ribicoff or Senator Robert Kennedy. The question-and-answer period left them even less satisfied.

Donner and Roche refused to tell the subcommittee how much their company spends on collision safety research, claiming it was impossible to segregate it from their other engineering and development programs. When asked about the Cornell report on the exceptional fragility of General Motors' door hinges, GM's engineering vice-president, Harry Barr, first said he was "not familiar with such data." After Ribicoff and Kennedy persisted with their questions, Barr suddenly recalled enough of the report to attempt to explain it away.

After one berating by Ribicoff, Donner and Barr inadvertently burst forth defensively with replies that indicated how remote General Motors' top management has been from the subject of vehicle safety and how few resources were being allocated to it. Donner said, "We got very concerned as we dug into this and found that we had nowhere to go." That is why "we wanted to see if we could get an institution like MIT to make a really in-depth study." Barr said that Dr. Huelke's investigations of one hundred and fourteen fatal accidents (financed by a grant of $15,000 from the U. S. Public Health Service) had given General Motors more useful information on second collision passenger impacts in General Motors' cars than the company had accumulated in the preceding ten years.

Senator Kennedy pressed to find out how much was spent for research such as that conducted by Dr. Huelke and whether General Motors had similar investigative arrangements elsewhere in the country. Donner and Barr declined to answer the first question, for obvious reasons. As for the second, Barr said, "We have not found another dedicated doctor that is doing this type of work." Kennedy asked whether he had tried to find people in other areas to do this kind of research. After much evasiveness, Barr simply stated: "No, I have not." Kennedy was visibly nettled by what he properly grasped to be the very low priority given crash safety research by General Motors. What followed was a rapid exchange of such electric intensity that the hearing room was hushed into total stillness.

Kennedy: What was the profit of General Motors last year?
Roche: I don't think that has anything to do—
Kennedy: I would like to have that answer if I may. I think I am entitled to know that figure. I think it has been published. You spend a million and a quarter dollars, as I understand it, on this aspect of safety. I would like to know what the profit is.
Donner: The one aspect we are talking about is safety.
Kennedy: What was the profit of General Motors last year?
Donner: I will have to ask one of my associates.
Kennedy: Could you, please?
Roche: $1,700,000,000.
Kennedy: What?
Donner: About a billion and a half, I think.
Kennedy: About a billion and a half?
Donner: Yes.
Kennedy: Or $1.7 billion. You made $1.7 billion last year?
Donner: That is correct.
Kennedy: And you spent $1 million on this?
Donner: In this particular facet we are talking about . . .
Kennedy: If you just gave 1 per cent of your profits, that is $17 million.

This tug of war sent the Ford and Chrysler representatives in the audience rushing back to their typewriters to make revisions and additions to their prepared statements. Both companies were more specific than General Motors in the role they visualized for the federal government. The industry, of course, would take care of the vehicle. Chrysler urged the establishment of a federal-financed center to look into accident causation, to study the "sociological and psychological factors" involved in operating automobiles, and to educate consumers to buy and use proven safety devices offered by the industry. Ford recommended a similar long-range program, sponsored by the Department of Commerce and contracted to private industry and universities, to study the driver, the highway, and law-enforcement—those weaker links of the chain linking the elements needed for safer highway travel. The Ford president, Arjay Miller, stated that at present "industry facilities for vehicle design and testing are the strongest links" in this chain.

During the two-hour hearing, Miller put on a long presentation which left little time for questioning. Learning of the no-nonsense treatment accorded General Motors, he prepared a three-page addendum outlining ten areas of increased activity by Ford in fulfilling "our responsibilities in the safety field." Ribicoff was intrigued by the way the automobile companies suddenly began pledging more attention to safety because of a brief public exposure at a Congressional hearing. But the pledges were vague, unenforceable, and designed to fend off any move for regulation. Safety remained solidly in the corporate embrace of the "trade-off."

Having helped focus Congressional attention on vehicle safety, the question now is how far the Ribicoff subcommittee will go to get at the roots of the problem and propose genuine solutions to it. An idea of the difficulties that any such effort will be likely to encounter can be imagined from knowing the continuing struggle to establish the first public tire safety standards in this country. In 1959 *The Wall Street Journal* published a front-page article entitled "Tire Troubles," which told of the tire industry's concern about the hazards of overloaded original-equipment tires and the inadequate recommended air pressures for the growing weight of the new cars. The article quoted an Akron tire engineer as saying, "Tire overloading has been a problem for the thirty years I've been in the business, but it started to become acute in the 1950's." The tire industry, it continued, had been trying to get the motor companies to buy larger tires to avoid this overloading. *The Wall Street Journal* described why it was bad to overload tires. "The constant flexing builds up terrific heat in the tire for the new cars. And heat is the worst enemy of a tire. It weakens the fabrics embedded in the rubber and saps the strength of the adhesive which holds together the various layers of fabric and rubber of which a tire is made." This leads to shorter tire life and blowouts long before the tread wears down.

Two years later, Karl Richards of the Automobile Manufacturers Association told the Roberts' subcommittee that "tire problems today are mainly concerned with improper use, maintenance, and replacement." Again it was the motorist's responsibility. Again there was no problem with the tires as they were received on the original vehicle.

About this time, New York State Senator Edward Speno began to receive letters from around his state complaining in some detail of new tires on new cars that mysteriously blew out after a few hundred or few thousand miles. The more Speno looked into the matter the more he learned of the inability of the tire buyer to know what he is buying. There were no reliable purchasing guides or any law anywhere dealing with tire safety standards. Any quality of tire could be sold, even those advertised for $7.95 as "perfect for in-city driving." Speno's legislative committee visited Akron, Ohio, home of four of the big five tire companies, on September 23 and 24, 1963. At a dinner given in the committee's honor by tire company leaders, Speno proposed the establishment of minimum safety performance standards for new automobile tires. Stunned silence greeted the end of his speech. One dinner guest spilled both his coffee and his after-dinner liqueur onto the man seated on his left. Speno had not only said something no one had ever said before, but it sounded as if he meant it.

The tire industry decided to cooperate with Speno in order to have a voice in negotiating the contents of the tire bill that was to be drafted. After several meetings with Speno and his technical consultants, tire company representatives, headed by those from Goodyear, prevailed upon Speno to limit the bill to standards for blow-out resistance and overloading. The sections on skidding and cornering standards were dropped. Late in 1963, the automobile industry told the tire companies crisply that there was to be complete and total opposition to any tire legislation. There followed what veteran observers at Albany called some of the most intensive and improper lobbying ever seen on those legislative battlegrounds.

Speno told the American Trial Lawyers Association in August 1964 how the tire industry began applying pressure. "In January," he said, "I received at my home a call from Akron from the president of one of the big companies, a very friendly call. It had to do with finances for my next election campaign and national public relations expenses. 'You're not serious about this legislation, Senator,' he said. I'm not categorizing the nature of the phone call. I'm just telling you it happened."

Another meeting was held between Speno and leading tire company representatives in Albany on February 19, 1964. Speno agreed to numerous modifications requested by the companies, including deletion of the overloading section which the automobile industry so violently opposed. They then surprised him by saying they would support the bill at the March 4th hearings. At that hearing, Speno was surprised again. The Rubber Manufacturers Association, the Goodyear representative, the Automobile Manufacturers Association, and automobile company spokesmen all stood up and totally opposed the bill. The Senate passed it, but the lobbying paid off in the Assembly where the bill was never brought to a floor vote.

On July 1, 1964, the Rubber Manufacturers Associaton (RMA) announced voluntary agreement among the tire companies to adhere to minimum tire standards promulgated by the RMA. The objective of this move was to take the steam out of any further legislative drives. The RMA standards were so obviously incomplete, weak, and unenforceable that both tire and automobile industries turned to another of their controlled agencies, the Vehicle Equipment Safety Commission (VESC) to write slightly more stringent standards that would have an official façade.

In September, the managing director of the Automobile Manufacturers Association, Harry Williams, recommended to the Speno committee in a letter and press release that it refer its tire legislation and all other automotive safety bills to the VESC which, Williams implied, was far more qualified to deal with such technical problems. The notorious background, purpose, and structure of the VESC as a tool of the automotive industry and as a palpable undermining of state legislative initiative is fully documented by the minutes of its meetings and its performance to date. Speno, who initially approved the bill making New York state the first to adhere to the compact creating the Vehicle Equipment Safety Commission in 1962, is so repulsed by its subversive effect on the integrity of the governmental process that he is considering a move to have the state withdraw from the compact.

Interest in tire hazards began in Washington after Senator Gaylord Nelson filed a bill in the Senate to establish tire safety standards. Complaints from motorists, automobile clubs, and tire dealers poured into Nelson's office. They applauded his statement of the need to assure motorists that the tires they are buying are safe. One California tire dealer wired: "You are right—many motorists are riding on a time bomb." The insidious aspect of this problem is that when the "bomb" explodes it is the driver who takes the responsibility.

Similar complaints were coming into the Federal Trade Commission, which finally decided to hold hearings in January 1965 on tire safety, size, grade, and quality. These hearings brought forth testimony from specialists in industry and government that visibly shocked some of the FTC commissioners. FTC chairman Paul Rand Dixon told the Senate Commerce Committee (which began its hearings in May) what the record had produced: "Our hearing contains substantial testimony as to the inadequacy of these Rubber Manufacturers Association standards. . . . The specific safety problems which were developed at greatest length during our hearing relate principally to the matters of tire size and the so-called practice of overloading, which are interrelated. Overload is the situation which exists when the curb weight of a vehicle plus the designed load capacity in terms of passengers and luggage exceeds the load carrying capacity of the tires with which the vehicle is equipped. The matter of tire size is directly related to the overload problem in that, all other things being equal, the size of the air chamber and the amount of inflation pressure therein determines the amount of load the tire can bear.

"Our record contains a number of statements to the effect that many original equipment tires mounted on new cars are inadequate to safely carry the passenger and baggage load the vehicle is designed to carry. One tire manufacturer stated that 'over the years, vehicle manufacturers, in an attempt to cut costs, have cut down the amount of tire they are designing on to their vehicles, and that some vehicles are overloaded when they are empty of passengers or baggage.'"

Repeatedly the problem of overload was traced back to the automobile manufacturers, who chose not to present themselves before the Federal Trade Commission. After it became obvious to the commissioners that cost-cutting and the car makers' obsession with the soft ride were the key reasons for the motorist getting an undersized tire, Commissioner Philip Elman wondered aloud whether the absence of the automobile companies hadn't turned the hearing into a performance comparable to Hamlet without the Danish prince.

A Goodrich executive explained how the automobile industry chooses tires for new cars. "For example, with a six passenger sedan, the weight of three passengers is added to the curb weight of the vehicle to determine the load that is to be used to select the tires." All the major tire companies and the Rubber Manufacturers Association refused to be drawn into any criticism of the automobile industry—their biggest customer—though some of the assistants to the spokesmen in the room were heard quietly cursing the automobile makers for forcing them into this predicament of trying to defend the indefensible.

Chairman Dixon later told the Senate Commerce Committee that the replacement tire market provided a great deal of consumer confusion and deception. "We believe confusion and deception are the results inherent in the existing situation where the approximately 950 different tire names currently marketed represent the products of approximately 120 private label marketers and 14 tire manufacturers; where tires may be designated as to quality, i.e., 'premium,' 'first line,' 'second line,' etc., regardless of the tire's inherent quality or safety; where the price of the tire has no discernible relation to its quality or safety level; and where many of the descriptive terms employed, such as 'ply rating,' '100 level,' and other grade designations, have no real meaning or definitive value in the absence of uniform standards. Testimony adduced at the hearing reflects that one manufacturer's 'first line' tire may be inferior to another manufacturer's 'third line' tire; and a manufacturer may supply a tire represented by him as a 'third line' tire to a private label marketer who is free to designate it as his 'premium' tire."

The commissioners listened incredulously as they heard John Floberg, secretary and general counsel of the Firestone Tire and Rubber Company, offer this steely assurance at the end of the hearings: "I submit that the best standard, the time-tested and proved standard and the appropriate free enterprise standard of quality should be the one that has in the case of tires, as in the case of other consumer products, worked most satisfactorily; namely, the discriminating and sophisticated taste of the American consumer." A leading National Bureau of Standards tire expert has said that he could not compare tires reliably for his own private purchase from the information available on the marketplace. Yet Mr. Floberg would impute such discernment to the average consumer.

There was only one candid statement submitted by a tire manufacturer. This came from Harry McCreary, Jr., chairman of the McCreary Tire and Rubber Company, longtime producers of replacement tires. McCreary argued for the need to inform the car driver, by a visible decal, of the net number of pounds of people and/or baggage which can be put into the vehicle before any tire becomes overloaded. "Then," he said, "if the driver insisted on piling in more people and/or baggage, he would at least know that he was skirting the danger area. As things stand now, the average driver simply doesn't give any thought to the matter—because no one has ever told him that he was placing himself, his passengers and every oncoming driver in a potentially dangerous situation."

McCreary told of the hold which the automobile makers have on the tire companies by virtue of their great purchasing power. "When Detroit snaps its fingers, Akron jumps through the hoop—backward, if necessary. . . . [The] decision as to what kind of a tire will go on those new cars is made in Detroit."

Henry Wakeland, automotive consultant to the Speno Committee between 1961 and 1965, gave the Senate Commerce Committee some documented illustrations. The committee purchased three tires labeled "Safety Special," manufactured by a Firestone subsidiary, and sent them to the National Bureau of Standards for testing. The bureau reported that the tires failed the endurance test well before the end, being unable to hold air. One of these "Safety Specials" was cut apart and showed tunnel-like voids all around the circumference. Referring to the absence of any public standards, Wakeland observed: "It is even legal to design tires this way, holes and all. Furthermore, when these tires blow out, there is not one police investigator in a hundred who would detect any tire problem. A blowout through one of those voids would have to be detected by an expert."

Wakeland then provided the committee with a clinching argument. The Automobile Club of New York (the state division of the Automobile Association of America) equipped twenty of their staff cars last year with brand-new premium tires of one of the best known names in the rubber industry. The tires were of a kind that had been advertised as the safest tires in the world. These tires retailed at well over fifty dollars each. He described what happened: "With the new tires in use, staff people began to have close calls in their driving, being unable to stop, and skidding unexpectedly. The Club tested several cars, comparing the premiums with much lower priced tires of competitive makes. The skids happened more readily and were between twenty and eighty per cent longer than skids with the rather ordinary lower priced tires. A Club representative told the Speno Committee Staff that the manufacturer took back the entire group of tires and he thinks it also pulled back stock from warehouses. The manufacturer actually changed his rubber compounding."

The tire company did not warn motorists to whom it had sold these tires and who are driving around on them. (The New York AAA preserved the anonymity of the company by not even advising its members to jettison those tires.) And as Wakeland concluded, "all of this is still perfectly legal in New York and everywhere else."

The Senate tire hearings were significant for future legislative thinking on vehicle safety. The attitude toward public law and public safety prevailing at the Department of Commerce was clearly stated by the Assistant Secretary of Commerce, J. Herbert Hollomon. There was no doubt about the strong need for tire standards, he stated, but the Department of Commerce preferred the voluntary, cooperative approach. "However," Hollomon said, "the Department would not object to legislation placing discretionary authority in the Secretary of Commerce to issue mandatory standards if in his discretion he determines that voluntary tire standards do not provide adequate safety requirements for the motoring public." The Secretary of Commerce, John Connor, a member of the General Motors' board of directors until his appointment to the cabinet post in January 1965, did not display much enthusiasm in establishing government standards. His blanket defense of the automobile industry's record and policy on vehicle safety before the Ribicoff hearings in March indicated that he had a detailed grasp of all the customary assertions. Alluding to his personal experience at General Motors' directors meetings, Connor was categorical in his statement to Senator Ribicoff. Regarding safety features, he said, "There is no lack of emphasis on the part of the manufacturers."

Senator Vance Hartke, who conducted the Senate tire hearings, heard Hollomon's conclusions with some wonder. He asked, "Why is the Commerce Department so reluctant to move in this field?" Hollomon reminded Hartke that the department welcomed Congressional authority to establish a research program to help develop better standards in cooperation with the tire industry, but the department did not want mandatory authority to set standards. His position, in sum, was that the "private government" of the tire and auto industry should be the preferred approach to public safety.

The Commerce Department's primary and overriding statutory mission is to "foster, promote, and develop" commerce and industry. It is the "house of business" in government. Given such a purpose, the department's leadership, its innumerable undisciplined advisory committees, and its omnipresent business constituency are generically unsuited to handle consumer protection laws. The consumer's interest would take second place to the interests of the business community. This is the reason why manufacturing interests always try to steer what consumer legislation they cannot defeat over to the Commerce Department. This is also the reason why they have fought any attempts to transfer the department's technical research institution, the National Bureau of Standards, to another department, or to give it independent status.

The automobile industry finally appeared on the scene of the tire controversy at the Senate Commerce Committee tire hearings in August 1965. Unfortunately, the committee asked the automobile companies and their trade association to appear together, as an industry, rather than individually. By assuming uniformity in viewpoint, the committee helped foster it and thereby lost the chance to explore company differences in tire specification policy. The most useful Congressional investigations into industry affairs have been those in which companies were questioned separately. The commerce committee accepted the idea that safety is not an object for competitive excellence but a subject of industry-wide collaboration such as in the case of the vehicle pollution question. A frequent corollary to this idea is that public regulation is unnecessary because of industry self-regulation.

The automobile executives arrived that August morning at the hearing room and filled two benches. A single statement was read for the industry by Harry Barr of General Motors. Afterward Barr himself answered questions from the Senators or gave them over to various friendly competitors for reply. The critical issues of undersized, overloaded tires, the consequence for safety of cost-cutting and what Henry Wakeland calls that "soft, squishy ride" were dodged. Barr's testimony consisted principally of emphasizing tire inspection and maintenance and the full capability of the states in handling tire matters under the Vehicle Equipment Safety Commission. Barr conceded that much more had to be done to inform the car owner about proper tire inflation pressures. He urged the committee not to look into past practice but to concentrate on the pending improvements the industry was about to make.

The hearing failed to compile an adequate record chiefly because Senator Hartke did not fill the promise of his known talent for incisive questioning. He simply did not do his homework and therefore came to the hearing room with little background or knowledge of the subject. The same was true for the other Senators on the committee. Unless Senators and Congressmen are willing to brief themselves properly, as Senator Mike Monroney has done in the aviation safety area, the automobile industry will continue to come to hearings with their programmed statements and cinematic performances and leave with automobile safety still subjected to unconscionable erosions.

It takes an impressive kind of political stamina for elected representatives to stand firm for an interest that has no organized constituency. But this has been the very nature of the consumer's safety interest. Without too much difficulty a legislator can succeed in identifying himself with a safety cause and soon find himself being maneuvered by private and allied government forces into sponsoring superficial laws of little consequence other than to cancel out what contribution government can make in fostering greater safety.

The automobile industry is in a particularly strategic position to force the subordination of vehicle safety in the overall hierarchy of legislative and executive programs. The industry knows that the political success of any administration more and more is being measured by its success in promoting economic growth, in sheer quantitative terms. However much talk there may be of increasing the national welfare by better distribution of income and opportunity, and controlling the safety and health hazards of a mechanized economy, the first and primary goal is to see that the gross national product goes up and up. There is little difficulty in establishing the important role of automobile production and sales in the overall economic picture. One look at the input-output tables prepared by the Department of Commerce will clearly illustrate this fact. Automobile production utilizes 21 per cent of all steel, 49 per cent of all lead, 61 per cent of all rubber, 32 per cent of all zinc, 13 per cent of all aluminum and 58 per cent of all upholstery leather sold in this country. One business in every six is classified as automotive; one worker out of every seven is employed directly or indirectly in connection with producing, supplying, servicing, financing or transporting the automobile. Automobile spokesmen never fail to cite these figures whenever they want something from government, or want to block the government from acting on certain measures.

During the House hearings on the excise tax cut in 1964, Richard Cross of the Automobile Manufacturers Association told the Congressmen: "Need I comment on the essential role of the automobile in the growth of the American economy? Fifteen per cent of our economy, one-seventh of our total economy, the bellwether, the leader of private enterprise, is our—that is your—automobile industry." At the same hearing, Congressman Charles Chamberlain of Michigan said: "It is essential to the continued health of the economy that all obstacles to its growth and stability be removed." Mr. Chamberlain is not the only politician who has got their message: Disturb or restrict the automobile makers and you jeopardize the entire economy.

As a privileged institution, the automobile industry has made an impressive record in Washington. Hearings reveal abuses, but legislation almost never follows. Senator Kefauver's lengthy hearings on its treatment of automobile dealers and the abuses of market power and concentration in the automobile industry spawned no laws to rectify the patent wrongs that had been so exhaustively documented. The industry's power is felt in the administration and enforcement of existing laws, as well. In the antitrust area there is sound doctrinal basis for taking action against one or more of the automobile companies, but it is not considered politically practical to do so. The Federal Trade Commission, which has known about odometer rigging for over three decades, never took action against the manufacturers for this deceptive practice. The Bureau of Labor Statistics is not at all satisfied with the evidence it is given by the automobile industry to determine improvements or deteriorations in auto quality for consumer price index adjustment purposes. The automobile makers permit only economists and marketing specialists, not engineers, to meet with Bureau of Labor Statistics statisticians. Selective information is given only to bolster claims of improved quality; the automobile companies put great pressure on the Bureau of Labor Statistics to accept these claims without their producing adequate data to support them. The industry then turns around and uses Bureau of Labor Statistics quality improvement credits as proof that the consumer is getting better automotive quality for his money.

The industry has been instrumental in pushing through Congress gigantic grants for more highways and in opposing the use of public funds for rapid transit and other surface transportation developments that would increase the efficiency, safety, and speed of the nation's transportation system. Like a Moloch, the automobile makers press for an increasingly larger share of everything economic. The result is that the American economy, the largest in the world, is being distorted by tendencies strikingly similar to those that operate in one-crop economies. It should be a matter of concern, not pride, that one of every five retail dollars in this country is being spent for automotive products. A modern technological society should be more efficient in getting around on the ground.

As expected, the automobile manufacturers want to sell more and more automobiles, regardless of the demand their production and use places on resources and consumer dollars, regardless of the gross imbalances in our land transport system, of the impact on land use and urban planning, and of all the other consequences of a flood of automotive products. It is clear that the sales success of the automotive industry is not simply due to the willingness of customers to buy, but also to public policy that ignores needs for rapid transit and builds the highways and provides other services that make possible the growth of the automotive subeconomy. It is also clear that the manufacturers are increasingly relying upon and encouraging a demand for automobiles which has little to do with a demand for transportation. General Motors' vice-president, William Mitchell, pointed this up succinctly: "The motor car must be exciting and create a desire and not become mere transportation, or we will have just a utility and people will spend their money for other things, such as swimming pools, boats, hi-fi sets, or European vacations." (Or, it might have been added, education, clothes, food, medical care, furniture, and housing.)

Such an attitude is not likely to give much attention to safety beyond the minimum demands for it in the marketplace. And even these minimum demands, relating as they do to observable operating mechanisms, are restricted by a highly concentrated industry which, as George Romney, then President of American Motors, said in 1958, has adopted a "common product philosophy" that has ended its "basic product competition." "Why should they promote customer interest in new product engineering possibilities that might eventually obsolete their existing production facilities?" asked Romney, emphasizing the limited consumer choice offered by the narrow quality of competition engaged in by automobile makers. What truth may remain in the classical economic notion that the public interest lies in the unhindered operation of the free market has been seriously compromised by a concentrated industry capable of substantially defining the standards of the marketplace.* Thus, out of the array of demands the public might make for the automobile, that of visible styling changes is greatly encouraged by the industry's promotion and advertising, while those of safety and non-pollution are not encouraged. According to Ford's Gene Bordinat, a new rear end on a car model costs its maker between twenty-five and fifty million dollars. Twenty-five million is more than the combined research and development expenditures of the industry on collision safety in the past fifteen years. If, as Ford's Donald Frey says, the customer cannot describe the kind of car he wants until the manufacturer shows him some ideas and innovations, and if, as GM's Kenneth Stonex admits, increased public awareness of automobile safety (stemming from the General Services Administration standards publicity) will produce faster adoption of vehicle safety features by his company, then there is a useful role to be played by both industry and government in informing the consumer fully about product safety. Yet the industry, by successfully blocking government efforts in this direction and by dominating the channels of communications through which the customer receives his information about automobiles, has obscured the relation of vehicle design to life and limb and has kept quiet its technical capability of building crashworthy vehicles.

The reference to "communications" pertains not only to the content of advertising and promotion engaged in by automobile makers, but to the impact which the massive sums spent ($361,006,000 in 1964 on auto advertising alone) have on the communications media's attention to vehicle safety design. It is more than coincidental that radio, television, newspapers, and magazines have so long ignored the role of vehicle design in producing the first and second collisions. In a rare exposure, *Newsweek* described the operations of the "two-hatters, who both sell automobile advertising and cover the news beat for their papers. After Chrysler's preview in San Francisco last year, Paul Masson, two-hatter for Hearst's *Journal-American*, filed

---

* In the sale of buses, buyer choice is almost synonymous with whatever General Motors chooses to offer. GM has over ninety per cent of the bus business in the country. Since 1957, the Southern California Rapid Transit District has desperately tried to persuade GM to improve the braking systems of its buses. It was not until 1965 with competitive bidding of a small Ohio bus manufacturer and the district's threat of public denunciation, that General Motors stated it would install better braking capabilities on new buses sold to this district.

glowing copy and then called attention to his stories by writing a letter to Chrysler's director of public relations. 'Our publisher is pleased to go all out,' wrote Masson."

The automobile companies do nothing that discourages this depreciation of journalistic standards. The *Newsweek* article reported how Chrysler flew more than three hundred newsmen to New York City. "They were bedded down at the Waldorf-Astoria, fed and watered grandly, and, of course, given a long peek at the firm's 1965 cars and trucks. The tab for all this chromium treatment—$400,000—was picked up by Chrysler." *Newsweek* made it clear that there were leading newspapers which did not permit "two-hatting." The article made no reference to magazines indulging in this nasty habit. But the same strains and inducements operate on all newspapers and magazines that rely significantly on automobile advertising. With all that money pouring into the till, it is not difficult to see automobile safety entirely in terms of the careless motorist. Some major magazines devote their news or feature sections to showing the reader the new model cars, which he could see just as well in the company's advertisements a few pages away. Several times a year *U. S. News and World Report* devotes cover page headlines to promotional stories about the automobile industry. *Reader's Digest,* the world's largest magazine, devotes several articles a year to automobile subjects. It has dealt with highway safety in terms of berating careless driving, advising drivers how to drive carefully and maintain their vehicles properly, and praising the quality and progress of automobile design. The *Digest* is no stranger to controversial causes, as its attack on cigarettes and its refusal to take cigarette advertising illustrates. When it comes to automobiles, however, it avoids criticism of the industry in spite of the judgment of its editors as to what constitutes a good story for its twenty million subscribers. For example, in the summer of 1963, an associate editor of the *Digest,* Walter Adams, had an idea for an article. "If we could point out to readers specifically what the various unsafe features of modern cars are, and if we could document our contention that these features are dangerous, we then could get at least some of these readers to looking for these features and avoiding them when they buy their new cars." Mr. Adams supported his point by citing the dangerous rear vision in his convertible and the reflection of the instrument panel on his windshield which "makes it hard to see the road and on a hot summer day has a sort of hypnotic effect that helps put [one] to sleep. My thought is that if only someone had pointed out such treacherous bits of design to me before I bought the car, I could have watched out for them and taken my money elsewhere. Most articles on safe automobile design take off on describing the author's idea of the ideal car. That gets us nowhere, because manufacturers can just ignore the whole business. I'd like to get an article on design they can't ignore because it sends the critical customer elsewhere."

Adams' sensible idea never developed into an article, but it was not because he could not obtain adequate information. Instead, the *Digest* published in early 1964 an article telling the country that today's cars are built better than they were in the old days. Apparently the magazine's publishers had sensed a widespread impression that this might not be so and had striven to correct it. Before and since, *Reader's Digest* has printed articles uncritically praising vehicle design and quality in the context of safety.

General Motors, has made a special effort to persuade readers of opinion journals, Ivy League alumni publications, and scholarly journals that its tremendous powers of decision over automobile design are held by something more than an old-line, acquisitive corporation. The series of institutional advertisements called "General Motors is People," with headlines like "Discoverer," "Originator," "Perfectionist," and "Safety is His Business," have appeared in outlets like the *Atlantic Monthly, Harper's, The Reporter,* the *Princeton Alumni Weekly,* the *American Journal of Sociology,* and numerous engineering school alumni publications. These ads do not sell cars; they try to sell General Motors as a worthy keeper of peoples' trust.

The result of continuing efforts like this has been the automobile industry's preservation of its hegemony over the design of its products—an independence unparalleled among the manufacturers of any other transport vehicle. Aviation, marine, and rail vehicles and equipment must adhere to public safety standards. These standards are as important for the principle they represent as for the safety performances that have been registered. The principle is that the rule of law should extend to the safety of any product that carries such high risks to the lives of users and bystanders. The automobile is the only product in America which continues to be sold year after year even though it kills thousands of people and injures millions more. If this continued marketing is evidence of the vehicle's importance, it also indicates how hard a bargain the automobile is striking with the American people. While the old diseases such as tuberculosis, pneumonia, and rheumatic fever are diminished as causes of death, the prominence of death by automobile rises. Today the motor vehicle is the leading cause of death among people between the ages of five and thirty and fourth leading cause of death in this country. Car accidents account for over one-third of people hospitalized by injuries in the nation; they are the leading cause of injury to ears and eyes and cause over twenty-five per cent of partial and complete paralysis due to injury. In 1964, 47,700 deaths meant the extinguishment of about one and three-quarter million years of expected lifetimes.

Only the federal government can undertake the critical task of stimulating and guiding public and private initiatives for safety. A democratic government is far better equipped to resolve competing interests and determine whatever is required from the vast spectrum of available science and technology to achieve a safer highway transport environment than are firms whose all-absorbing aim is higher and higher profits. The public which bears the impact of the auto industry's safety policy must have a direct role in deciding that policy. The decision as to what an adequate standard of public responsibility in vehicle safety should be ought not to be left to the manufacturers regardless of their performance. But the extraordinarily low quality of that performance certainly accentuates the urgent need for publicly defined and enforced standards of safety.

Two industry policies are especially inimical to a rational quest for safer automobiles. First is the all-pervasive secrecy that obstructs freedom of communication in the scientific and engineering communities. Company engineers are happy to benefit from the work of university engineering professors, but in return the university engineers are offered excuses about proprietary data, however purely technical or related strictly to safety it may be. Not only does this industry secrecy impede the search for knowledge to save lives—presumably a common dedication for all men—but it shields the automobile makers from being called to account for what they are doing or not doing. Secrecy preserves their control over how quickly safety innovations will be introduced. The perfect illustration of this is the curtain Ford has kept over its numerous prototype safety cars during the past decade—not to mention industry opposition to the New York state prototype car project and to a similar bill on the federal level introduced by Senator Gaylord Nelson. Secrecy permits the industry to enjoy a double standard of proof. For example, Liberty Mutual Insurance Company's demonstration safety cars have been criticized by auto company representatives on the legitimate ground that they were never crash-tested. Liberty's cars were scheduled to be crash-tested in late 1965, with public recording of the data by Derwyn Severy's group at UCLA. But the automobile industry had no plans to expose its vehicles to the same treatment. While it properly states that safety features have to be proven before adoption, it exempts from this stringent testing such features as sharp fins, glare-ridden chrome, hard-tops, wrap-around windshields, undersized tires, smaller brake drums, and front placement of fuel tanks in rear-engine cars (considered a dangerous collision hazard by many engineering authorities, whose findings are supported by mounting accident data).

The second policy inimical to the quest for safer automobiles is the industry's research and development commitment. Probably no other major manufacturing industry in this country devotes so few of its resources to innovations in its basic product. The automobile is not in line for any significant changes in the next two decades; this is the estimate of J. M. Bidwell of General Motors' research laboratories and is also the understanding that the Cornell Aeronautical Laboratory representatives carried away from extensive consultations with company executives and engineers.

Many scientists and engineers in government or outside the industry concur with William Stieglitz's observation: "It may well be that the evolutionary development of the automobile from the horseless carriage has gone as far as it can and that a totally fresh approach is required." This would mean innovation in an industry that has slowed innovation to a snail's pace, as shown by a glance at the list of "automotive highlights" since 1900 which *Automotive News* prints in its annual almanac issue. George Romney pointed to this problem before the Kefauver subcommittee in 1958 when he declared, "All companies in the automobile industry have the benefit of the vast research organizations of the supplier industries and companies, and that area of research vastly outweighs the area of research and improvement that is occurring right in the motor-vehicle industry itself." Romney cited among other illustrations power steering and improved application of steel to automobiles as supplier contributions. The automobile industry has also adopted as its own a number of important advances that came from military transportation research.

An idea of how meager a sum the automobile industry spends for safety innovations was given in 1958 by Andrew Kucher, vice-president for engineering and research at the Ford Motor Company. His was the only public estimate given up to the summer of 1965. Speaking for the Automobile Manufacturers Association, Kucher told an audience of motor vehicle administrators: "Because we are thoroughly sold on this philosophy, the motor vehicle manufacturers spend between five and six million dollars each year in safety-oriented research programs. This expenditure is aimed at solving basic problems and also is a searching for new and better solutions to old problems. You may be interested to know how this research effort is budgeted. One company, [Ford Motor Company] for example, estimates that about one-third of its annual safety research budget of one million dollars is devoted to the problem of safely packaging passengers. Another third goes to safety control of vehicle components, and the last third to projects such as lighting and development of general safety equipment. In individual company organizations, brake development programs cost between two hundred and two hundred fifty thousand dollars annually. Studies of vehicle controls and stability range from one hundred fifty to three hundred fifty thousand dollars in specific company budgets. Visibility and lighting problems each are accorded budgets in the fifty thousand dollar range." Even granting Kucher a margin for exaggeration, the sum of five million dollars amounted to less than one-twentieth of one per cent of the industry's gross sales in vehicles that year. Ford was spending $333,000 on second-collision research and at that time was assumed to be in the vanguard of the industry in such work. There is no evidence that any greater sums were spent in succeeding years.

In July 1965, after refusing to tell the Ribicoff subcommittee how much it spends on second-collision safety research, General Motors released a statement saying that it spent $193 million in 1964 on "safety, durability, and reliability." Into this swollen sum went vast and indiscriminate manufacturing, quality control, and many annual model-change expenses—none having any relation to improving the state of safety knowledge above existing levels, which is what the subcommittee's question pertained to. Nor did the General Motors' statement designate any category for second-collision research. Not to be outdone, Ford and Chrysler followed by stating that they spent $138 and $78 million respectively in the areas delimited by General Motors. Ford's breakdown was more specific and listed 1965 expenditures of $700,000 for its new automotive safety center and $300,000 for designing and building of prototype safety cars—indicating the outer limits of their research on crashworthiness. Considering such an allocation, it is understandable why the automotive safety center's director, C. R. Briggs, was being realistic when he told *Automotive News*, "You can't expect breakthroughs."

All these multi-million-dollar figures for safety and reliability did not fool anyone with any familiarity of the industry's actual commitments to the development and application of safety innovations. In 1965, General Motors' chief safety engineer, Kenneth Stonex, was still writing to individual physicians asking them if they could give him any data about maximum loads that a motorist can absorb should he strike the steering wheel or instrument panel. Ford was lending its new cars to Dr. Huelke to drive around for a week at a time so he could advise them that sharp edges or points inside the vehicle could hurt people. And Chrysler was dilatorily arguing that it was not getting enough police data on accident causation, while fully knowing that the Cornell data, the Harvard and Northwestern studies, and particularly the rapidly increasing variety and quality of human-simulation techniques, statistical and computer tools, and crash-testing permitted them many avenues for developing and evaluating safer designs.

Scientists in the Bureau of Public Roads estimate that the combined public and private support of highway traffic research (defined as the design and testing of safety measures and techniques) was eight million dollars at the most in 1964—the highest to date. This was broken down to two million dollars spent by industry, two million spent by state governments (mostly from federal disbursements) and private agencies, and four million spent by the federal government. Some accident specialists, like Dr. William Haddon, would place the true figure for high-quality research much lower. He does not think there are more than ten competent scientists working full time in traffic accident prevention in this country. These are the resources being devoted to discovering measures to prevent what Senator John F. Kennedy called in 1960 "one of the greatest, perhaps *the* greatest of the nation's public health problems." At the eight million dollar level, this country is spending about $166 in research for every traffic fatality, without taking into account the more than four million injuries every year.*

With some 1200 or less fatalities annually in civil aviation, the federal government spent between thirty-five and sixty-four million dollars each year from 1960 to 1965 on research and development for greater air safety. This was in addition to what was spent for safety work by the aircraft industry itself. Expenditure of sixty-four million dollars for 1200 fatalities means over fifty-three thousand dollars spent in safety research per fatality. The Federal Aviation Agency and the Civil Aeronautics Board spent about five million dollars to determine the cause of two Electra turbo-prop transport crashes in 1959 and 1960 and to find out how to correct the defect in other Electras.

Patently, such neglect of highway safety research is a rebuke to an affluent, technologically advanced society. The federal government's delay of decades in facing up to basic initiatives in vehicle safety is not without its price, for now the solution of the highway safety problem is fragmented and scattered among numerous federal agencies, each jealously guarding its presumed prerogatives and all either staunchly supporting or frightfully cowed by the automobile industry.

Federal activity in highway safety (apart from government employee safety programs) in 1965 consisted of (a) supporting research by the Bureau of Public Roads and the Public Health Service; (b) regulatory activity over the operational safety of interstate commercial trucks and buses by the Interstate Commerce Commission; (c) educational and state support activity by the Bureau of Public Roads, the Public Health Service's Division of Accident Prevention, and the General Services Administration (the latter by means of safety standards for government-purchased vehicles). These agencies with highway safety functions are quick to exclude the automobile itself from their area of responsibility. The Bureau of Public Roads and the Division of Accident Prevention have supported some university-based projects in accident investigation, tire skidding research, collision testing, and highway-

---

* This $8,000,000 for research should be compared with just one federal department's costs. In 1963, the Department of Defense reported that direct bodily injury, death and partial property costs of motor vehicle accidents involving active duty personnel amounted to $83,641,000. Moreover, $8,000,000 represents less than one-tenth of one percent of the direct costs of highway accidents in 1964.

vehicle communications systems. With few exceptions (the seat belt was one) these studies never yielded any policy recommendations affecting the vehicle; in fact, they produced virtually no policy recommendations at all. For the most part, the studies are not evaluated with the idea of translating knowledge into action. In the Division of Accident Prevention, the right to see these studies is granted at the discretion of the research grants chief. If he thinks an inquirer is not technically qualified to interpret the reports accurately, he can simply deny him access to the reports. The division has not even prepared summaries of these studies so that interested persons can learn what findings have been made as a result of this publicly supported research. One five-year grant for about $900,000 awarded in 1959 to a team of Harvard investigators to study fatal highway collisions at the scene was terminated after its fourth year for undisclosed reasons. There is a cloud over the published work of these investigators as a result and the Division of Accident Prevention has not done anything to dispel it, though to users of this information, it is essential that the division clarify its position. Whenever the Division of Accident Research is asked why it does nothing about known vehicle hazards, its answer is that it is primarily interested in the "human factor." If the "human factor" included executives of the automobile companies, the division's focus might have more immediate results. Unfortunately, the "human factor" is interpreted to mean only the driver.

The director of the office of highway safety in the Bureau of Public Roads, James Williams, and the chief of the division of accident prevention, Dr. Paul Joliet, say that the influence of the automobile industry on their operations restrains how far they dare go in criticizing or warning the public of vehicle design hazards. Both Williams and Joliet show adeptness in sympathizing with industry personnel on the one hand and critics of the industry on the other, depending upon which ones they are with.

The federal effort in highway safety in general and vehicle safety in particular suffers from the inadequate legislative authority of the groups that are required to administer it, from insufficient funds allocated to the effort, and from the lack of administrative consolidation that could launch a concrete program with a concrete purpose that would have the kind of high-level support that complex programs in atomic energy and space ventures have. But the highway safety effort has not received this high-level support (though

President Johnson's highway beautification program did recently.) On February 20, 1957, when he was still a Senator, Lyndon B. Johnson expressed on the Senate floor a thought that regrettably is still true. He called the "deadly toll of highway accidents" a problem whose "very familiarity has bred either contempt or indifference . . . We cannot abolish the automobile, but neither can we ignore the problems that it brings to us. There is a responsibility here which we must face." The Senator was proposing the establishment of an automobile and highway safety division in the Department of Health, Education and Welfare that, among other objectives, would "promote research into improved designs for automobiles . . ."

A federal research and development facility where problems of automobile safety could be comprehensively examined and solved is only the first stage of greater federal authority extending to the establishment and enforcement of safety standards and their continuous upgrading. This function in turn must form a part of a larger highway transport research and development program for more efficient and safe travel, by means of a more advanced integration of the functions of highway and vehicle. The Johnson Administration is expected to formulate gradually an overall national transportation policy which presumably will involve a closer coordination of air, land, and sea transport systems and a more rational allocation of public resources, especially in the direction of high-speed rail systems and more novel forms of rapid land transit between cities. This policy may lead to an examination of the present inefficient and disparate administrative arrangements for various forms of transportation. The advantages of taking the Bureau of Public Roads out of the Department of Commerce and making it into a separate entity (called, say, the Federal Highway Transportation Agency) directly responsible to the President should be seriously explored. It could be the first step toward creating an over-all Department of Transportation.

If the government is to be made capable of securing continually safer automotive design, it will require a sharply focused supportive constituency that is dedicated and skilled in pursuing the interests of safety. For until sufficient engineers, lawyers, physicians, and other specialists whose income and skills are pertinent to the building of the automobile or to its post-collision problems—until these people assume the roles of leadership that their superior knowledge makes available to them, legislators and administrators will continue to display "contempt or indifference." What must be squarely confronted is the blurring of the distinctions between government and business under the guises of "partnerships," "voluntary approaches," and "advisory committees." The growth of government power in Washington is far from being a zero-sum game with business; rather it presents business with an opportunity to use government to its special purposes. Thus, as in other consumer protection areas in recent years, there is considerable danger of Congress enacting the "no-law" law for automobile safety. The "no-law" law's chief purpose is to fill a genuine need with illusory matter. It impresses the remote public and relieves the nearby Congressman by a façade of controlling a consumer hazard problem. In reality, it omits the safeguards that would prevent the existing framework of private government, fostered by trade associations and standards organizations, from being made part of public administration. The "no-law" law is ambiguous or makes no mention of enforcement (like the seat belt and brake fluid bills), provides no standards for balanced representation on advisory committees (or for how and when they should meet), does not consider the issue of indiscriminate adoption of private safety standards, requires no periodic progress report to Congress on administration and enforcement, does not stipulate that prescribed standards must be technically justified in writing that is publicly available, restricts authorizations for funds to a nominal or zero level, and is peppered with the word "discretionary" as to the promulgation and issuance date of standards. "Regulated" groups are adept at becoming unpaid public servants, with the public defined as synonymous with themselves. The Interstate Commerce Commission has been delaying the release of a tire accident study until those groups at whom it is primarily directed pre-screen the material in detail and resolve any differences before it is made public.

The regulation of the automobile must go through three stages—the stage of public awareness and demand for action, the stage of legislation, and the stage of continuing administration. Since automobile safety ideally should keep pace with advancing technological capabilities, administrators have to do more than hold the line; they have to advance it. Without full disclosure, Congressional review, and participation by a consumer-oriented constituency of professionally qualified citizens, obsolescence and bureaucratic inertia will stifle the purpose of even a properly drafted law. Motorists may benefit from the efforts of dedicated and selfless champions performing this persistent vigilance, but these efforts will not be enough without a residual vigilance throughout the consumer public.

This vigilance can be kept up simply by understanding a few facts about automobile safety. First, safety measures that do not require people's voluntary and repeated cooperation are more effective than those that do. Second, the sequence of events that leads to an accident injury can be interrupted by effective measures even before there is a complete understanding of the causal chain. Apply these two cardinal principles of safety policy, proven in the control of epidemics and machine hazards, to highway safety and the spotlight turns on the engineering of the automobile. Furthermore, our society knows a good deal more about building safer machines than it does about getting people to behave safely in an almost infinite variety of driving situations that are overburdening the driver's perceptual and motor capacities. In the twenty to forty million accidents a year, only a crashworthy vehicle can minimize the effects of the second collision. Vehicle deficiencies are more important to correct than human inadequacies simply because they are easier to analyze and to remedy. And whether motorists are momentarily careless or intoxicated, or are driving normally when they are struck by another vehicle is entirely irrelevant to the responsibility of the automobile makers to build safe cars. Dr. Bernard Fox, a distinguished psychologist in the Division of Accident Prevention, after spending many years in research on the "human factor," concludes that the most economically, administratively, and technically feasible safety measure, and the one with the quickest and greatest results in saving lives and preventing injuries, is a crashworthy automobile. This is not a startling observation, except that it comes finally from a federal researcher who has stated his candid judgment.

A leading crash researcher and biophysicist, Dr. Carl Clark of The Martin Co. states: "Instead of the 40 mph barrier collision survival being a 'spectacular accomplishment,' it should be a routine requirement of proper car and restraint design. Indeed, without major modifications of car structure and size, by applying what we now know about crash protection, a fixed barrier impact of 45 mph should be experienced without injury, and crashes at higher speeds should be survivable." (A 45 mph crash into a fixed barrier, like a tree or stone wall, generates, for example, the same forces as a car striking the rear end of a stationary vehicle at more than 75 mph).

Engineers are not noted for making metaphors, but a safety engineer for one of the Big Three companies inadvertently offered an illuminating one to *Automotive News* (August 30, 1965) in describing his work: "It's like walking into a room in which there are a bunch of ping-pong balls on the floor. Then you throw another ball in the middle and try to keep track of what happens." That last ping-pong ball was safety. Dr. Donald Huelke, one of the few outsiders to be brought into the inner sanctums of design studios and given the confidence of the three or four safety engineers at General Motors and Ford, reported: "The auto industry has a small, dedicated group of individuals—almost a fifth column—working for car designs of greater safety."

One ping-pong ball among many presents a low order of probability. A fifth column indicates the activity is subversive of the dominant way.

At the basis of such symptoms and impressions is the unwillingness of the automobile companies to dedicate their engineering and investment energies to the kind of first line research and development that will produce the innovations that can make the automobile responsive to the safety requirements of motorists. Over the past decade in particular, the possibilities for completely new approaches to be translated into mass production hardware are almost programable given certain allocations of men and resources. The gap between existing design and attainable safety has widened enormously in the post-war period. As these attainable levels of safety rise, so do the moral imperatives to use them. For the tremendous range of opportunity of science-technology—by providing easier and better solutions—serves to clarify ethical choices and to ease the conditions for their exercise by the manufacturers. There are men in the automobile industry who know both the technical capability and appreciate the moral imperatives. But their timidity and conformity to the rigidities of the corporate bureaucracies have prevailed. When and if the automobile is designed to free millions of human beings from unnecessary mutilation, these men, like their counterparts in universities and government who knew of the suppression of safer automobile development yet remained silent year after year, will look back with shame on the time when common candor was considered courage.

Appendix A

HOW WELL ARE THE NEW AUTOMOBILES ENGINEERED FOR VISUALLY SAFE DESIGN? RATE THEM YOURSELF.

The visual design requirements listed below are some that can be evaluated easily as a car sits on the show room floor. A failure to meet one or more of these requirements means that needless hazards to life and limb have been engineered into the car.

Does the automobile you wish to rate meet each of the requirements listed below for visually safe design? If not, score it off by circling the corresponding number in box below.

Make of automobile : Model :		Encircle each unsafe vision design feature
A	:	:	1 2 3 4 5 6 7 8 9 10 11 12 13 14 15 16 17 18
B	:	:	1 2 3 4 5 6 7 8 9 10 11 12 13 14 15 16 17 18
C	:	:	1 2 3 4 5 6 7 8 9 10 11 12 13 14 15 16 17 18
D	:	:	1 2 3 4 5 6 7 8 9 10 11 12 13 14 15 16 17 18
E	:	:	1 2 3 4 5 6 7 8 9 10 11 12 13 14 15 16 17 18
F	:	:	1 2 3 4 5 6 7 8 9 10 11 12 13 14 15 16 17 18
G	:	:	1 2 3 4 5 6 7 8 9 10 11 12 13 14 15 16 17 18
H	:	:	1 2 3 4 5 6 7 8 9 10 11 12 13 14 15 16 17 18
I	:	:	1 2 3 4 5 6 7 8 9 10 11 12 13 14 15 16 17 18
J	:	:	1 2 3 4 5 6 7 8 9 10 11 12 13 14 15 16 17 18

1. The windshield wiper assemblies should *not* be bright chromium.

2. The windshield should *not* be tinted. (Standing outside, compare the appearance of your hands when the one is outside and the other is viewed through the windshield. If no tint is present your hands will look almost the same color and brightness.)

3. Stand in front and look through the car at objects behind it. There should be no major distortions, waves or other irregularities in the objects.

4. Each of the front turn signals should be at least 12 square inches in area.

5. Both front turn signals should be visible from every possible angle in front of the car. For example: You should be able to see them both while standing slightly in front and 6 feet to the side of the car.

6. There should be an outside rearview mirror.

7. Both red tail and brake lights should be clearly visible from every possible angle behind the car. For example: You should be able to see *both* the left and right sets of lights from a position 10 feet to one side of the car and slightly behind the rear bumper.

8. The top of the dash panel should be finished in a *dull black* or *non-glossy dark* color.

9. The instrument panel should *not be* darkly shaded by a wide long hood or deep covered well.

10. The numerals and pointers on the instrument panel should be large, of good contrast and readable at a glance.

11. The gear that the transmission is in should be instantly readable at a quick glance.

12. You should be able to identify all controls at a glance and to reach them easily.

13. The windshield should be free of distortions. These can be observed from the driver's seat by moving your head and noticing if outside objects bend or move irregularly. Move head up, down, and sideways.

14. The windshield should be free of internal reflections. These appear as ghost images around bright lights.

15. The windshield corner posts should be thin enough that with both eyes open an object 10 feet away, no matter how small, would not be hidden.

16. There should be no chromium on the inside of the windshield corner posts, on window trim or on the hood or fenders that can be seen by the driver behind the wheel.

17. There should be vision reference marks at the left and right front corners of the car. These may be fender ornaments or body contours that help the driver know the width and position of his car. They must not be shiny chromium. And they should be designed in a manner that does *not* present a hazard to any pedestrian struck by a vehicle.

18. In rearward view there should be no blind spots to interfere with backing or with perception at a glance of the location of other cars near you in freeway driving.

Form designed by Merrill J. Allen, O.D., Ph.D., Professor of Optometry, Indiana University, Bloomington, Indiana.

Appendix B

BOARD OF SUPERVISORS
COUNTY OF LOS ANGELES
383 HALL OF ADMINISTRATION / LOS ANGELES, CALIFORNIA 90012
GORDON T. NESVIG   CLERK OF THE BOARD

Members of the Board
BURTON W. CHACE
Chairman
FRANK G. BONELLI
KENNETH HAHN
ERNEST E. DEBS
WARREN M. DORN

180

On motion of Supervisor Dorn, unanimously carried, it is ordered that the following resolution be and it is hereby adopted:

WHEREAS, the Board of Supervisors is responsible for the health and welfare of the nearly seven million residents of the County of Los Angeles; and

WHEREAS, in 1947 the Legislature of the State of California, under an enabling act, conferred the authority to control air pollution in Los Angeles County upon the Board of Supervisors, and in 1948 the Board of Supervisors implemented this authority by activating the Air Pollution Control District; and

WHEREAS, medical science has accumulated epidemiological, experimental, and clinical evidence that levels of smog now experienced in Los Angeles County seriously affect persons suffering from asthma, emphysema and other respiratory ailments, affect significantly the breathing of normal subjects during high exposure periods, and produce significant increases in lung tumors in exposed animals; and

WHEREAS, the Los Angeles County Medical Association has affirmed repeatedly that air pollution constitutes a hazard to the health of persons residing in this community, and, because of the polluted condition of the air, physicians practicing in Los Angeles County advised during one year about 10,000 persons to move from the area; and

WHEREAS, scientists in the field of air pollution control, among the foremost being Dr. A. J. Haagen-Smith, have demonstrated conclusively that continuing occurrence of irritating, noxious, health-impairing smog in the Los Angeles Basin results from automobile emissions; and

WHEREAS, health and welfare in Los Angeles County is being jeopardized by the exhaust emissions of 3,500,000 motor vehicles, burning about 7,150,000 gallons daily; and

WHEREAS, the Board of Supervisors, since 1953, frequently has made known to the automobile industry the emergence of facts concerning the effect of automotive emissions upon air pollution conditions in Los Angeles County and the consequences to public health and welfare being experienced; and

WHEREAS, in 1953 members of the Automobile Manufacturing Association entered into agreements to pool all of their findings concerning control of air-polluting emissions from motor vehicles, and in 1955 they agreed to cross-license to each other any developments in controlling air-polluting emissions from motor vehicles; and

WHEREAS, at that time, and thereafter, spokesmen for the members of the Automobile Manufacturers Association asserted that as soon as they were convinced that motor vehicles contributed significantly to air pollution in Los Angeles County, and as soon as fundamental principles of control for motor vehicle emissions became known, these member manufacturers would undertake to have devices embodying these principles installed upon the vehicles they produced; and

WHEREAS, because of this representation by the automobile industry, millions of dollars have been spent to develop such devices by companies that are not members of the Automobile Manufacturers Association, such as American Machine and Foundry, Walker Manufacturing, American Cyanamid, Minnesota Mining & Manufacturing, Universal Oil Products, Arvin Industries, Ethyl Corporation, Norris-Thermador, W. R. Grace, Chromalloy, Holly Carburetor, Clayton Manufacturing Company, Oxy-Catalyst Company and many others; and

WHEREAS, in 1960, there was enacted in the State of California, principally as a result of the efforts of this Board of Supervisors, Assembly Bill 17 known as the Motor Vehicle Pollution Control Act, for the purpose of dealing with the problem of motor pollution on a state-wide basis; and

WHEREAS, under this legislation, within one year after the certification of two exhaust control devices, such controls would be required on new cars sold within this state; and

WHEREAS, on June 17, 1964, four exhaust control devices were certified, which started the time period running within which devices would become mandatory on new cars; and

WHEREAS, within two months thereafter the Automobile Manufacturers Association announced that automobiles of the 1966-model year would be equipped with exhaust emission control systems, which involved no new principles, but applied principles long known to the automobile industry; and

WHEREAS, if the Automobile Manufacturers Association had given the same attention to the problem in 1953-56 as they did after installation became mandatory, air pollution from motor vehicles would have ceased to be a problem in 1966, by which time vehicles with these control systems would have been produced and sold for ten years and hence most existing vehicles now would be equipped; and

WHEREAS, this was not done because of the aforesaid cross-licensing agreement and restraint of competition between the members of the Automobile Manufacturers Association; and

Index